HISTORY AND MEMORIES OF THE DOMESTIC VIOLENCE MOVEMENT

We've Come Further Than You Think

Gill Hague

First published in Great Britain in 2021 by

Policy Press, an imprint of
Bristol University Press
University of Bristol
1-9 Old Park Hill
Bristol
UK
t: +44 (0)117 954 5940
e: bup-info@bristol.ac.uk

Details of international sales and distribution partners are available at
policy.bristoluniversitypress.co.uk

© Bristol University Press 2021

British Library Cataloguing in Publication Data
A catalogue record for this book is available from the British Library

ISBN 978-1-4473-5632-5 hardcover
ISBN 978-1-4473-5633-2 paperback
ISBN 978-1-4473-5635-6 ePub
ISBN 978-1-4473-5634-9 ePdf

Cover design: Gareth Davies, Qube Design
Front cover image: Alamy/Iliana Suarez
Bristol University Press uses environmentally responsible
print partners.
Printed and bound in Great Britain by CMP, Poole

This book is dedicated:

To all activists on violence
against women across the world

To the survivors of gender violence with whom I
have had the huge privilege of working over the
last 50 years

To the memory of all those women who have been
killed, who have not survived

In particular, to Ingrid Escamilla Vargas, murdered
in Mexico in 2020

The cover of this book shows a 'Red Shoes' (*Los Zapatos Rojos*) protest. From 2009 on, the artist Elina Chauvet has initiated these demonstrations and installations, which have been held across South America and in other parts of the world.

The red shoes are left in public places, with each shoe representing a femicide: a woman murdered or 'disappeared'. The colour red symbolises blood.

The huge demonstration illustrated on the cover was held on International Women's Day, 8 March 2020, in the Plaza del Zócalo in Mexico City.

It was held particularly in memory (along with other femicide victims) of 25-year-old Ingrid Escamilla Vargas. In February 2020, she was killed and horrifically brutalised by her husband. (This book is also in her memory.)

Contents

List of poems

About the author

Gill Hague is Professor Emerita of Violence Against Women Studies, in the School for Policy Studies, University of Bristol, UK. In 1990, she co-founded, with Ellen Malos, the University's Violence Against Women Research Group, now the Centre for Gender and Violence Research. Gill has been an activist on gender violence since the early 1970s, producing about 135 publications on the issue, with eight books, including: *Domestic violence: Action for change* (with Ellen Malos); *Is anyone listening: Accountability and women survivors of domestic violence* (with Audrey Mullender and Rosemary Aris); *Disabled women and domestic violence: Responding to the experiences of survivors* (with Ravi K. Thiara, Ruth Bashall, Brenda Ellis and Audrey Mullender); *Understanding adult survivors of domestic violence in childhood: Still forgotten, still hurting* (with Ann Harvey and Kathy Willis); and *Honour-based violence: Experiences and counter-strategies in Iraqi Kurdistan and the UK Kurdish diaspora* (with Nazand Begikhani and Aisha K. Gill). Gill has also published three poetry collections. She has received two national awards for her life's work on violence against women.

Acknowledgements

My greatest thanks to all the violence survivors and activists, practitioners and researchers on violence against women, and to the women from the women's liberation movement, who talked with me and provided information for this book. It is immeasurably strengthened by their input which has made it, at least partially, a collective endeavour to celebrate the movements we all made.

Invaluable input, consultation and referral to key others were provided by Rebecca Dobash, and a quote to bring the book to a close was generously offered by Jalna Hanmer. Interviews (informal and lengthy) were conducted with Ann Devereaux (to whom extra thanks are due), Davina James-Hanman, Ellen Malos, Fran Wasoff, Jane Anderson, Lesley Welch, Lily Greenan, Liz Kelly, Margaret Davis, Nicola Harwin, Pragna Patel, Sarbjit Ganger, Subhaluxmi Mukherji, Teresa Parker, and six survivors who withheld their names. My deepest thanks to them all.

Those with whom I had important consultations or who are quoted in the text, to whom I am most grateful, included, most particularly, Alison Assiter and Jacky Gruhn; and also: Atuki Turner, Cath Kane, China Devereaux, D-M Withers, Eleri Butler, Emma Williamson, Evan Stark, Finn Mackay, Fiona Vera-Gray, Gail Chester, Hilary Land, Janet Bowstead, Judi Hodgkin, Kathy Willis, Leticia Mujeni, Marianne Hester, Mica Nava, Miriam David, Nazand Begikhani, Nicki Norman, Ravi Thiara, Sue O'Sullivan, Shahana Rasool and Trupti Jhaveri Panchal. Nicole Westmarland was especially helpful. Most of all, Nicola Harwin contributed to the project with tireless dedication, helping hugely with accuracy and information. A deeply-felt extra thank you to Fiona Vera-Gray for making invaluable additional suggestions on the text for streamlining and focus, which improved it greatly.

Organisations consulted included Women's Aid (England), Scottish Welsh and Northern Ireland Women's Aids, Asian

Women's Resource Centre, Brent, Musasa (Zimbawe), MIFUMI (Uganda), Cape Town Rape Crisis (South Africa), Special Cells for Women and Children (India), Older Feminist Network, Rape Crisis England and Wales, local refuge groups, AVA, Refuge, Southall Black Sisters and 70s-Sisters. Insights were contributed over time by the late Ellen Pence (in 2010 but her input was precious); and Aisha Gill, Anjali Dave, Annie Tunnicliffe, Audrey Mullender, Geetanjali Gangoli, Gwendolyn Sterk, Irene Fick, Jackie Barron, Kate Berry, Liane Bradbrook, Liz Bird, Lynne Miller, Marai Larasi, Margaret Cerullo, Marla Erlein, Marsha Scott, Nancy King, Nira Yuval-Davis, Nishi Mitra, the late Pat VT West, Rissa Mohabir, Rachel Bentham, Sarah Mason and Tais Cerqueira Silva. I am deeply indebted to them all. Particular extra thanks for reading drafts and contributing to content and editing, to Alison Assiter, Cassie Hague, Ellen Malos, Jacky Gruhn, Janet Bowstead, Lily Greenan, Nicola Harwin, Nicole Westmarland, and especially Dave Merrick who has helped way beyond what I could have expected.

I am most grateful to the anonymous survivor for her poem in Chapter 4, and to Liz Kelly for permission to use a modification of her original tapestry analogy. My sincerest thank you and best wishes to Jane Rose and Immaculate (Uganda). Many thanks to the Policy Press, and in particular to Victoria Pittman and Shannon Kneis, for commissioning and then guiding the production of this book with sympathy and warmth. And similarly to Annie Rose of Newgen Publishing. An enormous thank you to Cassie Hague for painstaking expert help with referencing and the preparation of the manuscript. Also to Keiran Merrick for invaluable help with the cover. And personal love and thanks as ever to my late mother and father, Dorothy and Tom, and to Dave, Keiran, Cassie, René-Francois, Liza, Alison and 6-year-old Ezra.

Finally, my sincere gratitude to all the survivors of violence, including domestic abuse, rape, and 'honour' violence, with whom I have worked for so many years. You have taught me more than I can ever say. Your stories, resilience and bravery are what support and inspire this book and our struggle.

1

Introduction

We've come further than you think

Violence against women is endemic across the world. One third or more of the world's women experience abuse, violence or hurt, at the hands of men during their lifetimes. What's more, these are often men who they know and who may profess to care for them. This upsetting statistic comes, not from a feminist polemic, but from the World Health Organization, the most august health body globally.[1] Wherever we live, we hear, on an almost daily basis, about women being killed, about violence in the name of so-called 'honour', sexual violations, rape – the distressing list is endless. Gender-based violence, as it is frequently called these days, is endemic in war and conflict, with reports – again almost daily – of terrifying sexual violence against women in conflict zones.[2] And if you look up and down your own street, you can be sure that, in some of those homes, maybe including yours, domestic abuse will be happening.[3]

It is easy to be overwhelmed by the magnitude of violence against women, to feel that things will never improve. But this short book takes a different tack. For 50 years now, the most recent manifestations of the long campaigning struggle by women, and some men too, to combat gender violence have been underway across the world. The gains have been huge in terms of women who have been assisted, services provided, policies put in place, research done, professionals trained, public awareness raised – and resulting social change. We can see that violence against women is shatteringly common everywhere. But we can also see that there have been many steps forward in building a safer and more just world for both women and children. Thus, the intention of this book is to show there is hope. There are actually changes everywhere, even if they are small in some places. As in the very first words of this book: *we've come further than you think.*

What is meant by the terms 'domestic violence' and 'violence against women'?

Domestic violence, frequently intimate and sometimes extreme and long-term, occurs widely across the world – in fact, in every country. Most frequently (although not always), it is committed by men against women. Domestic abuse includes physical violence and belligerence, and importantly sexual violence. It also includes psychological and financial violence and abuse, and the coercive control of some women by their partners.

Violence against women is wider than domestic violence, of course. Its range is staggering and deeply disturbing. It includes rape by strangers or acquaintances, sexual assaults and attacks (sometimes with implements and weapons), sexual murder and relentless sexual violence in war.[4] And it encompasses 'honour'-based violence and killings, femicide (murder of women on grounds related to their gender), forced and early marriage, woman trafficking, personal imprisonment, sexual slavery, maiming, genital and other mutilations, and both physical and sexual torture. If you are tempted to think this list is extreme, have a look at the website and statistics put out by the United Nations.

The aims of the book

The movements against violence against women in different countries have taken up the task of challenging these highly distressing issues, head-on. The main aim of this book is to showcase these efforts, and the domestic violence movements specifically, so that we can maybe learn from them. Commissioned as a shorter book only, it is not possible to deal fully with all forms of gender violence, especially sexual violence (outside domestic abuse). Rather, the book focusses specifically on the movements against domestic violence. It places them, though, in the context of both the gender-based violence movements as a whole, and other wider social movements. It especially celebrates the early passionate days.

Thus, the book highlights under-recorded, radical, women's history from the late 1960s onwards, and some of the advances that have been made. It is the tenacious struggles of women activists, in the countries of the UK and globally,[5] sometimes followed later by the work of policy-makers and service providers, that have led to these advances, and to changes in attitudes and social provision. (Both the inter-personal abuse of men by men and by women, and violence in same sex and non-binary relationships, have received helpful policy and research attention too, as a development of these initiatives.[6])

Most importantly, the book is illustrated with direct reference to the first-hand recollections gleaned from those who 'made' this history. Since this original generation are now moving towards the end of their lives, including the author, it is important to add to the records sooner rather than later. We have moved far in this huge endeavour. It is remembered here – while many who built it are still here – as a service to the future.

What is needed is a collective, collaborative effort

What is really needed in recalling this important history of women's struggle, and of related attempts at transforming the world, is a collectively-written, collaborative effort. This would enable different, possibly contradictory, voices to be raised, including those of violence survivors, to build a textured account, produced co-operatively. After all, much of the work was done in groups and campaigns, often with the intention of combatting individual self-enhancement, and encouraging instead the collective. This larger collaborative endeavour would be for the future.

Rather, this book is designed as a starter, to record and celebrate, briefly, the women's movements and their struggles against domestic and other forms of abuse, and to highlight some of the transformative politics developed. However, so very many activists, researchers, survivors and service providers have generously and enthusiastically contributed that it has turned into at least the beginning of a collaborative project, the beginning of a collective remembering of our shared past.

A short book only: not a detailed or academic account

From the start, it needs to be noted that this is a condensed, broad brush-stroke book. It does not, and cannot, contain detailed accounts of all the complicated minutiae of the movements against violence against women, of exactly what happened when to whom, or of the complexities of both agreements and disagreements. For those seeking such detail, this book can, I hope, act as a 'pump-primer'. It is written in as light and accessible a style as possible, given the subject matter. While it does contain details of services and policies, it is designed as a relatively easy, and, in places, poetic read. The book is referenced throughout in the endnotes, but it is not meant to be an academic work.

A participant analysis

This history is written by an insider, a participant in the social movements and struggles highlighted. It reflects on something to which I as the author and others like me were, and are, totally committed. However, it is not an opinion piece. It is based on long-term activist involvement, on wider research, on study of the literature, and on specially conducted interviews and consultations.

My qualifications to write it are that I have been involved in women's and other political issues since the late 1960s, taking an active part in the building of the women's movement, from then on, and in other movements before that. Over the nearly 50 years since, I have been a gender-based violence activist, practitioner, researcher, and, later, Professor of Violence Against Women Studies at the Centre for Gender and Violence Research, University of Bristol, UK, of which I was one of the two founders (with Ellen Malos) in 1989/1990. (This Centre has always aimed, where possible, to link with activism and to raise the voices of survivors.)

It has been my huge honour to have met and worked with many inspiring violence survivors and activists in countries across the world, over this time. I am encouraged that many of the pioneers of feminist work on violence against women in this country, and elsewhere, have been happy for me, their long-term colleague, to take on the task of compiling this short book.

How the book was developed

Overall then, the book discusses political transformations from the 1960s on, focussing on the women's movements against domestic violence mainly, with some attention to sexual violence and wider forms of gender abuse. These reflections are derived from, and combined with, memories and interviews, an element of personal memoir, a selection of poems, and boxes highlighting issues or anecdotes.

As the author, I was pleased, to talk in detail with some older feminists from the beginning of the movements in the late 1960s/early 1970s. More widely, I was grateful to be able to conduct about 20 lengthy interviews/discussions, supplemented by about 30 further consultations, with those who 'were there', who carry the memories, expertise and information. Those interviewed are named in the footnote and, more fully, in the Acknowledgements.* They included key feminists, activists,

---

* Consultations and quotes were offered especially by Rebecca Dobash and Jalna Hanmer. Interviewees included: Ann Devereaux; Davina James-Hanman; Ellen Malos; Fran Wasoff; Jane Anderson; Lesley Welch; Liz Kelly; Lily Greenan; Margaret Davis; Nicola Harwin; Pragna Patel; Sarbjit Ganger; Subhaluxmi Mukherji; Teresa Parker; and various survivors. Those especially consulted included Alison Assiter and Jacky Gruhn; and further, Aisha K. Gill; Atuki Turner; Cath Kane; D-M Withers, Emma Williamson; Eleri Butler; Evan Stark; Fiona Vera-Gray; Finn Mackay; Gail Chester; Gene Feder; Harriet Wistrich, the late Harriet Wordsworth; Hilary Land; Jackie Barron; Judi Hodgkin, Kate Berry; Kathy Willis; Liz Bird: Leticia Mujeni; Marianne Hester; Mica Nava; Miriam David; Nazand Begikhani; Nicole Westmarland; Nicki Norman; Nishi Mitra; Ravi Thiara; Shahana Rasool; Sue O'Sullivan; Tais Cerqueira Silva; Trupti Jhaveri Panchal. Also Women's Aid (England); Scottish Women's Aid; Welsh Women's Aid; and Asian Women's Resource Centre, Brent; Cape Town Rape Crisis; Musasa (Zimbabwe); MIFUMI (Uganda); Older Feminist Network; Rape Crisis England and Wales; Refuge; AVA; Southall Black Sisters, Special Cells for Women and Children, India; among many others.

policy-makers, service providers, researchers and survivors of abuse, from the period. Women's Aid (England), Scottish and Welsh Women's Aids, Women's Aid Federation Northern Ireland, Rape Crisis England and Wales, and various gender violence projects in this country and internationally were consulted, including Southall Black Sisters, Asian Women's Resource Centre, the founders of AVA, and MIFUMI. Organisations like Older Feminist Network, Women's Aid and London 70s-Sisters in the UK asked for contributions from their members.

Consultations were conducted with various projects for Black and minority ethnic women and with activists from the women's movement. I also consulted with those with specific expertise on transnational feminist collaborations and on meeting the needs of different groups, for example, disabled abused women and survivors experiencing violence/killing in the name of 'honour' or their relatives. Many organisations in the field have recently passed their 40 year – or even 50 year – mark. I was able to draw on written material and exhibitions produced to celebrate these anniversaries (for example those of Scottish and Welsh Women's Aids and Southall Black Sisters), and also to consult relevant books, archives and papers, and previous histories.

What the chapters contain

This introductory chapter lays out the rationale and scope of the book. It is followed by Chapters 2 and 3 which give a brief account of some of the projects and strands of the wider women's liberation movement that ignited with huge zeal, in the 1970s. Chapter 4 looks at the early development of the passionate struggle against male violence (within the wider movement), with specific focus on domestic abuse.

Chapter 5 expands this history, briefly covering the history of combatting rape and sexual assault. Chapters 6 and 7 both look at the sometimes inspiring and radical practices and politics of the early refuges and the domestic violence movements. Between them, Chapters 8 and 9 address changes in the 1990s and 2000s, mainly in the domestic violence sector, but also regarding sexual and 'honour'-based violence and other harmful practices.

Chapter 9 also covers campaigns, legal victories, global initiatives, and wider strategic advances. Chapter 10 then discusses international responses and the role of the domestic violence shelter movement in other countries. Chapter 11 looks at the history of activist-oriented gender-based violence research and at transnational feminist approaches avoiding Western dominance. It is followed by a short end word (Chapter 12).

The word 'Black' is capitalised throughout when it applies to people and projects. This practice has been followed less in the last several years than it was in the past. However, the recent Black Lives Matters initiatives have led to the renewed use of capitalisation in many media outlets from 2020 as a sign of respect, and so it is adopted here.[7] Attention to the Black women's movement against gender-based violence and issues for Black and minority women are integrated throughout, rather than being separated off into a specific dedicated chapter. (Various Black activists in the movement were consulted about this, with opinions varying as to whether the 'specific chapter' approach would highlight the issues or alternatively [for a slight majority] might 'ghettoise' them as a kind of add-on.) Issues related to lesbians, to disabled women, working class women and others are also, where possible, integrated into the discussions, rather than separated.

Overall, this period was one of pioneering women's history and activism, but it is disappearing from our view. Many young workers in the present domestic violence sector, for example, have no idea about the history and feminist struggle which led to the services and policies which they now operate. Thus, the book begins to fill the gap. It highlights innovative political moments in this powerful history with – at its core – the raising of marginalised voices, especially those of abused women and of the valiant women activists who have worked on these issues for so long.

The wider social movements from which the women's movements arose

The struggle for women's liberation was embedded in the social and political ferments of the 1960s and 1970s. In this period, new social movements proliferated in many countries, and frequently resulted in the raising of previously unheard voices. The women's movements, and the struggle to combat the violence from men that women so often experience, grew out of this, not only in Western societies, but worldwide. It is important, then, to recognise this grounding. It seemed for a while as if attempts at social change were everywhere.

There were transformations in the Left, the Black liberation struggle, student movements, gay liberation, and the massive mobilisation in many countries against the Vietnam/American War.[8] This was the period of the expansion of movements and wars for national liberation across the globe (for example, in Angola, Algeria, Zimbabwe, Mozambique, and many more), and of resultant de-colonisation, as the flags came down on the British and other empires.[9]

Simultaneously, the great Uruguayan author and activist, the late Eduardo Galeano, was writing in his masterwork about 'the open veins of Latin America', often plumbed and drained by their dominant Northern neighbour.[10] There were the various solidarity movements, including with Allende supporters in Chile, the Sandinista movement in Nicaragua (a little later) and anti-apartheid in South Africa. And there were campaigns on the Palestine/Israeli and other Middle Eastern conflicts, and the continued (sometimes exultant, sometimes deeply problematic) development of the Cuban revolution.

In Western countries and some others, fresh ways of living and challenges to the status quo were well underway by the end of the 1960s. For example, in the UK countries, new life experiences opened up before many of the post-war generation, particularly but not solely the more privileged. In just a few further examples, the radical movements encompassed community action and activism, the Irish struggle in the North of Ireland, poor people's movements, anti-psychiatry, the peace movement, and challenges to class discrimination. There were radical bookstores, political opposition and strikes, the development of workers' rights, and the building of the trade unions in new ways, including for women.

During the 1960s and 1970s, experiments in new music, film and art challenged what had gone before. Poetry tended to throw away structure, sometimes became 'concrete', and further developed its frequent role as a contribution to liberation struggles. There were movements in theatre, as previously pioneered by Bertolt Brecht, to get rid of its fourth wall, the one between the play and the audience, and worldwide expansion of Augusto Boal's Theatre of Oppressed.[11] It was within this swirling political and broadly progressive context that thousands of women activists took up the cause, and the women's liberation movement burst into prominence.

Conclusion

From that time on, those of us who have committed considerable sections of our lives to political transformation have tried to build challenges to the status quo and to oppression in all kinds of ways, especially for women. These attempts have often been wonderfully successful. But they have not been without failure, conflict and horror at the way things have developed in some places. Nevertheless, the trajectory of this book is transformative in intent and realistically optimistic, drawing on the author's lifetime work on gendered violence. It does not avoid the subsequent loss of some of the advances made, which started out so bravely and positively. But brave and positive they were. It is worth remembering them and learning from them.

The book aims to be part of this remembering, part of these multi-stranded attempts, to make the world a better place. Perhaps, human beings together can make something finer. The violence against women movements are unashamedly part of that effort. Let us begin, then, with a look at their midwife, the women's liberation movement itself.

2

Everything seemed to change at once: women's liberation and the women's movement(s) from the 1960s

The great mobilisation of women began with a vision supported by action. The vision was of a world transformed.

Violence against women researchers,
R. E. Dobash and R. Dobash[1]

The women's liberation movement (WLM) seemed to leap into the world for those of us who were engaged in making it. One minute we were not part of it. And then we were. It was indeed the 'great mobilisation of women'. For many of us, our lives changed forever.

These next two chapters provide a brief overview of the history of this unprecedented mobilisation, including memoir and memories. They cannot claim to be comprehensive. Instead, they provide a short 'précis' about the hugely complicated social movements of women that encompassed women's liberation, with a focus mainly, but not solely, on the UK.

For more detail

For readers who would like more detail, fearless writings by dedicated feminists were produced as the women's movements in different countries were actually unfolding. There are very many fine books and archives on the subject, referenced throughout these chapters. The detailed section on sources about women's liberation at the end of Chapter 3 expands this list with a wide range of important works, including the historical work, for example, of *Sisterhood and after* and *HOWL*. Between them all, they provide precious memories and a record of the astounding contributions made by feminist writers and activists from the late 1960s on.

As a starter, they include *Sisterhood is powerful: An anthology of writing from the Women's Liberation Movement* (1970) edited by Robin Morgan, *The body politic: Writings from the Women's Liberation Movement in Britain 1969–1972* (1972) edited by Michelene Wandor, *Sweet freedom: Struggle for Women's Liberation* (1982) by Anna Coote and Beatrix Campbell, and *No turning back: Writings from the Women's Liberation Movement* (1981) by the Feminist Anthology Collective.[2]

And so it started

At the end of the 1960s, as noted in the last chapter, the anti-Vietnam War movement, and the civil rights, peace, New Left, student and Black movements were all flourishing. The national liberation movements in colonised countries had burst onto the scene, transforming world history. The Black Power movement was taking urban areas of many Western countries by storm (and, especially, although not solely, in the US, meeting violent repression as experienced, for example, by both the women and men of the Black Panthers).[3]

By the late 60s, women members of many of these movements (by no means only in the West) began to talk about how their voices were commonly silenced and ignored. They started to suggest that separate meetings for women were needed, often said to have been modelled (to some extent) on the women's version of the Chinese *Speaking Bitterness* groups (set up after the 1949 Chinese Revolution). At these new meetings, they talked about the way women were being treated, identifying the thrill and pain of shared personal feelings and experiences.

And so it started. Building on the various other social movements, women's liberation in different countries first began, probably in the US and Canada, in the late 60s.[4] The idea spread quickly to Europe and elsewhere. The term itself, 'Women's Liberation Movement', may have been brought into the light, according to many commentators, as an initiative of women who were part of SNCC (the Student Non-Violent Coordinating Committee), the pioneering and militantly activist civil rights organisation in the US which also embraced Black Power.[5] SNCC had always contained powerful women like, for example, Fannie Lou Hamer.

Then, many other women banded together and took it forward. The whole thing felt completely new at the time to the enthusiastic participants who sometimes characterised their changed awareness as like putting on a pair of 3D glasses. The 3D, they joked, showed the true nature of their lives and how women were treated by men, when previously these issues had been largely ignored or invisible to them. Some of them called it BF, or 'before feminism', transformed radically and comprehensively to AF, 'after feminism' and a new life.

Background and memoir

The late Betty Friedan, in her ground-breaking 1963 book, *The feminine mystique*, had talked, in terms of educated middle class, mainly white American women, about 'the problem that has no name'.[6] And the great French writer, trail-blazer and feminist, Simone de Beauvoir, had long since written her magnus opus, *The second sex,* back in 1949.[7] In it, she identified how life was largely defined in terms of men, and women were in the position of being 'the other'.

Thus, the women's movements were indeed new, but had precursors. Women resisting their subservient position have always existed, pretty much everywhere, but a more pronounced struggle was particularly evident in the late 19th and early 20th centuries. This was the era of the fight for the Vote for Women in many countries, and for better treatment in general, including in terms of domestic violence. The period was sometimes called the first wave. While use of the word 'wave' can be inaccurate and confusing, the activists in the 1960s/70s often called the women's liberation movement 'the second wave', and so it has remained. Since then, there have been further waves as young activists have taken up the beacon. A key component of them all has been the now well-known concept: 'The personal is political'. This has been such an important part of feminism that it needs to be flagged up at the very beginning.

The author on the display board too

The women's movements have always suggested that the author of a piece of writing should not be an invisible observer, positioned in the ether somewhere. Rather, the idea was transparency. The author's position in the world should be up for display to build accountability. And this has become de rigueur. Thus, as part of this quest for transparency, and since this book is specifically designed to contain a component of memoir, I include a little of my own history. For those not interested in such personal memoir, please skip forward to the next section, 'Where did the movement in UK countries come from? Fertile roots', or the one after, 'The new passionate movement'.

Personal memoir

On a personal level, then, I was living in Montréal, Québec, when the women's movement began, and was politically active in radical community action, setting up co-operatives and campaigning as an active white ally of the Black liberation movement, an awkward position to negotiate at times during the Black Power era. I was part of a free-living, politically active international community in which only a couple of members were white. I had stayed in the haven of Mexico City with exiled revolutionaries from Latin America, and, in Montréal, I moved among a group of politicised young women and men from Latin America, Egypt, the Caribbean, Vietnam, South Africa and elsewhere, including African Americans in flight (literally) from the violently racist US of the day.

The times were exciting and hard, with student uprisings, and political and social turmoil everywhere. In 1968, for example, the much-remembered Montréal Congress of Black Writers, guarded by Black Panthers in their uniforms, was addressed by Stokeley Carmichael, Miriam Makeba and C.L.R. James. (Eldridge Cleaver was meant to attend, but was said to have dropped underground the week before.)

Later, in 1970, I remember people hiding in cupboards, when the Canadian Government imposed the War Measures Act (in response to the actions of the Front de Libération du Québec). All civil liberties were suspended, with tanks and thousands of soldiers on the streets. Friends were imprisoned or deported to hostile regimes, and to probable persecution or death. Overall, we fought corporate developers and the police, and some of us took big risks (smuggling banned left-wing political items, or people who were fleeing, through the US border, for example). Initially my friends and I felt that the new women's groups which appeared in about 1969 were indulgent – a distraction really from the sometimes dangerous issues around which we were campaigning.

But I quickly learned better. I joined groups and campaigns, finding my own identity in the power of women's voices raised against injustices – in making a movement of our own. I took an active part in women's liberation, back in the UK, from 1971 on, also worked for the rights of excluded communities, for example children in care, and devoted myself to the violence against women struggle when it started.

Where did the movement in UK countries come from? Fertile roots

The women's liberation movement in the UK's countries grew out of complex and fertile roots. The generation that made it was mainly born at the end of the Second World War and after the Holocaust. They/we were fortunate to live when we did in Europe, especially those of us, who, due to the huge expansion of universities in the UK in the early 1960s, had access for the very first time in our family histories to higher education. We grew up as more or less the first generation who did not face conscription into the armed services, or have to either go to war or face the impacts of war at home.

We were also the very first generation in history where women were able substantially to control their child-bearing, with contraception available in a brand new way for wives. Increasingly, it was available for women who weren't married too. Unbelievably, to begin with, women in heterosexual relationships could avoid getting pregnant unless they wanted to. Although this could lead to difficult or abusive pressures from men, the lives of women could be transformed, and many were. It was a development our mothers and grandmothers, tied to child-bearing, could not have dreamed of.

It wasn't all glowing. In Britain after the War ended, there were the growing revelations about the horror of the Holocaust, its aftermath, and anti-Semitism. There were also deep fears about the imminent threat of nuclear bombs being used which we often felt was real and very likely. To grow up in the 1950s was to face a period of intense austerity (in my case, food and clothes rationing till age nine, with food rationing eventually ending in 1954). Bananas were more or less unknown at first, and viewed as priceless treasures when they started arriving. There were bomb sites all around where my family lived in London, and post-war trauma and poverty.

In a personal anecdote, my mother (unimaginably to me) had been bombed out twice in the city, the second time after marrying, but she was alone, with my father in the War away at sea. She lost both homes in totality and almost everything she owned each time, but escaped very narrowly with her life. Our first rented (and unheated) childhood home in the mid-to-late 1940s was a flat which had three-inch wide cracks in the ceiling, opening up to a scary, unknown black space above. They were the result of bombing which had completely destroyed the rest of the terrace. I would crouch underneath them, aged 4, keeping a strict eye on the ominous darkness through the cracks, regarding them with silent terror. After 70 years, they still populate my nightmares.

As time went on, things got better in the post-war period. There was the beginning of prosperity for many, a recovering country, but also continued social rigidity and strict division of gender roles which we never really questioned. Almost no one did back then. Slowly, in the 1950s, came almost universal male employment (women often working within the home). There were welfare provisions courtesy of the 1945–1950 Labour Government and new material inventions (for example, the exciting beginning of TVs, record players, washing machines and fridges). Crucially, there was medical care free at the point of delivery, the redoubtable NHS. My friends and I knew we had been the new welfare state babies. The government had given us free orange juice and cod liver oil, after all. Born at the end of the horrors of world war, we very often felt that we were inheriting a different, new world and we were its vanguard. Almost everyone at the time believed strongly and optimistically in 'progress'.

By the 60s, there was the burgeoning of new progressive political movements and a resurgent different sort of radical Left that felt attractive. There were full grants, including fees, for those who went to university (still a small minority despite the huge expansion). And there was the acceleration in the breakdown in Britain's entrenched class relations to some extent, including some opportunities (many lost now) for working class young people to move, like my own partner, into a different world of higher education and jobs.

It began to seem that endless new adventures and social developments opened up before many of us in the UK's countries and elsewhere. And it was also a period when conservative ideas about sexual relationships were breaking down. There was recreational drug use, new music everywhere and exciting possibilities for how (mainly heterosexual) young people could behave (women as well as men, despite men being mainly in control, and the existence of something we often felt, but only later learned to call 'sexism'). Many of us could see injustices in the world and wanted to make it better, and we felt we had the freedom to do so. It was fertile ground for women's liberation.

The new passionate movement

The new passionate, enthusiastic movement that resulted from all this was totally fresh, but also learned from, and was embedded in, what had gone before. How women's liberation and feminism were defined and understood varied widely, both then and now. In her 2015 book, *Radical feminism*, Finn Mackay states that: 'feminism as a social movement can be defined in a very broad sense as a global, political movement for the liberation of women and society based on equality for all people'.[8] Many commentators emphasised the importance of the word 'liberation' as something which was more transformative and revolutionary than equal treatment. Transformation implied hoped-for (and fought-for) changes for women in almost every area of political, cultural, societal and economic life.

In the nearly 50 years since that time, the feminist movements have diversified and have resulted in huge changes for women in many Western countries and across the world. Those who lived through the historical period previous to the 1960s can attest to the subsequent changes in the position of women in general, in many places. Anyone tempted to dispute the gains made could perhaps try going back to live as a woman in the UK countries in the 1950s.

The improvements for women must, however, be considered alongside setbacks, backlash and the ongoing sexism, misogyny, and attacks on women that continue today, as recently highlighted by the high profile #MeToo and #Time's Up movements (themselves only possible because of the previous decades of work on men's abuse of women). But, looking back, the gains have been extraordinary, and so was the movement itself. Social movements can give rise to visionary and hopeful ideas[9], and this was certainly the case. In those early days, the women's movement was full of excitement and zeal, a heady mix, with new realisations, personal transformations and campaigns emerging in rapid succession.

Consciousness-raising

Being part of women's groups was foundational to women's liberation – and a new way of organising was quick to emerge. This was the Consciousness-Raising (CR) Group, evolving directly out of the new movement. Used as an organising tool, this type of group went on to make a remarkable contribution to building social change. The idea was to share personal experiences and, together, to develop new understandings and analysis about women's subordinate position and about both social and political issues. Thus, practice fed directly into theorising, and theorising led back into practice and action.

Esteemed feminist, Jalna Hanmer explained in a 2010 interview for *Sisterhood and after* that:

> The reason you had to be in one of the groups – was because the groups met. That *was* the women's liberation movement. ... It was all about being in a group and women talking about their personal situation – what was wrong with it, what could be done about it – to try to bring about changes to a more satisfactory life.
>
> They were all required to talk because that is the way you discover your oppression. It made a lot of sense. And it actually worked as a system. Because women *didn't* understand why they felt so bad, they couldn't see why ... they *didn't* understand why they couldn't do the things they wanted to do. It was just a kind of terrible mystery. So it was only by talking about it that there began to be some understanding. And it was really understanding about oppression. And where did the oppression come from. And who is oppressing me. And how can this be overcome. These were really quite basic life questions that we were grappling with.[10]

The first-ever women's consciousness-raising group is thought to have been set up by the pioneer 1960s radical feminist group, New York Radical Women (later to become Red Stockings in 1969). In 1967, a first group was held (which involved the late Shulamith Firestone who subsequently wrote her feminist classic, *The dialectic of sex: The case for feminist revolution* published in 1970[11]). CR groups then multiplied rapidly in the US and in other mainly, but not solely, Western, countries. In the UK countries, CR groups were formed, also in the late 1960s, with the first possibly in Hull.

In London, a group in Tufnell Park started in 1969, with the participation of left-wing women from the US, campaigning against the Vietnam War. Various other groups were set up in London and Leeds also in 1969, and then in Bristol. Quite rapidly, several groups in London joined together into a larger group to form the Women's Liberation Workshop which loosely coordinated women's liberation activities in the city from then on. They published the much-prized magazine, *Shrew*, and also the separate *London Women's Liberation Newsletter* from 1969 till 1978.

Some Black women's groups and left-wing organisations criticised the CR method as too introspective, when vital fights needed to be fought, against racism and the fascist National Front of the time. This was a fundamental and important critique. But CR groups were never meant to be just discussion or therapy-type groups. The aim ideally was to lead to action. At the group meetings, there would often be a theme to provide focus. Women would share intimate personal experiences and insights, sometimes talking about these things for the first time ever. The idea was to develop awareness of discriminatory and unfair situations that women members faced in order to fight to change them. CR led to the development of collectively-derived personal, political and social analyses of women's lives and of understandings of how these were inter-related.[12]

Women interviewed for this book spoke about CR groups being enlightening and exhilarating, as if their eyes were suddenly opened. Two long-term feminists who separately discussed the book with me used almost the same words about how they suddenly realised, almost like a lightning bolt over and over again (as different subjects came up), that: "You were not alone. It suddenly all made sense." The groups were women-only of course, and were safe spaces where participants could (at best) feel confident and relaxed, and could work together to make something new and challenging to society.

Thus, women began to explore their own histories and to develop the idea of shared resistance. These realisations could be entirely life-changing, exploring what was often (at the time) uncharted territory. The political realisations made extended to issues like the structure of the nuclear family, its impact on women and children, and the position of men in society. Some groups talked about living under a capitalist system, racism, supporting strikes and political actions, class differences and anti-lesbianism, leading the way to both new campaigns and transformed lives. Everything came up for discussion, from the most intimate issues for women to the widest.

For myself, I was in several CR groups over the years in Canada and the UK, and I remember how new issues came up all the time that we had never thought about in such a way before. These could range from poor treatment by male colleagues, to women being trapped looking after the children, to abortion (and support for those who had had one), to unequal pay. (In 1970, women in the UK earned only about 65 per cent of what men did.)[13] There were quite often reflections on sex and how women could achieve sexual fulfilment.

There might be discussion of our deepest emotions and personal traumas, and how they were affected by issues from the behaviour of men towards women on the streets, to pornography, sexual violations, rape and violence against women. We might also discuss who precisely cleaned the toilets in our (frequently collective) houses, wearing make-up or not, and personal hygiene issues, especially men's, perhaps. The idea, though, was that the discussions were always anchored by our own experiences. As time went on, some groups began to consider moving towards lesbianism and to being 'woman-identified', as some of our (many) badges at the time used to say.

This type of approach endures in some long-term women's groups, including a CR group, originally at the Institute of Education, established in 1976 and still very active. Members have lived their lives side-by-side and now grown old together, a priceless gift for all, perhaps. When consulted for this book, one of its members, long-term feminist and cultural historian, Mica Nava, said: "We gave each other courage." She added: "CR meant different things in different places. For some groups the focus was on being mothers, or on politics and raising consciousness elsewhere, or sexuality. There wasn't one form of consciousness-raising at all."

Carrying on the women's liberation flame, CR features in the work currently of groups like the Older Feminist Network and London 70s-Sisters, and some of the women's groups set up as part of the #MeToo movement. The organisation Extinction Rebellion also uses methods like this sometimes. It could be that a return to this technique of sharing experiences and then organising (much as in participatory action methods) would be of benefit to other progressive and feminist causes today. Revisiting CR could be a grounded and thoughtful way forward.

On the one hand: patriarchy

CR was a direct manifestation of those dramatic words, 'the personal is political'. This concept was a far-reaching and complex one that actually required a lot of thinking about, and that helped to bring passion and commitment to the making of political change. The understandings which participants developed in their groups were about the way that male control across society very often resulted in women being diminished or contained in myriad ways. As women's liberation gradually identified the wide (sometimes called 'hegemonic') nature of such control and dominance by men, there began to be talk about the term patriarchy.

Feminists have gone on talking about it ever since. They generally used, and use, the word in a broad way to imply male domination and power, rather than in its original usage of a patriarch controlling his individual family and family line. However, it is not utilised in a simplistic way, either. For many years, feminist analysts have been pointing out that patriarchy cannot be viewed as one entity, permeating people's existence in a single way.[14] It's a complicated and ever-changing phenomenon, operating differently in different contexts.

The term has been in and out of fashion, but has almost always been thought of as being attached to structures of power, including in terms of social class and unequal wealth, but which focussed on the dominance of men across the world. While some people object to the word, what it succinctly references has proved very resistant to change. In 50 years of campaigning action by many women, much of it has led to successes, and to the enormous advances made since the women's liberation movements emerged. But patriarchal relations across the spectrum of society and the world have tended to endure, as discussed by Miriam David[15] and others, even if sometimes in modified or decreased forms.

Even after a half century of women's activism, if you look at the membership of governments across the world or at, say, high-level global meetings, world religions, trade union bosses, those in power in the media and local authorities, CEOs of companies, the armed forces, the controlling bodies of multinational corporations, what can be observed about women? Well, of course, what you quickly see is that they are scarcely there. Despite some noted improvements and the dogged fights put up by women in all these sectors, male domination and power remain, even if considerably dented. The people who control the world still tend to be mainly men. It is not hard to discern.

On the other hand: collectives and new ways of organising

In response to these gathering realisations back in the 1960s and 1970s, the early women's movement took to organising and campaigning. It was an extraordinary outburst of new activity and action. The organising groups that were set up almost always used a new way of working, which was also prevalent in other social movements of the time. This was collectives. Pretty much everything was done in collective organisations where everyone had an equal say – or as equal a say as possible. No one was the boss or had power over anyone else.

This magnificently brave way of doing things was everywhere. Quite quickly, there were women's collectives to produce newsletters, to make music, to discuss sexual abuse in families, to struggle against role divisions in domestic labour, to set up conferences, to write plays, to publish books, to organise marches and campaigns, and to challenge the government. The list was endless. Communication was unrecognisable to how it is now. There were telephone trees (to contact each other), but no printers yet, with photocopiers few and far between, and too expensive for multiple use. So – vitally at the time – there was also collective organising of who did the duplicating/mimeographing which was usually smudged and purple, as the fingers of those doing it often were, too.

There was an attempt within this to challenge traditional ways of doing things, including how to hold meetings and to make decisions. Possibly boring procedures operated by much of the Left and the union movement were often jettisoned. While someone almost certainly jotted down some notes, there were to be no more rigid procedures, minutes of meetings, motions, amendments or 'any other business' sections. The women's groups evolved new ways of collective decision-making. Chairmen became chairwomen or chairpersons, taking the role on a rotating basis, or disappeared completely. Everyone had to take responsibility.

This led to exciting new ways of doing things co-operatively, and many innovations were invented in how to organise, and then tried out. These included, for example, how to be sure everyone spoke in the meeting (hard), how to make decisions collaboratively and not just by majority (hard), how to get the actions decided upon actually done (hard), and so on. Everything was taken on, often enthusiastically and in ways that had not previously been attempted – and everything was up for grabs. Real steps forward in collective organising were made.

There were also some critiques, famously for example, in the pamphlet 'The tyranny of structurelessness' by American feminist, Jo Freeman.[16] This still-quoted work was distributed like wildfire through the movement from 1970 on, sometimes officially published in different publications, but sometimes bootlegged without permission or credit. It is worth saying that this admittedly was how things tended to be done at the time. Formal publications were often to be frowned on, as tainted by the dead hand of editorial, monetary and possibly male control, and of officialdom and repression.

The pamphlet discussed issues about structure-free collectives, including the frequently-experienced difficulty of how – even if there was no one in charge – informal hidden leaders emerged and took control, sometimes without anyone realising, and with no official channel through which to challenge them. Power differentials between women of different social classes, sexualities, ethnic backgrounds, education levels, degrees of confidence and life experiences were difficult to sort out. However, collectives remained in action then, and some remain now, albeit sometimes with a reintroduction of some jointly agreed procedures. (Collectives in the violence against women movement are discussed in detail in Chapters 6 and 7.)

Groups and campaigns erupt almost daily

Quite quickly, then, this new women's movement of the late 1960s/early 1970s (mainly in the West initially), with its exuberant commitment to collective working and CR, gained passionate adherents. Things seemed to change by the day. A torrent of events, groups and political actions erupted, with new ones emerging all the time. Meeting someone who had been involved for a whole two years, I remember my women's group at the time being totally overwhelmed with awe at such unimaginably long experience of so many changes.

Some of the earliest political actions were protests against the objectification of women in the Miss World contests of the time. These protests attracted international publicity in 1968 in Atlantic City in the US, in actions coordinated by the famed American feminist, Robin Morgan, and were followed in 1970 by similarly passionate Miss World protests in the UK at the Albert Hall, London. Also in 1970, the Ruskin History Group Women's Conference (organised by women like Sally Alexander, Sheila Rowbotham and Anna Davin) was held at Ruskin College, Oxford. The Ruskin conference has gone down in history as the key, formative moment in the women's movement. It led to an explosion of CR groups and, importantly, developed the first 'Four Demands' of the movement: 1) equal pay, 2) equal education, 3) free contraception and abortion on demand, and 4) free 24-hour nurseries. These were formally adopted at the second national conference in 1971 in Skegness.

The movement quickly developed Women's Centres where collectives and groups could meet, and pregnancy testing was often held. Groups, frequently operating from these Women's Centres, were set up in towns and cities around the country in quick succession. This led to a dizzying variety of campaigns (and sometimes to complexities within and between them), and to passionate debates and huge zeal-full leaps forward.

Women's liberation was critiqued almost from the beginning (sometimes by itself) as being mainly made up of educated and relatively privileged women (often white, as discussed later). But there was also an ongoing working class women's history which prolific feminist and socialist historian, Sheila Rowbotham (mentioned above as an organiser of the famous Ruskin conference), has highlighted. (Two of her most important books were *Women resistance and revolution* (1972) and *Hidden from history* (1973), both devoured eagerly by many in the movement.[17]) In 1968, there had been the historic Women's strike at the huge Ford factory at Dagenham where women machinists went on strike for equal wages with men. In a very successful action, the factory was brought to its knees.[18]

They won an improvement in their pay grade, with participation by the well-known veteran Labour MP, Barbara Castle, Minister of Employment at the time. Mind you, they had to strike again in 1984 to access the next pay grade. But their struggle was unprecedented in 1968 and paved the way for the Equal Pay Act of 1970, supplemented by the Sex Discrimination Act of 1975 forbidding discrimination between men and women at work. While equal pay for equal work has still not been achieved, these Acts have been massively important for women.

In 1971/1972, another important struggle by women workers was the Night Cleaners Campaign, led by May Hobbs, a militant cleaner, working for a contract company. This was a brave and ferocious fight in which the women's movement was very involved, to improve pay and conditions for office cleaners and to increase unionisation. After a remarkable struggle, it was victorious. Hobbs wrote a book of her life.[19] Modern day night, and other, office cleaners are once again un-unionised and, very often, face terrible pay, zero hours' contracts, and damaging work situations. The crucial importance of unionisation for improving working conditions for women (and men), and the heroic actions of women like May Hobbs to fight for the rights of women workers, could be revisited and learned from today, when so many unions have been decimated, and workers left unprotected and facing discriminatory working conditions.[20]

Back in the times of the women's liberation movement, groups of women campaigned tirelessly, tending to favour (at the time) direct action to having any truck with conventional electoral politics. Women often lived together in co-operative shared houses. Childcare was frequently also shared. Crèches at meetings were commonly run by anti-sexist men (although this changed as time went on, and women-only events evolved). Back then, there were no child protection checks and policies, or health and safety rules. Or, if there were, no one knew about them. It seems that it mainly worked out OK, though. The children often had wild and wonderful times.

Feminist newsletters, presses and books

A plethora of women's newsletters developed at the time. These newsletters were distributed both locally and nationally to spread the word. They were produced by much unpaid volunteer work and complex duplicating, usually in the afore-mentioned purple ink on sporadically working (and then doggedly not-working) mimeograph machines. The most influential was the national internal newsletter, *WIRES* (Women's Information Referral and Enquiry Service), which played a critical role in spreading information about the movement from 1975.[21] Until *WIRES* started, there was the *News from Women's Liberation* (1972–1975). Also, there were the *London Women's Liberation Newsletter*, the *RevRad Newsletter*, the *Libertarian Women's Network Newsletter*, lesbian and Black women's newsletters, and many local ones, for example, the *Leeds, Nottingham* and *Bradford Women's Liberation Newsletters*.

A remembrance of those times: a group of local feminists used to meet monthly for a whole day to produce the *Bristol Women's Liberation Newsletter* in someone's house. I have a memory, in the early 80s, of a friend's young son (who used to come along to the production days) adroitly choosing the 'Women's Liberation Newsletter' in a later game of 'Guess the Object'.

Everyone tried and tried and tried, but none of us were remotely able to guess it. Cheers from all as he revealed the answer, and he was bright with pleasure at his triumph.

Alongside newsletters were magazines and journals, in profusion, including *Spare Rib*, the best known across the UK, which was read very widely. *Spare Rib* occasionally triggered huge controversy, for example, over anti-Semitism and anti-Zionism in 1982. Totally iconic then and now, *Spare Rib* ran from 1972 for 21 years. It is archived at the British Library. There was the also iconic *Ms Magazine* in the States, still publishing, and particularly associated with the legendary feminist, Gloria Steinem.

In the US, too, *Off Our Backs* was a long-running and influential feminist publication between 1970 and 2008, and *Sinister Wisdom,* a lesbian literary and art journal is the longest-running lesbian journal (from 1975) to date. In the UK, there was the socialist feminist collective and magazine, *Red Rag* (from 1972/1973). There were *Scarlet Women, Outwrite, Catcall,* the lesbian-focussed *Sappho, Trouble and Strife* (a bit later), and many others. These were rapidly followed by the setting up of women's, lesbian and Black women's presses and printing collectives which specifically published books by women to chronicle the new movement.

One of the first of these new books was *Wedlocked women* by Lee Comer (Sanders) which was published by ground-breaking Feminist Books.[22] There were also, among many presses, Sheba Press, OnlyWomen Press, and, famously, both Virago established in 1973, and the Women's Press established in 1978. Later, came women's bookstores like Sisterwrite in Islington, London, together with feminist fiction and a cornucopia of women's writing.

In North America in the 1970s and 1980s, there were a great many feminist presses, and they included the Boston Women's Health Book Collective which published the still much-loved *Our bodies, ourselves*, with four million copies sold since 1970.[23] Wonderful new feminist novels were produced by women like the late Marilyn French, and ground-breaking African American writers began to emerge at this time, although not necessarily identifying with feminism by name. They included the late Toni Morrison, Alice Walker, the late Toni Cade Bambara (writing a few years later), and of course the late phenomenal Maya Angelou.

A notable (somewhat later) press was Kitchen Table Women of Color Press established by long-term American lesbian writer and teacher, Barbara Smith. The Press published the key collection, *This bridge called my back: Writings by radical women of colour* (in many editions).[24] Kitchen Table was set up at the suggestion of the much-celebrated Black lesbian feminist activist and poet, Audre Lorde. Her collection *Sister outsider* showcased some of her many incisive writings.[25] She died in 1992, and is still deeply admired and missed. She was one of the most magnificent.

Adding to the Four Demands amid a multitude of conferences

National UK women's liberation conferences were held from the 1970 Ruskin conference on, and were hugely important to the movement, until the final (somewhat acrimonious) one in Birmingham in 1978. They debated very serious issues, and also were occasions to meet up and interact with feminists from across this, and other, countries. There was always an atmosphere of excitement and exhilarating possibility, despite furious debate and disagreement, often. I have light-hearted memories from both the Bristol Women's Liberation Conference (1973) and the Edinburgh one (1974) of women challenging convention by stripping to the waist to dance at the (women-only) evening discos, or to swim, swimsuit-free (in the swimming pool of Bristol Student Union, for example). A friend describes standing at the door of the disco trying valiantly to deflect the oncoming male security guards who wanted to know what was going on. She succeeded.

More seriously, at the 1974 conference in Edinburgh, the 'Fifth Demand' for legal and financial independence for women was added to the original four. This campaign, colloquially called 'YBA Wife', followed on from the Family Allowance (later renamed Child Benefit) Campaign. It was built on painstaking research and activism by feminists like Ruth Lister and Mary McIntosh, Hilary Land, Angela Mason and Katherine Gieve. They organised a new campaign about the way that women were structurally disadvantaged and that marriage itself held them in inferior financial and legal positions. The new Demand highlighting these issues was then formally adopted by the women's liberation movement at the Edinburgh conference. Related to this, a memorable slogan of the time was 'You start off sinking into his arms and end up with your arms in his sink'.

Lesbian liberation

In Edinburgh, too, the 'Sixth Demand' was formally adopted. This was for rights and recognition for lesbians an end to discrimination, and also for sexual freedom and the right of a woman to define her own sexuality. This comprehensive demand was the culmination of a triumphant campaign by lesbian feminists for recognition and support. Lesbians had initially had to struggle to be part of women's liberation. In the States, for instance, the 'Lavender Menace' group, originally formed at the suggestion of author Rita Mae Brown, mounted powerful guerrilla-type actions to highlight the exclusion of lesbians from the 1970 Congress to Unite Women in New York. There was much discussion of being lesbian in the early days in the UK countries too, and a great many groups contained both lesbian and heterosexual women. This issue ignited in the early 1970s and, as time went on, lesbian feminism formed a strong 'movement within the movement' in North America, and also in the UK.[26]

D-M Withers (2018) suggests that: 'During the feminist revolution of the 1970s, the lesbian community emerged as a newly visible, politically energized group, determined to speak and to be heard as women who loved women.'[27] Recalling this crucially important move forward for the WLM, Lynn Alderson and Sheila Shulman wrote in 1983 about 'Writing our own history: When lesbians came out in the movement'.[28] The first National Lesbian Conference was in 1974, developing from, and giving rise to, a plethora of lesbian groups, presses, networks and campaigns. From 1982, the Camden Lesbian Centre, later joining with the Black Lesbian Group, was the first of many lesbian centres that were then established. Lesbian Line was set up in 1977, followed by other specialist lesbian helplines. (Lesbian feminism is further discussed in the next chapter.)

The independent Black women's movement

Black women started autonomous Black feminist groups in the 1970s, often as a result of dissatisfaction with the women's liberation movement and of feeling they did not 'fit' in it. While some mainly white groups did take on issues of racism in solidarity, others were seemingly oblivious and failed to deal with the racist oppression that Black women faced. Overall, Black feminists taking up women's issues had often been already involved in the wider and very active Black movement. They had been struggling perhaps against immigration and deportation policies, against imperialism and colonialism, poor treatment in the health service, unfair and racist housing and employment practices, discriminatory treatment of Black children at school, public and police harassment of Black men, and Black women too, on the street, and active, deadly fascist groups. Naked racism was everywhere, resulting in wide-ranging vibrant Black movements and the Black Uprisings in 1981 in Brixton (London), Toxteth (Liverpool), Handsworth (Birmingham), Chapeltown (Leeds), Moss Side (Manchester), Bristol (in 1980) and elsewhere.

An independent Black women's movement (separate to some extent from both the Black and women's movements) began to evolve in response to this widespread and pervasive racism and also to women's subjugation. Redoubtable activists, including the late Olive Morris, and Gerlin Bean, Liz Obi and Stella Dadzie, among others, some associated with the Black Panthers in the UK, set up pioneering initiatives. These included the Brixton Black Women's Group, set up in 1973, leading later to the Black Women's Centre, the first-ever such centre in the UK's countries, with both feminist and anti-racist, anti-imperialist principles.

In 1978, they established OWAAD, the Organisation of Women of African and Asian Descent, dealing with anti-imperialist and national liberation issues in Africa and Asia, as well as the UK. Taking a position independent of white feminists, this leading and umbrella organisation campaigned widely, from 1978 till 1982, on issues including deportation, immigration, aggressive policing of young Black people, school exclusion of Black children, domestic violence, and Black women being used as subjects for unproven contraceptive testing.

Separate conferences for Black feminists began in 1979 with the first pioneering OWAAD conference. OWAAD also produced a newsletter, *Fowaad*. Many Black women's groups were formed and flourished from then on, in various cities, and the important book, *Heart of the race* (1985) by Beverley Bryan, Stella Dadzie and Suzanne Scafe documented the impact of the autonomous Black women's movement.[29] Fighting racism and sexism together in this way meant that some Black women rejected the word feminism as white-identified. These issues are also discussed in Chapter 3.

Campaigns, demonstrations, music, art: more and more of everything

Further new groups set up included those established by Latin American, African-Caribbean, Jewish, Turkish, Chinese, and South Asian women, and many others. Some women developed lesbian liberation in relation to other identities with the proliferation, for example, of Black lesbian, Asian Lesbian, Jewish lesbian, or Irish lesbian groups, campaigns, newsletters and networks. Other groups challenged discrimination against working class women with many discussions held (and some conflicts erupting) about the meaning and impact of social class.

Some groups worked for equality for disabled women (alongside the disability liberation movement), and, later, for women with learning difficulties and mental health challenges. But, in general – and although many organisations like the *London Women's Liberation Newsletter* collective did their absolute best – the movement was often somewhat careless about access issues for disabled women, a discriminatory and ill-informed attitude which was directly challenged by the pioneering organisation, Sisters Against Disablement (SAD) from the early 1970s.

In this spectacular range of activity, the changes were almost daily and seemed to cover all areas of life including, importantly, challenging violence against women, discussed in later chapters. There were feminist art projects, 'teach yourself self-defence' groups, and genital self-examination groups to break down inhibitions and to teach women about their cervixes and clitorises. Performance actions and events were common, including those of the very irreverent agitprop SisterShow in Bristol. Unannounced, for example, SisterShow women would burst into a room hosting a serious women's conference discussion on difficult (and perhaps rather boring) issues. They would gleefully hurl heaps of mixed up, irrelevant words, scrawled on bits of paper, into the midst of their serious academic sisters – and run out again. Their sisters would likely be left, rooted to the spot, and mouths open in surprise.

This particular story was related to me by Pat VT West, a leader of SisterShow, in hospital a few days before she died in 2008. It was a powerful conversation that I will, of course, always remember – and with warmth and laughter. We both laughed completely helplessly then, even though she was crushed with terminal pain.

One of SisterShow's actions features in the following poem, written in the mid-1990s. The main male speaker at the event described was the late and admired John Berger, and one of the women was Pat.

Women in art: a public debate

A quarter of a century later,
and they're still talking about it –
how those crazed women
appeared from nowhere
in big hats,
and hurled radishes.

Just as some noble, sane men,
were valiantly explaining
'the nude in art'.

And yes,
they had contritely and
authoritatively discovered,

in full support of
the women's liberation
cause of course,
that men
were the 'doers' in Art
and women merely surveyed.

With what sagacity
the clever men spoke,
supporters of feminism to a man –
and very comfortably off.
And in they burst, those two women,
tore off most of their clothes,

across the righteous male droning,
painted their bodies
lewdly with thick paint,
hugged the wise men
with paint-encrusted arms,
rubbed bright wet pigment

into the carefully selected suits.
And legged it to safety,
making it clear to everyone,
even after a quarter of century,
just who the Women's Revolution
actually belongs to.

There were feminist poetry collectives, Black and lesbian film collectives, discos, dance projects and events, and the production of women's or lesbian plays. Feminist theatre groups included (among many) the ground-breaking Women's Theatre Group (later Sphinx Theatre), Gay Sweat Shop, Cunning Stunts, Beryl and the Perils, Sadista Sisters, the Theatre of Black Women (producing pioneering Black women's theatre for the very first time), and Monstrous Regiment (named after a diatribe against the 'monstrous regiment' of women in 1588 by reformer, John Knox).

Musicians formed women's music groups and feminist bands, producing feminist songs and entertaining women at many events, protests, benefits and social get-togethers. For example, there were weekly discos at London's Drill Hall Theatre, which also hosted the fabulously innovative annual lesbian feminist pantomime. Feminist bands included the Northern Women's Liberation Rock Band, Ova, the Slits, Stepney Sisters, Jam Today, Frankie Armstrong, the Guest Stars and many others. Holly Near was, and remains, a highly influential American feminist singer, along with women like Alex Dobkin, Meg Christian, Cris Williamson and the long-term Black activist, Bernice Johnson Reagon with her group, Sweet Honey in the Rock. The entirely iconic Michigan Womyn's Music Festival in the US started in 1976 (and ran till 2015).

Women's demonstrations played a key part in the women's movement, especially the yearly celebrations on International Women's Day on 8 March. These led on from the first historic and exciting Women's Liberation March in the UK on 6 March 1971. There were also marches of women workers, of lesbians, of Black women, marches for women's equal employment, for nurseries, decent housing – the list was endless. Especially perhaps, there were demonstrations for abortion on demand, following on from the previous 1967 Abortion Act (which provides for abortion in laid-down circumstances). The Women's Abortion and Contraception Campaign (WACC) operated in the early 1970s.

Then in 1975, the vibrant National Abortion Campaign, NAC, burst onto the scene. In the next few years, feminists had to defend the Abortion Act several times against Private Members Bills, seeking to restrict it, and against other attacks. Abortion legislation continues to be vulnerable to attack in this, and other mostly Western countries (where it exists). In 2021, this is most particularly the case in the US with abortion rights being entirely reversed in several states. But the NAC in the 1970s and 1980s in the UK was stunningly successful and packed with dedicated activists, fending off (in the main) various restrictive amendments to the Act. Its archives are at the Wellcome Library in London.

Women and Manual Trades (Women on the Tools) was set up in the UK in about 1975 (and still continues), supporting women workers entering traditional male occupations like construction. Similarly, women's workshops were set up to teach furniture-making and carpentry to women, which many still do. There was a huge amount of work by women attempting to reform the trade union and labour movements in terms of women's issues, which has also continued ever since. The Working Women's Charter was a campaign for women's rights at work which gained wide support. Its launch and 14 demands were met with exhilaration in 1974 (though few have yet been achieved).

In 1976 came the famous Grunwick strike at a London film processing plant, started and dominated by women of South Asian descent, who had been fired for trying to organise a trade union. They were led by the late, redoubtable Jayaben Desai. The strike was a pivotal moment in labour movement history. After a hard fight to be taken seriously by mainly white male trade unionists, they eventually gained support across both the union and labour movements, with many workers collecting money and arriving at the plant en masse to picket in solidarity and to support the women strikers. Grunwick changed the face of UK trade unionism, for a while at least. And struggles for the rights of Asian, African and African-Caribbean workers gave rise to specific Black trade union groups, for women as well as men.

Later, there were organisations like Women in Black, which has been supporting women persecuted in other countries and campaigning for peace and justice since 1988. The redoubtable organisation Women against Fundamentalism (of all types) was set up in 1989. Members of both groups have continued steadfastly taking on these difficult issues for 30 years. In 1984, Women Against Pit Closures, consisting of miners' wives joined by feminists, supported the 1984–1985 Miners Strike. And then there were the many women's peace camps of the early 1980s, and the huge efforts feminists put into fighting war.[30] This culminated in the famous Greenham Common Women's Peace Camp which, from 1981, campaigned against the installation of Cruise nuclear missiles at the Greenham US Air base, Berkshire. In 1983, the Embrace the Base protest included 30,000 women joining hands to encircle the base. The camp lasted for 19 years.

Regular Women's Group meetings in one small city from their Women's Liberation Newsletter, September 1983

Angry Women	Women and education
Asian women's group	Women and housing group
Black Women and Wages for Housework	Women and Ireland campaign
Black women's group	Women and Troops Out (Ireland)
Campaign for women's rights	Women's karate and self-defence
Co-counselling	group
Consciousness-raising group	Women's voice readers group
Disco collective	Women in moving pictures (WIMP)
Incest survivors	Working class women's group
Latin American Women group	Women against pornography
Lesbian disco	Women against media myths
Lesbian women's group	Women's health group
Mothers for peace	Women against racism and fascism
Motherhood group	(WARF)
National Abortion Campaign	Women in manual trades
Newcomers weekly welcome meeting	Women in social work
(introducing new women to the WLM)	Women's self-help therapy
Polytechnic women's group	Women oppose the nuclear threat
Pregnancy Testing at the Women's	(WONT)
Centre	Women's therapy group
Radical feminist meeting	Women's history group
Rape Crisis Line	Working with girls group
Socialist feminist group	Women writers group
Wages for Housework	Women's workshop collective
Well women information group	Working with girls group
Women's Aid	Women's book collective
Women against Deportations	University women's group
Campaign	Newsletter collective
Women and Art group	Women's Centre Steering group

Finally in this inevitably partial remembrance, challenging violence against women was a huge effort in the women's movement. The subject of the final 'Seventh Demand', it gave rise to pioneering initiatives like rape crisis, Women's Aid, and Reclaim the Night, fighting to make the streets safe for women. These are discussed from Chapter 4 onwards.

A dazzling array

In sum then, over the 1970s and since, innumerable campaigning, action and discussion groups were set up. It was such a dazzling array that it is hard to comprehend it all. In a final set of examples to illustrate the breadth of it, these included groups on women's health and mental health, feminist therapy and counselling, women's poverty, claiming benefits, where to find separate lesbian feminist living spaces, and fighting racism, fascism and anti-Semitism. There was *Shocking Pink* magazine (published for and by young women), Black women's comedy and international women's partnerships. Then, there were groups on child-rearing and motherhood, pregnancy, bringing up boys, women in philosophy, feminist history, women and immigration, women and religion, women in social work, women in the media, non-monogamy, how to not be in couples – and on and on and on. Just a few short years before the movement, there had been none of it – nothing.

The Seven Demands of the women's liberation movement

In summary, in the UK, the Seven Demands of the women's liberation movement (building on the original four) were:
- equal pay;
- equal education and job opportunities;
- free contraception and abortion on demand;
- free 24-hour nurseries;
- financial and legal independence for all women;
- an end to discrimination against lesbians; a woman's right to define her own sexuality;
- freedom from intimidation by threat or use of violence or sexual coercion, regardless of marital status and an end to all laws, assumption and institutions which perpetuate male dominance and men's aggression towards women.

A last anecdote from those times: during the London National Women's Liberation Conference in 1977 where the final Seventh Demand was adopted, someone in our feminist house was responsible for the food. We all sterilised the bath (really well) and made the red cabbage salad in it, full to the top. Kneeling to lean over it, we mixed and stirred it vigorously (in very long plastic gloves, be reassured) with our arms.

3

Women's liberation: strands, debates, transformations

This chapter moves on to reflect briefly on second wave feminism more widely and on the strands within it. All feminists in the women's liberation movement, from the beginning, developed understandings about the personal being political and about male control of society and often of women's lives. They also analysed the position of women as wives and mothers in the post-war period when the nuclear family had been much encouraged in many countries after the destruction of wartime. However, there were various streams that evolved within this, sometimes in opposition to each other, sometimes overlapping. The big ones were radical and revolutionary feminism, socialist and Marxist feminism, and liberal (sometimes called equal rights) feminism. These were expanded with the development of autonomous Black women's and lesbian movements, further discussed later in this chapter.

Thorough analyses of the main strands of feminism have been developed in a wide range of very useful books and websites. These include, separately, Alison Jaggar and Rosemarie Tong on the various types of feminisms, Michèle Barratt and Mary McIntosh on socialist feminism, Shulamith Firestone and (more recently) Finn Mackay and others, on radical and revolutionary feminism, and Sheila Jeffreys and others on the lesbian revolution.[1] Almost all commentators on feminism now include discussion of these different types. There were also other strands of activism and activity like cultural feminism, eco-feminism, anarcho-feminism, Irish, Jewish, Black and other identity-based feminisms, theoretical approaches to feminism, and so on.

So what distinguishes different strands of feminism?

Liberal (or equal rights) feminism was, and is, a mainstream reformist movement, trying to seek reforms in the existing social structure. A good example is the long-running NOW (National Organization of Women) in the US, established to fight for women's rights. NOW was particularly evident during the struggle throughout the 1970s to introduce an Equal Rights Amendment into the US Constitution. This important struggle had many years of success, followed by setbacks, backlash, much resistance from the right wing, and finally defeat. In general, NOW continues to be very active, campaigning currently for immigrant women's rights, for example.

Liberal equal rights feminism has been very successful in influencing social change through conventional methods in many countries. In the UK, this includes work with parliament, and the local and central governments of the four UK countries for women's rights. Liberal feminism has sometimes been viewed by other feminists as insufficiently challenging of the status quo, although it has resulted in many improvements in women's lives. Undoubtedly, equal rights – a liberal claim – remain hugely significant, and liberal values are presently under threat in many countries.

Radical feminists tended strongly to emphasise patriarchy as their main focus of analysis, and to concentrate particularly on campaigning against violence against women and against pornography and prostitution. A further commitment they almost always promoted then, and continue to do so, is the importance of women-only spaces. Ground-breaking (even all these years later) and superb works were produced by radical feminists in this period, some, but by no means all, in the US.

Among these American works are such famous books as *Sexual politics* (1970) by the extraordinary Kate Millett, *Gyn-ecology: the metaethics of radical feminism* (1978) by Mary Daly, *The dialectics of sex: The case for feminist revolution* (1970) by Shulamith Firestone, the extreme radical feminist pamphlet, the SCUM Manifesto

(1967) written by Valerie Solanas, and *Of women born: Motherhood as experience and institution* by the esteemed poet, Adrienne Rich. All of these great pioneers are sadly no longer with us, and we mourn their loss. A collection of huge importance was the afore-mentioned *Sisterhood is powerful: An anthology of writing from the Women's Liberation Movement* (1970) edited by Robin Morgan, and, in this country, *The female eunuch,* very influential in its time, was published in 1970 by academic and media personality, Germaine Greer.[2]

As women's liberation developed, **revolutionary feminism** grew out of radical feminism (to which it is closely related), most especially in the UK, but elsewhere too. It may have been first formally proposed by well-known feminist activist, Sheila Jeffreys, in a paper at the 1977 London National Women's Liberation Conference.[3] This new strand of feminist thought and activism tended to take particularly committed positions as regards male power, viewing men as a 'class', and moving away from both personal interaction with men and involvement with male-dominated social structures. As long-term gender-based violence professor, Marianne Hester[4] explains: "Both radical and revolutionary feminists took women's experience as the starting point. However, revolutionary feminists in addition problematised 'men'. While women's experience was central for feminist theorising, it was not enough. It was also crucial, in their view, to study the male supremacist context."

From such revolutionary and radical feminist viewpoints emerged ideas about political lesbianism (choosing women as a conscious choice). These new approaches gave rise, over time, to separatism: women ceasing to interact with men wherever possible and living entirely separately. Such ideas were pioneered by the Leeds Revolutionary Feminist Group in a key paper on political lesbianism distributed around 1981,[5] although political lesbianism, itself, and living mainly with women, had been practised by many from the early 1970s.

Many projects developed at the time for women to live and operate separately to men. Lesbian feminist living situations, hoping to be utopias, were set up, like the (sometimes huge) rural Womyn's Land projects in different countries. Separatism did not necessarily mean coming out as lesbian. Choosing to be committedly and proudly celibate, or broadly woman-identified, were much discussed and practised. Nevertheless, a famous slogan of the time was 'feminism is the theory, lesbianism is the practice'.

Key radical feminist writings were contributed by Sheila Jeffreys, Sue O'Sullivan, Gail Chester and many others.[6] For example, Jeffreys, in her 2018 book, *The lesbian revolution: Lesbian feminism in the UK 1970–1990*,[7] and other authors, have discussed how lesbians played a key part in the WLM. Lesbian feminists came together, and created new theories, language, ideas and a whole new way of life in the 1970s. A previously non-existent feminist milieu developed quickly in which extraordinary changes were brought about, specifically, by the contributions of lesbian feminists, some emerging from the gay liberation front (which included both men and women) and some politicised for the first time through women's liberation.

Developing theories about sexuality and heterosexuality (as also noted later) were the greatest theoretical achievements of lesbian feminism, according to Jeffreys, elaborated further by Black lesbian groups and campaigns. Lesbian feminists created strong emotional, social and political communities, which, it is important to note, often (although not always) nurtured all feminists, not only lesbians, and were crucial to the wider movement. These passionate theoretical and activist contributions by lesbian feminists and political lesbians may have been somewhat lost and overlooked in recent years, and deserve surely to be revisited and revitalised.

Socialist feminists tended to incorporate concepts of patriarchy into their view of women's oppression but also to emphasise a class analysis of society. They pointed out the need to revolutionise, not only patriarchal relations between men and women, but also social relations between those in power and those being exploited and damaged by that power. Socialist feminist academics and activists Michèle Barratt and the late Mary McIntosh, in *Women's oppression today*,[8] their classic 1980 text of the debate about Marxism and feminism, developed various analyses in which they suggested, along with other feminist social theorists, that patriarchy should not be viewed as an essentialist, unchanging force for subjugating women.

Rather, they pointed out, a more flowing analysis is needed of the changing interactions of class, gender and racial divisions.

At the very beginning of the second wave movement, Juliet Mitchell's original and pioneering work, *Women: The longest revolution* (1966), alerted left organisations to the need to take on the struggle for women's liberation.[9] The concept also developed, later, of 'non-aligned' left-wing women who did not wish to identify with a particular socialist group, but who still subscribed to socialist views, as well as to the women's liberation movement. (The last section of this chapter talks briefly about feminism and the New Left.)

Socialist feminists developed theoretical ideas about how the social arrangements needed to produce goods under capitalism significantly determined women being in inferior positions. This was particularly because their domestic work in the family was essential to enable (mostly male) labour power – men going out to work – that made capitalism function. Socialist feminist analyses tended to suggest that individual men were not necessarily responsible (and were likely to be also exploited by the workings of capitalism).

These were, and are, difficult issues to untangle, and this short book can only touch on them. The debates about patriarchy and socialism in the women's movement of the 1970s and 1980s between radical and socialist feminists were many, and often bitter at the time for some protagonists. However, the different approaches were sometimes presented in a stereotypical way. For example, socialist feminists might be caricatured as believing capitalism and the class struggle were solely to blame, and radical or revolutionary feminists as maintaining determinedly that all men were to blame. But it was certainly far more complicated than that.

Radical and revolutionary feminists almost always saw patriarchy as socially-produced and non-biological, and were anti-capitalist and against repression by the State, as well as being invested in combatting male power. Many socialist feminists believed that male domination was ages-old, predating capitalism and they often enthusiastically worked in women-only spaces. The main strands of feminism developed and changed constantly, and each held their own national conferences. I was involved in an 'Oxford + 4' conference in Oxford, four years after Ruskin (which felt like an insurmountable age during which everything had been transformed). This conference was many months in the planning, and we literally had to figure out what we had to do day-by-day.

The most experienced member of our group was Mary McIntosh, or Mary Mac, as she was often called, much-respected campaigner for lesbian and gay liberation and socialist feminist, who sadly died in 2013. It was a 'Feminism and Socialism' conference on the Four Demands (very broadly), specifically discussing new proposals for the fifth and sixth demands (to be taken later to the Edinburgh conference). Full to capacity, the conference was mainly activist-based. There was much attention to the campaign for the Troops Out movement in the North of Ireland (set up in 1973), and to the imprisonment of the Price sisters. The two sisters had been convicted for an IRA bombing in London and were midway (alongside their male colleagues) through an astonishingly long hunger strike (1973–1974) which finally lasted 200 days, prolonged by force feeding.[10]

Several of us from the organising group lived together in a feminist collective house in Oxford, and were involved in local campaigns, including establishing a nascent Women's Centre and a woman's helpline, as well as our CR group. We were committed 24/7 to the new movement and were enthusiastic about women-only projects. We identified as socialists and, also at the same time for most of us, as radical feminists. (Some of us said we were both feminists and socialists, rather than socialist feminists.)

Thus, there were both conflicts and overlap. Some commentators have claimed that the different strands all had more in common than is sometimes suggested, especially in terms of gender-based violence work, as noted by well-known feminist activist professor, Liz Kelly.[11] In fact, during the first phases (at least) of the women's liberation movement, many active women couldn't quite see the difference and felt that their own positions encompassed all of it, in complicated ways.

This 'we have more in common than not' perspective has certainly been my own experience, working closely over many years with women who identify as radical and revolutionary feminists, as socialist feminists, as political lesbians or as liberal feminists, all of us collaborating closely, and in a committed and deeply heartfelt way, in activist work on violence against women. In these groups, often besieged from all sides and supporting the most vulnerable of women, the arguments felt distracting and scarcely relevant. Rather, the practical struggle against some of the worst and most brutal manifestations of women's oppression came to the fore.

Transformations, conflicts and divisions

Even so, while there were new developments all the time in the women's liberation movement, there were also sometimes harsh conflicts which could be painful for those involved. A few of them are mentioned here. All of the strands of feminism believed that the structure of the nuclear family, together with the fact that domestic work and childcare were widely viewed as women's work, constituted major causes of women's subordinated position.[12] As a result, a complex discussion grew up in the 1970s about the role of domestic work in society, known as the 'domestic labour debate'. It led to much useful academic and practical analysis within both the socialist and radical feminist traditions, as outlined in Ellen Malos's edited book, *The politics of housework* (1980).[13]

There were conflicts from the beginning, however, with the split-off organisation, Wages for Housework. Deriving from the Italian progressive and feminist movements, renowned Italian feminists, Maria Dalla Costa, Silvia Federici and others, developed the idea that wages were due to housewives for the work they did. The Wages for Housework movement in the UK was led by Selma James, and developed its associated campaigns, WAR (Women Against Rape), Black Women for Wages for Housework, Wages Due Lesbians, and the English Collective of Prostitutes. Always very vocal, its advocates consistently made themselves clearly visible, and conflicts developed quite quickly. The rest of the women's movement often viewed Wages for Housework as leading to an individualistic, narrow or impractical approach, and advocated a broader analysis. The conflicts have continued. However, always a militant and international organisation, Wages for Housework is still going strong.[14]

Other combative disagreements within the women's movement (which also continue), revolved around pornography and prostitution. Some feminist organisations condemned all pornography as violence against women, as proposed by the late renowned Andrea Dworkin who played a key and very influential role.[15] They characterised the more extreme types of misogynist pornography as undisguised hatred of women and documented the often extremely distressing violence used by men for sexual gratification. Others resisted this position, finding some lighter pornographic images acceptable and not harmful to women, and believing that further bans to those already in place might increase State repression. This is a highly simplified juxtaposition and readers are recommended to consult relevant writings. (The conflict was epitomised at the time by confrontations between then existing organisations like the Campaign against Pornography, on one side, and Feminists against Censorship, on the other.)

Feminist views of prostitution tended to crystallise around, on the one hand, it being seen as violent subordination and exploitation of women, often dangerous and frightening, in which the women concerned are used by men in whatever way the men want. On the other hand, prostitution is viewed by some as a choice made by women in their struggle to support themselves and their children against impoverishment, a view frequently promoted by sex worker organisations demanding recognition and good working conditions. The argument can be simplified to wanting to make prostitution *illegal* for clients (but not for the women) as a damaging and misogynist practice, versus wanting to make it entirely *legal* to enable regulation and protection of the women's rights.

Either way, sex workers are clearly entitled to employment rights. SWARM is a collective founded and led by sex workers who believe in self-determination, solidarity and co-operation. UK-based, they are part of a global sex worker-led movement advocating the full decriminalisation of sex work. The English Collective of Prostitutes also was, and remains, very active on this issue. They tend to oppose viewing prostitution as abusive and exploitative. Activists on violence against women, however, often take the opposite position, being exposed, perhaps, to the extreme violence that women working in prostitution and pornography frequently endure. In my own time working with survivors of violence who were earning money as prostitutes, we supported more women who had been abused and violated than I can recall. One woman was hit hard with an iron bar as punishment for 'poor service' and nearly killed. Another was knocked senseless as she walked along the street, chatting. The attack, which came without warning from behind, was by her pimp.

We also supported women with split and damaged vaginas and with severe psychological trauma, women deliberately cut and tortured, and women living permanently in hiding due to extreme violence in their work. In the refuge where I worked there was one occasion where five of the women living there were fleeing (ineffectively in the end, as it turned out) from the same violent pimp, a 'big man' in the 'industry'. On the other hand, I remember one woman leaving the refuge and earning about £500 in one night (this was 30 years ago) which she said was the easiest and most money she could get for her children, and therefore worth the danger and hassle.

Back in the 1970s and 1980s, disagreements about these and other issues sometimes erupted as we all tried to build the movement of women for the first time. Different groups might quickly jump onto the moral high ground which they might then defend, with total belief in their 'rightness' against other (seemingly less enlightened) women. Class differences led to conflicts and challenges from working class women, and there was the evolution of some separate working class feminist organisations. Being lesbian versus being heterosexual, and whether lesbianism was the superior way forward, sometimes resulted in hurtful arguments. Ditto whether to have children or not, and, if you did, whether to take them with you to meetings.

On occasion, these arguments could manifest in deeply personal ways. In one example I knew about, a group of women lived together in a collective house where the working class members insisted that the middle class members had to do all the domestic labour, absolutely everything, day in day out, 24/7, to correct for class privilege. And no arguing about it. In another, a new mother was not allowed to breastfeed as childcare was meant to be collective, even though no one actually knew anything about babies. Some heterosexual women I knew felt wretched and hid their sexuality guiltily from their feminist sisters. Lesbians described experiencing ignorance, discrimination and heterosexual privilege within the movement every way they turned. Some women always attracted to women could feel undermined by political lesbianism entered into as a conscious choice.

Overall then, in the 1970s and 1980s, the divisive issues of men, of social class and of both women's and lesbian separatism were much debated in the UK and elsewhere. Disagreements about men's relationship to feminism (perhaps as 'pro-feminist' or anti-sexist supporters) and about whether women should leave them behind were common. On a less individualised level, Adrienne Rich popularised the idea of what became widely known as 'compulsory heterosexuality'.[16] This is the concept that heterosexuality is so normalised, automatic and assumed under patriarchy that other sexualities like being lesbian are marginalised, and vilified. In response to these ideas as discussed earlier, separate movements of lesbians within the wider women's struggle evolved.

Black women and intersectionality

Since the beginning of women's liberation, Black women have formed powerful organisations, often to fight both sexism and racism at the same time, and some of these have built towards an independent Black women's movement, as noted in the last chapter. It has become commonplace to suggest that the movement was dominated by white and middle class women, at the beginning at least, as briefly discussed in Chapter 2. I would contend that this is partially true of course, but that there were many women's collectives and groups (including ones I was involved in) which were mixed in terms of ethnicities, sexualities, class backgrounds and age. The best of these groups (again I was lucky to be in some of them) tried to take on issues of racism and other types of discrimination. They campaigned for individuals facing racist treatment for example, and joined in campaigns against racism against women more generally. These kinds of groups were committed to fighting injustice and supporting Black struggles. The situation was perhaps not always as extreme or one-dimensional as some later commentators have indicated.

However, from the beginning, it was undoubtedly true that many Black and minority ethnic women described feeling overlooked by the women's liberation movement. There were disagreements, including over the main movement Demands which were sometimes seen (particularly on abortion) as focussing on white women. Despite some mixed groups and attempts to promote involvement from different ethnic communities, the majority whiteness of many feminist events was much noted. As a result, Black women self-organised independently, and also combatted racism within existing groups.

Addressing the American movement mainly, esteemed long-term activist and scholar Angela Davis wrote in one of her key works, *Women, race and class* (1983), about the way that women's liberation was impeded by an overlooking of race and class.[17] A further key contribution was made by the American theorist and educator, bell hooks (who spells her name in lower case).[18] She used the powerful phrase pioneered by the great anti-slavery campaigner Sojourner Truth in her perennially renowned speech of 1851, 'Ain't I a Woman'. hooks took these words and produced her highly influential work, *Ain't I a Woman? Black women and feminism* (1981). It contributed, with her later book (of many), *Feminist theory: From margin to center* (1984), to both theory and awareness about the lack of diverse voices in popular feminism. hooks argued that achieving equality for women was impossible and idealistic while racism remained. She advocated for something more embracing of all women, which acknowledged and took on differences, and, like Angela Davis and many others, she urged feminists to consider the relation between race, class, capitalism and gender.

Building on this, an important move forward came a bit later with the now common adoption of the theory and practice of intersectionality. This was first developed by Kimberlé Crenshawe at the end of the 1980s to explain the situation of African American women.[19] The concept gives a theoretical understanding of how different types of 'oppression' such as racism and sexism, as well as discrimination on grounds of class, disability and sexuality, interact and intersect in the forming of someone's identity. The idea is that intersectional feminism takes on the way these multiple complexities all interact together.

A highly regarded theorist of race, class and gender is Patricia Hill Collins who took theories of intersectionality further. She developed the idea of a 'matrix of domination' involving intersections of race, gender, socio-economic status, age and sexuality. Hill Collins discusses how Black feminist thought can be produced only by Black women since structures and themes of oppression experienced by Black women are the foundation of the theories resulting (sometimes described as Black 'standpoint' feminism). These ideas are debated in her books, including, most famously, *Black feminist thought: Knowledge, consciousness, and the politics of empowerment*. A recent work is *Intersectionality* (2016), written with Sirma Bilge.[20]

Intersectionality can appear a bit hard to understand. It is perhaps important not to 'over-academicise' the concept, so that it becomes clothed in other similarly complex words. Rather, it can be viewed, not as something just for intellectuals, but instead as a tool of activism, a tool of change – indeed a tool of liberation. The aim is to take on the reality of how experiences and identities actively intersect and interact together, and have real-life impacts – rather than to just 'add' one form of discrimination to another. Simultaneously, as ideas about intersectionality evolved, so have specifically focussed Black or lesbian feminist theory and practice.[21]

Moving on: identity politics

In general, passionate arguments continued through the 1980s, including the 'being lesbian or heterosexual' issue, women's separatism, cultural and eco-feminisms (and how they fitted in, or didn't) and identity politics. This last term is a broad and contentious one. However, women defining themselves according to particular or multiple identities (and sometimes conflicting with women of other identities) became an especially marked trend in the movements in many Western countries as time went on.

Towards the end of the 1980s in the UK, identity politics developed more and more (as discussed further later in relation to the violence against women movement). At the same time, the movements declined, to some extent, under the influence of changing conditions, of Thatcherism in the UK, Reaganism in the US, and similar backward steps elsewhere. But activism and women's service provision continued. It was never the case that feminism was over. Claims at the time of the existence of something called post-feminism have been misleading, as elucidated by many, including prolific feminist academic, Sylvia Walby.[22]

More recently, exciting new waves of feminism have erupted one after the other, steered usually by young women. Hostile conflicts have also continued to some extent (erupting around queer theory, for example, and around transgender rights).

Women in the academy

Since the early days, a huge body of feminist scholarship and literature has been produced, and the women concerned have been pioneers of something new. This large volume of admirable academic, literary and cultural work produced by feminists has been extraordinary. In addition to the feminist scholars highlighted throughout the text, there were the famed French theorists, Luce Irigaray, Julia Kristeva and Christine Delphy, and feminist thinkers like Elizabeth Wilson, Diana Leonard, Angela McRobbie, Susan Himmelweit, Stevi Jackson, Alison Assiter, Maggie Humm, Annette Kuhn, Mica Nava, Anne Phillips, Nira Yuval-Davis, Nancy Chodorow, Sandra Harding, Nancy Hartsock and the world-renowned work of Judith Butler. But this is just a tiny selection of the feminist theorists who have transformed the academic canon in their subjects.

Their successes have not been without struggles and setbacks, as the academic institutions, usually dominated by men, fought back about divisions on lines of gender or sex. The interestingly unusual book, *Reclaiming feminism: Challenging everyday misogyny* by Miriam David, noted earlier, is a melding of memoir and history about feminists in the academy.[23] David records how the new women academics in the universities had to fight every inch of the way, often being put down, ignored or patronised, by the academic establishment, on their way to (partial) recognition.

Pioneering journals like *Feminist Review* (from 1979) charted the unprecedented rise of feminist scholarship and developed new feminist agendas. A key resource, the journal presented socialist and feminist theories, especially around issues of class, race and sexuality. Complex schools of feminist theory have developed over the years, including feminist standpoint theories, Black feminist theorising, and both post-modernist and post-structuralist approaches.[24] At the same time came the ground-breaking setting up of university courses on issues affecting women, and then the formal establishment of Women's Studies units and degrees in higher education. The National Women's Studies Association was formed in 1977. The development of these pioneering programmes continued apace in the later 1980s and 1990s. However, Women's Studies[25] (now frequently renamed Gender Studies) has decreased in prominence in recent years in the UK, but flourishes in many non-Western countries.

Grass-roots activists have sometimes been critical of women in the universities, certainly in the past, during the second wave days. Some characterised academic women as remote from radical struggle and as powerful or privileged, since they might have had relatively well-paid and secure jobs, as many did. Often, though, they didn't (facing temporary contracts and constant job losses). The critique has also been made that, as time went on, some theoretical, philosophical – and especially post-modern – developments in feminist ideas became too elitist and impossible to comprehend for those outside the academy, like feminist activists 'on the ground'. There is no doubt truth in this. Not being able to understand a word of what your sisters have written can be viewed as speaking of academic privilege. However, it is also the case that complex intellectual work may be hard to do in a way that others outside its field can fully understand. Women in the universities have continued to undertake heroic and complex endeavours in often adverse situations. Many also melded this work with their activism.

A word on the wider women's movements across the world

The women's movements have in no way been limited to the West. They extend across the world in a rich tapestry of campaigns and activism. It is not possible to do this huge subject justice in such a brief account as this. But, just a few examples are mentioned here. Back in the 1970s, as the movements evolved in the West, feminist action simultaneously evolved in countries like India and Iran where there has been a lengthy history of militancy. In India, for instance, there has been a long tradition of direct action by women – physically taking on perpetrators of violence, for example. Activists sometimes held up placards in front of where the man concerned lived, or jumped up with such placards as he was addressing a public event.[26]

While different cultural understanding, words and tactics may sometimes be used, Indian women's political activity and struggle for change have continued. They have often challenged the multiple ways that men dominate both social and political life, and also religious traditions in the country. The powerful Indian women's movements have responded with a huge number of strategies and interventions, sometimes successful, according to interviewees from Bombay/Mumbai.

These interviewees explained that they have also sometimes been defeated by ingrained male domination, cultural issues, the unequal impacts of neo-liberal, globalised development, and serious violence against women. And this list is not even to mention the enduring painful impacts of previous British colonialism and Partition. Nevertheless, the Indian movements, consisting often of outspoken women's advocates, have defiantly stood their ground. Another issue is that, while International Women Day celebrations have become more muted in recent years in the West, massive, dynamic events occur annually in India (and in other countries of the Global South), which amazingly involve thousands and thousands of women (as also discussed in Chapter 9).

In another example, the history of the vibrant African movements is characterised by women who have fought the patriarchal status quo in a dizzying array of cultural contexts. Obioma Nnaemera in 1998 stated that:

> The feminist spirit that pervades the African continent is so complex and diffused that it is intractable. Not too long ago, a colleague asked me to provide a framework of African feminism as articulated by African feminists. My … response was: 'The majority of African women are not hung up on articulating their feminism, they just do it.'[27]

She went on to suggest that there are many feminisms and movements, and no single monolith, as different women's battles are fought across the African continent, for example, on decolonisation, female genital mutilation, bride-price and girls' education. The same is true elsewhere, for example, in the Near and Middle East. Western ways of doing things tend not to apply, and cultural contexts take different complicated forms.

Meanwhile, a complex international feminism has developed, as part of the post-colonial movement and often concerns itself with advancements in women's rights. Key events, among many, have been the various global conferences of women, for example the World Conference of Women in Beijing in 1995 with its Global Platform for Action, and other worldwide initiatives (some of which are noted in Chapter 9). Women fighting in the Global South to improve their situations have had real successes (even though the advances made have not always been able to be maintained). There are now women working on women's issues in almost every country. I have had the personal honour of working with such phenomenal activists all over the globe.

Women's liberation and the New Left

While the focus of this chapter is on women's history, there was always a close and sometimes contradictory relationship between women's liberation and the left-wing, progressive movements. In the 1960s/70s, there was the development of the New Left – a more libertarian Left (than previously) which often organised separately from the old leftist organisations and parties. There were attempts to do things differently in many countries around egalitarianism, social equality and social justice (although not without conflict and sectarianism).

In the UK, the then-existing, traditional Communist Party changed somewhat in the early 1970s, partly due to being forced to, by incoming left-wing feminist activists. The Party began to take on issues for women, as did the Labour Party. Suddenly many more feminists started to join up, for a while at least. Some left-wing organisations (like the International Socialists, now the Socialist Workers Party, and the IMG, the International Marxist Group) gradually developed both women's wings and women's publications (for example, *Socialist Women*) and also campaigned for women workers through the labour movement. There were also anarchist leftist organisations, some of which gave rise to anarcho-feminism. Of course, some of these left organisations took on feminist challenges with more acceptance than others. Many feminists in these groups battled endlessly on the issues for women, and still do.

From the mid-1970s onwards, there were direct attempts to build bridges and to bring together feminism and the Left. The key one of these was 'Beyond the Fragments', a late 1970s initiative of Sheila Rowbotham, Lynne Segal and Hilary Wainwright, which led to much discussion and an action network.[28] (Their book of the time, *Beyond the fragments: Feminism and the making of socialism*, was republished in 2013, with a new introduction taking on more recent challenges to feminism and the Left.) There were also long-term women's organisations like the National Assembly of Women, formed in 1952, and broadly affiliated with the Left.

In the period, there was the continued evolution, alongside anti-sexist initiatives, of anti-racist and anti-fascist organisations and of anti-apartheid work, of leftist and feminist challenges in the trade union movement, and of struggles against war. There were also ongoing developments in anti-imperialist organising, in solidarity work, in support for previously colonised countries and national liberation struggles, and for Palestine fighting often illegal aggression and attack. In all of these, feminists were intimately involved.

Later, in the UK's countries, there were challenges to religious fundamentalism, to the persecution of Muslim and Black, minority ethnic and refugee communities, and to neo-liberalism, with strong feminist participation and sometimes leadership. We have also seen, in recent years, both the smashing – and the sometimes exciting development, almost always now with women playing a key role – of left-wing movements in various parts of the world. The long-standing Black Lives Matter movements, for example, led by women in many places, have spread across the world from 2020 in response to police brutality against Black people in the US and elsewhere.

This book is not the place to discuss these developments further. However, one observation is that organisations in the Left frequently have quite vitriolic disagreements with each other. As someone committed to the humanitarian and progressive view of society that the Left at best embodies, I offer here pleas for avoiding sectarianism. There is the possibility, rather, I would strongly suggest, for concerted and warm-hearted efforts by left organisations to try not to fall out with each other – to not engage in endless splits – when perspectives may differ little as far as the wider world is concerned. Of course, it is also important not to minimise real and significant disagreements, which have practical implications for left-wing organising, and so need to be practically addressed.

These pleas recognise the transformative work of left activists, parties and organisations across the world for social liberation and justice. My personal belief remains that people in the Left are, or could be – one would hope – the most humane and compassionate of people, who might be able to avoid arguing fiercely. At their best, left parties and groups have developed in tandem with the women's liberation movement and the Black women's movement and, in tolerant and mutually constructive ways, collaborate on campaigns for women safety, rights, freedom and liberation.

Memoirs and memories

As those of us who were part of the women's liberation movement grow older, the task has arisen of continuing to record and commemorate all that we did, what we changed and what we couldn't change. Many women of the period are writing inspiring memoirs or histories, for example, *In our time: A memoir of a feminist revolution* by Susan Brownmiller (2000), and a 2007 memoir, *Making trouble: Life and politics* by Lynne Segal.

Further examples include feminist novelist and poet Michèlle Roberts' 2007 memoir, *Paper houses: A memoir of the 1970s and beyond*, and, also in 2007, Mica Nava's *Visceral cosmopolitanism* which contains some personal reflective memoir. Sheila Rowbotham's 2019 memoir, *Promising a dream: Remembering the sixties,* is a perceptive and poignant memoir, and Miriam David's afore-mentioned work provides memoir as well as a history of feminists in higher education.[29]

Further books, archives and references

Some of the key books written as the women's liberation movement happened are listed near the start of Chapter 2, or are referenced throughout these last two chapters (for example, among many, key work by Shulamith Firestone, Kate Millett, Angela Davis, Robin Morgan, Kimberlé Crenshawe and bell hooks). Books written more recently include, among many, the comprehensive, easy-read 2015 book, *Radical feminism* by Finn Mackay noted above, *Feminisms* (1998) edited by Sandra Kemp and Judith Squires (and dealing with the period since 1980), *The feminist memoir project: Voices from Women's Liberation* (2007) edited by Ann Snitow and Rachel Blau DuPlessis, and *The feminist revolution* by Bonnie Morris and D-M Withers, published in 2018.

This recent work is packed with wonderful reproductions of posters, leaflets, memories, campaign publicity, women's movement ephemera and buttons worn. An important paper by Jill Radford (1994) is 'History of the Women's Liberation Movement in Britain: a reflective personal history'. And a helpful 1990 book, edited by Michelene Wandor, is *Once a feminist: Stories from a generation*. But these are just a few.[30] For further references (a selection of many), see the endnotes.

Historical archival resources are available from Feminist Archive North based in Leeds, and Feminist Archive South based in Bristol. Specialist libraries include the stunning Glasgow Women's Library, preserving women's history in Glasgow and Scotland, which also houses the Lesbian Archive. The Lesbian History Group additionally provides a website of archives. The two major UK libraries are the historic Women's Library in London (now operated through the London School of Economics) and the Feminist Library, originally the Women's Research and Resources Centre, founded in 1975 specifically to record the history of the women's liberation movement. It now has a permanent home in South London after years of moving and insecurity. Both of these are treasure troves of resources, but have had to survive evictions, attacks and property appropriations until recently.

Other archives and libraries include the Women's Liberation Music Archive, the Women's Art Library (at Goldsmiths College), the Black Cultural Archive, and the comprehensive oral/written history resource in the *Sisterhood and After* collection of the British Library, coordinated by Margaretta Jolly. Jolly has produced a 2019 book of the project, named *Sisterhood and after*, too.[31] The project *Unfinished Histories*, also through the British Library, celebrates alternative women's theatre and histories, and held an exhibition, *Unfinished Business: The Fight for Women's Rights*, in 2020. An important website and collection to celebrate the women's liberation movement, named HOWL (History of Women's Liberation), has been developed since 2019. It is a priceless resource acting as a hub, preserving the movement and foregrounding women's personal stories. Since 2014, the FLA (the Feminist and Women's Libraries and Archives network) has provided an umbrella network.

Feminist organisations carrying on the flame include the Women's Resource Centre in London, established in 1984 and providing an invaluable network of support to women's organisations in support of women's human rights. FiLia acts as a key, central hub and organises large annual feminist congresses. Older Feminist Network and London-based 70s-Sisters also share archive memories of the period. All of these initiatives preserve our history (or herstory as some feminists prefer), together with other admirable libraries set up by feminists and historians, including online materials and websites. The many exhibitions, websites and initiatives in progress to celebrate the 50th anniversary of the women's liberation movement are presently providing important memories and resources.

A concluding word

Women's liberation was and is a movement of extraordinary challenge to the status quo. It is worth celebrating the way that many of us stood up, often so bravely and with such passion and zest, to construct feminism from the bottom up. What we built, and go on building, has continued over the last 50 years, developing in different ways in different communities, and involving new groups of diverse young women, each generation.

This book concentrates mainly on the early days, but, in more recent years, there have been new waves of different types of feminisms. There has been the development of local 'Feminist Networks' in towns and cities, and a re-invigorated Fawcett Society. There are now new journals like *Feminist Dissent* (from 2016), the #MeToo campaigns, initially at least led by Black women, new policy networks for girls and women, and resurgent equal pay for equal work struggles by women in the media and elsewhere.

The women's liberation movements led – although not without conflict and backlash – to impacts and increased opportunities for women and girls in almost all areas of society in Western and many other countries. Without being 'essentialist' and falsely lumping women together as a homogenous group, it is still true that women's positions have got better in many countries (even if in uneven and sometimes contradictory ways).

The women's movements planted the seeds, characterised by endless inventiveness. It was a privilege to live through it. But it is true that the wild hopes and dreams of total liberation and of a transformed world for women have remained (with isolated triumphs) just that – hopes and dreams. Nevertheless, the progress was real. Some of the most important developments concern violence against women, not yet addressed in this summary. They form the dedicated subject of the rest of this book. In conclusion, while there is still a long way to go, the women's liberation movements in the UK and across the world contributed to wide-ranging advances. They also resulted in transformed lives for many of those who lived and breathed them, from the 1970s on. For many of us, they were our finest days.

4

The violence against women movements burst into life

The task of transformation was enormous, but the spirit and energy of the time was of equal measure, and so began the struggle for change.

R. E. and R. Dobash[1]

The rest of this book focusses specifically on the history of the movements challenging violence against women and girls, and domestic violence in particular, since the late 1960s. However, the epigraph/quote above leads directly on from the one that starts Chapter 2, as a deliberate continuation: the wider women's movement was the foundation. Thus, the reason why the previous two chapters were devoted to the women's liberation movements, including the Black women's movement, in various countries is that the struggle to take on male violence against women was embedded from the start within them. They were its wellsprings.

Activism has always been the backbone of challenging the abuse perpetrated by men and experienced by women. That was the case in the 1970s and 1980s. And it is the case now. Those who are committed to the issue can perhaps be proud, despite the continued incidence of high levels of gender-based violence, to be part, now, of a loose-knit and diverse global movement, spanning the countries of the world. In fact, in almost every nation currently, there is at least some activity to combat male violence. It is to this that we now turn.

Refuges (shelters), rape crisis centres, and many other services and campaigns were set up both in the UK countries and elsewhere in the early 1970s, as part of this worldwide effort. All these years later, the movement takes complex forms, and is active to varying extents, in different regions, countries and cultures – but is there, almost everywhere, nonetheless. As we take on board diversity and difference, and varying degrees of power between women, as indeed we must, it is possible, these days, to make wide links and build solidarity on violence against women. The links and solidarity can, at best, stretch across the vast diversities between women around the world (as has been my experience working with activists and survivors in many different countries). And it is then possible to join together across all those differences to challenge the various types of violence and abuse which jeopardise and harm women (and children) everywhere. A strong claim but one with some accuracy.

It wasn't always like that, though. This chapter focusses mainly, but not solely, on how things developed in the early years in the UK countries. Readers of this overview who require more detail might like to refer to the Women's Aid federations and to groups like Refuge and Southall Black Sisters (especially their various 40th anniversary celebration documents), as well as books from the historical period by Rebecca and Russell Dobash, Liz Kelly, Amina Mama, Susan Brownmiller and others listed in the section on 'Books and resources for wider reference' at the end of this chapter.

The first glimmerings: taking on violence against women

From the 1970s onwards, then, a new feminist focus on violence against women emerged in various countries, often influenced, sometimes unconsciously, by other social movements. These included, as noted before, the Black liberation movement, the anti-Vietnam War struggle, freedom struggles in the 'Majority' World of the Global South, the (then named) gay liberation movement, the worldwide student rebellions and the oppositional 'counter-culture' of the time. Suddenly and enticingly, visions of transformation and human liberation were in the air.

It is also important to note that progressive legislation in the UK countries in the 1960s which freed women a little – liberalising divorce, family planning and social security, and improving women's housing rights – helped to make the subsequent changes possible. At the beginning, though, there were just small beginnings, the first glimmerings at the start of the 1970s. Awareness of domestic violence, sexual abuse and rape then began to develop, as part of the women's liberation movement. In the UK, for those who were involved at the time, they built on what they learned from their own personal experiences, and from talking to other women about what theirs had been.

An analysis began to take shape of how the wide-ranging oppression of women that women's liberation was identifying was reinforced by violence. In those early days, it took us a while to fully understand that we were up against something big – and that it was all linked together. The rage we often felt at the time, and the unfairness to women that we saw around us, were crucially linked to the way many men (once you knew to look) could clearly be observed, or experienced, as acting in controlling ways towards their families, girlfriends and wives.

This, we then figured out quite quickly, could include through rape and sexual dominance by individual men, and through abusive or aggressive behaviour in intimate relationships. Such behaviour was magnified in impact by women's general economic dependence on men, often as housewives. This was compounded by discriminatory housing tenures (as late as the 1970s, women were refused mortgages in their own names) and by the inferior legal position of wives across society at the time (despite the legislative improvements of the late 1960s).[2] All these seemed to reinforce each other. It was a bit like a 'perfect storm' of difficulties swirling impenetrably around many women. And underlying the perfect storm, we began clearly to see, was the violence committed by (some) men.

Actively taking on the violent abuse that many women experienced came from these realisations. New agendas were suddenly everywhere to be seen, as gender violence activists emerged out of the women's movement and attempted to change – well – everything. Almost daily, women, newly feminist, came up with fresh insights, thinking and action in a way that had not previously been possible – or even conceivable. For many of those early activists on violence against women, as noted in previous chapters, those days were the defining ones of their lives, including the women who, just a short time later, found themselves moving on from discussions of male violence and consciousness-raising about it. Quite suddenly, it seemed, they were actually setting up (with little or no money) practical working projects on domestic abuse, rape and sexual violence.

There is an emphasis in this chapter, as in the book more widely, on the example of domestic violence (which includes sexual violence from intimate partners). However, the next chapter will reflect, as well, on other forms of sexual abuse and rape. It is vital not to minimise the importance of issues of wider sexual violence in favour of domestic abuse. Rather, they are all linked together.

Domestic violence and abuse: history and passionate moves forward

Throughout known history, there appears to be an endless parade of rape and sexual attacks against women. The continent of Europe, for instance, is named for rape victim, Europa, who was raped by Zeus. Further, as far as we know, men in almost all societies have always chastised, punished and violated their wives and daughters. It has traditionally been widely viewed as a man's accepted right and duty to do so. In the 20th century, domestic and sexual violence tended to be kept more hidden in many countries as matters of family shame. But, almost everywhere, it was the woman, rather than the man, who might be gossiped about and judged, for both domestic violence and rape, behind cupped hands.[3]

Those who remember the 1940s and 1950s in the UK can recall the moral censure, the embarrassment, the shame and the almost total silence about domestic and sexual violence. The silence was perhaps more marked among the middle classes, but firmly there, nonetheless, across class and social boundaries. A short 1996 book, *The silenced pain* by Claudia Wilson and myself, reported a small research study on domestic violence between 1945 and 1970 in the UK.[4] For a long while, potential interviewees for this study were deeply reluctant to come forward or to talk, often having endured a lifetime of domestic violence in shame and complete silence. Although the silencing of abused women does indeed remain common, it was a deeper, heavier silence, back then, than can be readily comprehended these days.

Two women quoted in the study said:

> I did leave a few times with the children. But it was so frowned on ... You couldn't leave your husband. It wasn't done. I would have been so ashamed if anyone found out. And if I left, how would I support them? I had no way at all of supporting them ...

> The way the violence ruined my life, undermined my whole personality. I'm bitter that my life was gone and wasted, I lost it, it's over and wrecked, I am so profoundly saddened.

The adult son of the second woman added in his own interview: "The impact was devastating. I can't even begin to articulate the agony and endless despair she suffered without telling anyone. It affected her whole being." In the interview, the pain hung tangibly in the air.[5]

The women interviewed remained deeply saddened and scarred by the violence they had endured from the 1940s on. They spoke movingly and extremely painfully for the first-ever time about these distressing experiences – just as they were reaching the very end of their lives. The study found that: 'These women, in their waning years, were painfully aware of the irreplaceable loss of their right to a peaceful life ... the ever-lasting loss of trust ... the great tragedy that had imbued their adulthoods'.[6]

It really was the case that, until the women's liberation movement, women experiencing domestic and sexual violence did not have any place – literally – to turn. There was often nowhere at all to escape to, no one to talk to, and no one to help them, except perhaps each other. Women have always found some support from other women. But there were no refuge or shelter organisations, few housing alternatives to marriage, almost no criminal justice responses, no counselling centres, no good practice guidelines, no support or advice, little wider public awareness. Women in violent relationships rarely had any way out.

Challenging the very fabric of relations between women and men

Then, the new women's movement gave rise to the interlinked rape crisis and domestic violence movements, the main service provider of the latter being Women's Aid. The connection between present-day provision and the direct action and feminism of the 1970s is a quite straightforward one, although it is sometimes overlooked or forgotten today. Services on violence against women are now widespread, but all of them derive in one way or another from their foundation in activism.

For domestic violence, it began when women who had suffered abuse started coming to the new Women's Centres, set up by the women's movement, requesting help (sometimes having been sent by local council social services and housing departments).[7] This was the case in Bristol, for example, where women escaping violence began arriving at the first Women's Centre (in the house of one of the activists, Ellen Malos), asking for support and assistance. The women coordinating the small Centre weren't sure what to do. They decided that they should take the women and children in, and provide them with an emergency place to stay in the basement of the house. And these types of things were happening everywhere. All across the UK's countries, tiny actions of help and compassion were taking place, often in someone's back room, as a response to women arriving, having been violated.

The women concerned who were trying to escape from domestic violence were not feminists (usually). But they found out, somehow, that there were these other unknown women around – and that, almost out of the blue, these other women might offer assistance. And so they threw their fates to the winds to try to get help. These were acts of almost unimaginable courage and trust by the women concerned, with their children.

As they arrived, they would have no idea what might then happen to them – and neither would the women opening their doors. From the perspective of nearly 50 years on, it was staggeringly courageous for all concerned. And, of course, violent husbands could come knocking at those doors, quite likely, and quite soon – and they often did.

Political actions and meetings specifically on domestic violence then began to be held, sometimes involving both women who had experienced violence and those who had not, working closely together. Out of these came the idea of setting up proper projects. These were conceived of as separate safe houses or refuges/shelters to which women who had suffered abuse could escape, and from which they could perhaps begin to construct new lives, free of violence. Astonishingly quickly, the new women's groups managed to achieve this seemingly scarcely possible task. Actual refuge projects were cobbled together somehow (and sometimes with the help of sympathetic local government workers). Abused women immediately came to them – *immediately*. As soon as they opened, the women and children were there.

The idea was, more or less, a new and revolutionary one. Apart from a few precedents in the 19th century during the first wave of the women's movement, such a thing had rarely been done before. The new women's initiatives confronted – in a concrete and undeniable way – men's rights and power within the family. And the (male-headed) family was the heart and bedrock of how personal, family and sexual relations were organised in society. Women were taking unprecedented action to leave their husbands who they had probably, at the time, promised to 'obey'. They were suddenly trying to get themselves out of violent marriages and partnerships, often without warning.

Not only were they doing this – extraordinary at the time – but then they were doing something even more extraordinary. They were going to live together with groups of other women in safe houses run by women. It was a quite remarkable and entirely unpredicted development, stunning in its fearlessness and daring.

In addition to all this, the refuges that were set up were at secret locations to which women experiencing domestic violence from their husbands or partners could escape – and more or less disappear.

At first, many men, husbands, women, agencies like the police, and indeed society as a whole, could scarcely believe it was happening. But it was.

Suddenly, in a significant way, the very fabric of personal and sexual relations between men and women was being challenged.

Refuges are now commonplace, and challenging domestic violence is part of criminal justice work and popular culture. It is almost impossible to conceive of what it was like when all this first started happening, beginning from a base of pretty much zero services and zero societal interest. The brazen – and brave – challenge of it was, and is, without doubt, something to celebrate. This short book is part of honouring the women involved, the work they did, the support and help they provided to other women – the pure audacity of it. The new actions taken by women, for and with other women, on both domestic and wider sexual violence, were a shock all round. They were unprecedented. They were breath-taking.

New services, new beliefs, new ways of living

From then on, everything speeded up. The setting up of new projects kept on happening, on an almost daily basis. Feminist activists in the countries of the UK (as in various other countries) put almost infinite amounts of energy, zeal, physical work and commitment into trying to get the new centres and services for abused women going. Groups worked tirelessly on a volunteer basis initially. But any service which was established was continually overwhelmed with women and children needing refuge space. The extent of the need was painfully clear. The new refuges still kept on and on filling up as fast as they appeared. And everyone involved knew that this was merely the tip of the iceberg of domestic violence.

Rebecca and Russell Dobash have played key roles in the movement from those days. In retirement, they still do. In their 1992 book, they described how, 'There were no set ways of doing things, nor any textbook theories or professional philosophies … responses were developed through direct contact with the women in terms of their own needs. New issues arose constantly. New solutions were created daily'.[8]

They pointed out that being new in one's own historical period, as the activists on domestic and sexual violence were, often means that there is a freedom to create something unique, something fresh and previously untried in the society in question. And that is what the women taking action on violence against women did, without a doubt.

However, it means, as well, that, while constructing something brand new, which is already so hard to do, there is likely also to be incomprehension and often criticism on a general level. For something as contentious as violence against women, this is almost certain to be magnified. Whenever services specifically for abused women have been first established anywhere in the world, it seems they are belligerently opposed. This was certainly the case for the domestic and sexual violence activists in both the UK and other countries in the 1970s and 1980s. They had to fight their way forward, often pitting themselves against steely, usually (but not always) male resistance and community suspicion.

Women setting up refuges/shelters and support projects based their decision-making on feminist principles, working to create an egalitarian situation with the women staying there. This immediately differentiated these new women's projects from local councils and from traditional social work and housing initiatives. The idea was to assist women and children in leaving violent homes and certainly *not* to then replace abused women's possible servitude in their relationships with their husbands with another form of servitude (rule-bound council homes or hostels for instance).[9] Rather, there were few authority figures in a refuge.

During the preparation for this book, Pragna Patel, Director of Southall Black Sisters, recalled:

> The refuge movement was so vibrant then. And political. In practical ways and political ones too. It was a merging of compassion and empathy and real practical support. The projects were more organic

then, and new and more holistic, I think … It was
CR that taught us:
Women can do it …
Women will do it …
And women are doing it.

Liz Kelly, feminist activist and researcher on violence against women, talked, also for this book, about how everything was done, not as an individual effort – but as a co-operative and totally committed 'we'. All the groups worked enthusiastically to make something new and different.

She discussed being on a near vertical learning curve as Norwich Women's Aid was being set up, learning new skills, like how to accomplish needed practical carpentry or how to mend electrical wiring in the new refuge. At the same time as performing such tasks for which they likely had very little preparation, the group members were constantly taking women and children into the house, working out how best to support them, and finding out more and more about domestic violence and abuse. The women volunteers concerned had to do everything from scratch. What's more, the accommodation being occupied might have been in poor condition and, quite likely was a previously unused property. In the refuge where I worked myself, we sometimes joked about our jobs being to stand firm with the women living there, but mainly to unblock the drains (which, in reality, we did rather poorly).

Some of these ideas are discussed more fully in Chapters 6 and 7, including the fact that Women's Aid refuges, like the emerging rape crisis centres, were all collectives. A radical practice was that the women coming to stay in a refuge were regarded as collective members. Equality, sharing, and everyone taking responsibility were the order of the day. There was a sense of solidarity in relationships between those providing and those using the services, and an emphasis on autonomy for the women and children staying at the refuge. Women shared their experiences together and could, at best, develop self-respect, self-determination and a new future, with committed support provided for a while in the (temporary) refuge situation. A lot of the time, it worked out really well, with lives transformed.

Occasionally it didn't. But it was all being done in practice, not just in theory – women joining with other women across vast differences to become strong and, together, to overcome male violence. It was, and is, an exhilarating concept.

Refuges and Women's Aid

Famously, the first known refuge of the period in the UK (and possibly the world) was set up in 1971 by an organisation called Chiswick Women's Aid, whose spokeswoman was Erin Pizzey. While some other women's groups were also dealing with domestic violence at the same time, public consciousness of the issue was moved in a profound way by the media publicity and hype surrounding Chiswick. Very quickly, other refuges began to be established, one after the other, by groups of dedicated feminists who communicated around the country, and began the idea of building a whole network.

It was not long before Erin Pizzey, who was a committed and powerful entrepreneurial figure, publicising the plight of abused women, had disagreed with the rest of the Women's Aid movement. These disagreements were often over her views as to the causes of the violence, which she developed along the lines of some women being 'violence-prone',[10] and her antipathy to collective and co-operative ways of working. By 1974, Chiswick Women's Aid had unilaterally split away from the rest of the Women's Aid movement to go it alone. There was some acrimony, with interviewees for this book recalling attempts by Pizzey to take over other refuges or prevent them being set up, to criticise them in public, and to combat feminist and left-wing views with which she bitterly disagreed.

In 2020, Pizzey was featured in a book which suggested that she had perhaps not received the prestige due to her, as the feminist pioneer of the issue.[11] It is true that she was indeed an outstanding and original pioneer and deserves concomitant respect. The domestic violence sector almost universally acknowledges this. But it is not the case that she was a feminist or an activist for the wider movement, and she was never involved in campaigning for the vital legal protections on domestic violence that were achieved in the 1970s.

Pizzey now works with the men's rights movement. She left Chiswick Women's Aid in 1983, and its successor, Chiswick Family Rescue, was renamed Refuge in 1993. Now a member of Women's Aid, it co-operates with the rest of the domestic violence sector. Refuge has repudiated Pizzey's more women-blaming perspective on male abuse. They now run wide-ranging refuges, publicity campaigns and support services, including on issues for Black and minority women, guided by their long-term Director, Sandra Horley. (For more on Refuge, see Chapter 8.)

Back in the 1970s, the new groups proliferated rapidly. Scotland quickly had seven independent groups, the first being in Edinburgh set up in 1973, followed by Glasgow in 1974. More than 40 refuges came into being just in 1974 alone, across the whole UK, with new ones being set up all the time. As well as providing safe and secure accommodation for women and children escaping violence in the home, the new groups campaigned about and publicised the issue of domestic abuse for the first time.

In 1974, they established the National Women's Aid Federation (NWAF), which later became the federation specifically for England, Wales and Northern Ireland. The first refuge in Northern Ireland started in Belfast in 1975. Scottish Women's Aid was set up as the federation for Scotland in 1976 with a National Coordinator from the beginning. After getting a tiny amount of funding, NWAF also began tentatively to employ National Coordinators, and both federations held national coordinating conferences from then on. (It was at the first conference of NWAF that the split with Chiswick Women's Aid took place.)

By 1975, more than 80 groups were part of NWAF alone, when just a couple of years before there had been none. Almost all of the refuges set up in both Scottish Women's Aid and NWAF used the words Women's Aid in their individual names (for example, Newcastle Women's Aid or Cardiff Women's Aid). The federations coordinated these local groups regionally, and mounted national campaigns around domestic violence. In 1978, to encourage regional autonomy further, NWAF divided into three separate federations, Women's Aid Federation Northern Ireland, Welsh Women's Aid and the Women's Aid Federation of England.

The name of the latter was shortened to WAFE for many years, but it is now often known just as Women's Aid. This account focusses more on this federation because of its large size, but the other three are featured too throughout, and provide vital services in each of their countries. (It is important to avoid Women's Aid in England, now known as the national domestic violence charity, being seen as actually the national representative for the whole UK, which it isn't.) Back in the 1970s, more and more domestic violence services were set up, often, with very little in the way of facilities. The extent of the need became more and more painfully clear. In 1975, a government Select Committee on Violence in Marriage recommended that one refuge space be provided per 10,000 of the population, an aim which remains unmet to this day.

In other countries, refuges – or shelters as they were more frequently called – were established at about the same time as in the UK. The first feminist shelter in the US was probably in St Paul, Minnesota, in 1974, and the first shelters in Canada which had a feminist perspective were started by Interval House, Toronto and the Ishtar Transition Housing Society in Langley, British Columbia, both in 1973. In Australia, the first shelter was Elsie House in Glebe set up in 1974.

Funding

As they developed over the next years, refuge groups found that they needed to have paid staff. It was too much for volunteers to do everything. They also needed money and budgets in order to administer and run the projects they had enthusiastically established. So they began to apply for some funding and to employ workers (refuge workers and, as time went on, children's and outreach or follow-on workers too). The main collective meeting, which included the unpaid members, paid workers, volunteers and women from the refuge, was usually then called the 'Support Group'. It could be said that these groups were no longer equal collectives since they now included some paid workers. But they continued to work as equally as they could and to be regarded as collectives by their members.

From the first national conferences on, the Women's Aid movement had to struggle with contradictory difficulties, as the projects battled to finance themselves and get funding for the first time. They struggled around how you got it, and then how to stay true to your ideals, once you had it. The hard question was (and continues to be) how much a women's organisation can be simultaneously both a political campaigning body against male violence and a provider of services to abused women. There is plenty of left-wing literature saying it cannot easily be done, as well as right-wing literature saying it should not be attempted – especially, perhaps, the campaigning part. Providing services almost automatically entails a degree of negotiation with the establishment in order, among other things, to secure resourcing with which to do it. This is likely to be unacceptable to many of those in a campaigning movement who are dedicated to resistance to the State and to political action.

In the movement of the 1970s, this debate crystallised around how to provide sensitive, independent domestic violence services and to keep them autonomous, free of outside interference, while obtaining much needed support from government and other bodies. The federations attracted some grant-aid for their central offices fairly quickly and, by the end of the decade, Women's Aid groups usually had some sort of financing. In the early 1980s, more groups obtained both properties and funding from official government bodies and programmes like the (long since replaced) Urban Programme, from local authority housing and social services committees, and from housing association special projects and joint funding schemes. Without exception, though, this was inadequate and precarious.

Some feminists, like Ellen Malos, have spoken ironically of this as 'supping with the devil'[12] (especially in terms of the later multi-agency projects on domestic violence), as radical and feminist ideas were put under pressure by the demands and restrictions imposed by funders, and by criminal justice and local authority bodies. But it seems the 'supping' had to be done as there had to be funding if the services were to expand and consolidate.

Continuing to grow

Throughout the 1980s (into the 1990s), domestic violence services continued to develop. From providing safe space as their main mission at the beginning, refuge groups began to offer wider community services too. New organisations and outreach projects joined the initial refuges. Gradually, too, with training and input from the movement, the police and criminal justice system began to improve – at first, only a bit – their initially poor or non-existent responses.

As new streams of funding became available (although it was always a struggle to get them), the collectives needed to take on issues of negotiation with stakeholders, accountability as employers, management structures, monitoring and evaluation. While much of this assisted good practice, the women's organisations found themselves, more and more, being sucked into 'the system'. (Daily working practices and pioneering principles of refuge groups from the early days are discussed and celebrated in detail in Chapters 6 and 7.)

WAFE, itself, closed briefly due to loss of funding in the mid-1980s. It restarted in Bristol in 1987, as a result of the dedicated work by a small holding group, including long-term activist, Beryl Foster, to establish it with a new legal status and funding. A fresh membership structure was set up with a representative National Coordinating Group to oversee the federation and make decisions. While WAFE, like the other federations, was a membership organisation responsible to its members, a new National Office was also established to help carry decisions out. Nicola Harwin, National Coordinator and later CEO, from 1987 till 2012, was a key figure in WAFE's development from this time onwards. A feminist activist since 1970, she was one of three workers (all working together in one small room) who were employed to set up the new office from scratch, to re-affiliate 300 local groups to the new membership structure and to put on a national conference for them all, just three months later.

From this tiny base, they built the organisation up, employing many more workers over time, moving to larger premises, developing new projects and setting up different streams of work and departments within the collective. These included very active training, publicity and policy departments. Other important WAFE officers, among many going forward into the 1990s, were Linda Delahay, National Housing Officer, and Hilary Saunders and Thangam Debbonaire (now a Labour MP), who were National Children's Officers at different times. Similarly important contributors, also among many, were Jane Hutt in Welsh Women's Aid and Fran Wasoff, first coordinator of national Scottish Women's Aid (in the mid-1970s).

Scottish Women's Aid and the other federations had National Offices working as collectives, together with management boards drawn from member groups (in a similar way to WAFE). Working together, all the federations were very active through the 1980s, building the sector, coordinating the network of refuge and outreach services for both abused women and children, and engaging in research and campaigning work. By the mid-1980s, many of these services had been established as grass-roots women's projects for nearly a decade.

Some of the many things the Women's Aid federations achieved as they moved through the 1980s into the 1990s included publicity and awareness campaigns, relevant research, ring-fenced funding for refuges (sadly, no longer the case), and services like Survivors' Handbooks. They developed creative structures to facilitate groups remaining collectives for as long as they could, with clear divisions of roles and, for example in WAFE, a 'matrix' of women working on different projects, but as equals. All the federations gradually worked out ways to meld their feminist principles and values with delivery of services and with taking responsibility for efficient employment and management practices.

As the domestic violence and abuse services expanded and diversified, they built on specific improvements in legislation and policy (outlined in Chapter 9) to assist survivors. In the late 1980s, WAFE set up the first National Domestic Abuse Helpline, which continues to this day (now with Refuge). National Helplines were similarly set up in the other UK countries, as noted further in later chapters. The four federations set up All-Federation meetings from 1987 to coordinate work between them, which they still do. Overall, together with other violence against women projects developing at the time, the federations continued expanding through the period into the 1990s, and with contagious commitment and zeal.

Meeting the needs of women from Black and minority ethnic communities

Women's Aid, and much of the developing domestic violence and abuse sector, attempted through the 1970s and 1980s to work in anti-discriminatory ways. Domestic violence services often took, and continue to take, an active role in combatting racism, heterosexism, discrimination on grounds of disability and class, and other forms of inequality and injustice. In fact, many refuges began to develop their first Equal Opportunities Policy back in the early 1980s, and these equality and diversity policies have developed considerably ever since. Interviewees from different backgrounds spoke of how the refuge groups they had known (or worked in) strove to serve mixed communities of women (providing interpreters when needed, for instance). This was especially in the cities, where Black and minority women would often use them as a matter of course.

However, as for the women's liberation movement more widely, the services were challenged as having a sense of white entitlement (often unconscious, perhaps) and for not being attentive enough to – or even accurately aware of or concerned about – the needs of women from Black and minority ethnic communities. This term is frequently shortened to BME or BMER communities, with the 'R' referring to refugees. (Alternatively, BAME and BAMER might be used, with the A standing for Asian, although these terms have been critiqued.) The acronyms are used by agencies as they prefer, and these preferences are reflected where possible in this book.

It became clear, as time went on, that many minority women could not access refuge space which took on their needs in a meaningful, informed way. The Black women's movement, which developed autonomously as discussed in earlier chapters, began to challenge the domestic violence movement to improve their services to BMER women, and simultaneously to establish their own projects. Organisations and refuges specifically for

Black and minority ethnic women were established mainly from the 1980s on, some members of Women's Aid and some independent. These specialist projects aimed to counteract white bias and racism, and to provide for particular cultural and religious needs. Women from Black and minority ethnic communities could also use the more generic refuge network, which of course was open to them, but might be poor at meeting these needs. But they could at best be offered a choice.

Projects for African, African-Caribbean and Asian women began to operate, and some existing refuge groups also set up specialist BME services as part of their wider provision. A strong development was the gradual establishment of a loosely coordinated network, specifically, of South Asian domestic violence projects. Some of these specialist projects were empowerment and support services without housing provision, and some provided refuges and safe accommodation.

The new South Asian network and projects in the 1980s could usually provide support in different languages and culturally sensitive services (for example, around food and cultural, religious and community customs). Entirely new in their conception, these projects broke new ground. They provided – and provide – expert support and services to women of South Asian descent including British women and also new immigrants, around issues like forced marriage, 'honour' violence, immigration and lack of access to public funds, as well as domestic abuse.

A few examples of BME projects set up in the 1980s include Roshni in Birmingham (set up in 1979), Hadhari Nari in Derby (1986), Shakti in Edinburgh (1986), Roshni in Nottingham (1987), Ashiana in Sheffield (1981), Ashiana in London (1989), and Hemat Gryffe Women's Aid in Glasgow, founded in 1981 as the first Asian, Black and minority ethnic Women's Aid Group in Scotland.

Important pioneering projects like Southall Black Sisters and the Asian Women's Resource Centre, Brent, were set up as far back as the end of the 1970s, and the London Black Women's Project was established as the highly respected Newham Asian Women's Project (NAWP) in 1981. In Chapters 8 and 9, these specific ground-breaking projects are covered further, together with the expanding Black women's domestic violence movement, the further development of specialist BMER services after the 1980s, and the challenges they have faced and face. In terms of the wider movement and Women's Aid, the building of anti-racist practices and of challenges around other minority issues are discussed towards the end of Chapter 7.

Books and resources for wider reference

Further resources on violence against women, in addition to those noted at the beginning of this chapter, are available, at the time of writing, in the various 50th anniversary exhibitions and websites of the women's liberation movement. The feminist archives listed in Chapter 3 are also an excellent resource, including, those produced by the British Library. Key texts[13] from the historical period are those by Rebecca and Russell Dobash, especially *Violence against wives* initially published in 1980, a pioneering and crucial work, as well as their later 1992 book, *Women, violence and social change*. A few other examples[14] include *Surviving sexual violence* by Liz Kelly (1988), *Against our will: Men, women and rape* by Susan Brownmiller (1975), *The hidden struggle: statutory and voluntary sector responses to violence against black women in the home* by Amina Mama (1996), *Violence against women in South Asian communities* (2010) edited by Ravi Thiara and Aisha K. Gill, and *Domestic violence: Action for change* by Ellen Malos and myself (2005, 3rd edition).

Useful American resources[15] are *Feminist perspectives on wife abuse* edited by Kersti Yllö and Michele Bograd (1988), *Violence in the lives of black women* by Carolyn West (2003) and *The source book on violence against women* (2001) edited by Claire Renzetti, Jeffery Edleson and Raquel Kennedy Bergen. Key journals include *Safe: The Domestic Violence Quarterly* (which recently became online only) from Women's Aid in England, and both *Violence Against Women* and the *Journal of Gender-Based Violence*, published in the US and the UK respectively. The many organisations in the domestic violence and sexual violence sectors and their websites feature a huge number of useful reports, practice guidelines and research studies. An oral history project on *Uncovering the Stories of Women who Pioneered the Refuge Movement* by Colchester and

Tendring Women's Aid, together with other local refuges and the London Black Women's Project, began in 2016.

To conclude

This chapter takes the history up to the end of the 1980s. The wider organisational history of Women's Aid and the domestic violence movements from the 1990s on is continued in detail in Chapter 8. Chapters 6 and 7 focus, rather, on the huge contributions of their extraordinarily radical and innovative early politics and policies. They have much to teach us.

The chapter ends with a poem contributed to the book by a survivor of domestic violence:

I can't get better
(by a domestic violence survivor)

I can't get better. I can't forget
Or if I do, it jumps back again.

Go away. It wasn't fair.
It was my life. My only chance.

That was it. You made it a nightmare
I'm too damaged and hurt

I can't get better. It wasn't fair
I can't forget. Not ever.

5

Taking on rape and sexual violence, as well as domestic abuse

Domestic violence includes sexual violence against women by their male partners, sexual attack as part of physical domestic abuse, violent sexual practices, rape in marriage, sexual violence from family members, and so on. But sexual abuse and assault by men stretch much wider in a panoply of harmful sexual practices experienced by women. Some commentators, including Liz Kelly, have pointed out that the focus of the gender violence movement as a whole has tended to be often filtered through the lens of domestic abuse. With less attention given to issues of wider sexual violence, there can be an unhelpful skewing in responses. Thus, in recognition, while this book is specifically about the struggle against domestic violence, it does contain some specific coverage of sexual and other types of violence, both throughout and in this dedicated chapter.

All forms of woman abuse sit on a spectrum of gender-based violence and cannot really be separated from each other. Thus, it is key for this history of challenging domestic abuse to include attention to the sexual violence movement more widely. From the beginning, the two major focusses of the violence against women movement were sexual abuse and inter-personal domestic violence by men. The new campaigns around both were often entwined.

The hardest issue: combatting sexual violence for the first time

Let us, then, take a step back, once again, to those early passionate days of the women's liberation movement, and return to reflect on rape and sexual assault. As for domestic abuse, these painful issues were suddenly in the public eye in the early 1970s as they had rarely been before. Rape groups, helplines and campaigns on sexual violence began to develop at more or less the same time as Women's Aid, or perhaps a little later. Like the domestic violence projects, they were part of women's liberation and were a leap of faith into the unknown at the time, conducted with profound commitment by those concerned.

For rape and sexual violence, this new awareness seemed to be happening for what felt like the first time in history. Until then, there had tended to be an all-embracing, disapproving, but broadly unconcerned culture regarding rape, and very often women victims/survivors of rape were the ones who took the blame. The result was that the voices of victims tended to be silenced (as still is the case today, but to a lesser extent). All women knew about rape and sexual attack, of course. They very often lived in fear of it. But, in general, sexual violence was an unspoken, hidden subject, pretty much everywhere in the world, resulting almost universally in shame and often rejection for the women and girls (and sometimes men), who were raped and violated. It was the victims who were commonly the ones vilified or shunned. Then, feminists from the burgeoning women's liberation movement in various countries broke the silence.

This was taking on the sharp end of women's oppression indeed – the hurtful, shaming, life-wrecking outcomes for women being subjected to rape, to sexual brutality, and in extreme cases, to sexual torture and mutilation. At worst, this includes lethal sexual violence by men. To be clear, this means sexual practice and exploitation that result in death. These distressing issues were suddenly being exposed to both women's movement and public attention.

Pioneering work on rape in marriage and femicide

A book that changed the landscape (then and now) was *Against our will: Men, women and rape*, by American feminist, Susan Brownmiller.[1] The book elucidated the anti-woman attitudes that permeated our societies, and the judgemental way that victims of rape were treated when seeking justice. Diana Russell who died in 2020 was another key American gender violence activist and scholar. Writing widely on rape, she published her influential book, *Rape in marriage*, in 1982, which built on much previous activism. Before this activism of the 1970s and 1980s, rape occurring in a marriage had rarely been considered as even possible.

Russell also developed (with others) the concept of 'femicide' to mean women killed for reasons connected to being women (also referred to, in terms of campaigns, in Chapter 9). Well-known UK activist academic Jill Radford joined with Russell to edit the later ground-breaking book, *Femicide: The politics of woman killing* in 1992.[2] Back in 1976 in Belgium, Russell had also pioneered the first feminist International Tribunal on Crimes Against Women, a four-day global women's speak-out denouncing all forms of sexual violence, patriarchal oppression and violations of women and girls. Attended by 2,000 women from 40 countries, it was addressed by Simone de Beauvoir.

At the beginning: small confidential groups on sexual violence

In the 1970s in the UK countries and elsewhere, women initially started talking about sexual violence and rape in small, confidential groups. In particular, sexual abuse survivors began, tentatively often, to speak out. It all then took off. Incest survivors groups were set up to discuss sexual violence in the home, mainly against girls in families, with women sharing their present or past experiences. And activists then began to come together to develop brave ideas about militantly campaigning on sexual violence and rape, both inside and outside the home. The women in these first rape and incest groups stepped out of the mould and made courageous moves into the unknown.

The rape crisis movement

They began to both campaign and to establish nascent rape projects to support women survivors, usually with no money, but with zeal and enthusiasm and endless energy from all participants. Women came together in dynamic groups to set up these new collectives dealing with rape (with the first one possibly being as early as 1973). The groups worked alongside, or overlapped with, incest survivors groups, across the UK and also in other countries. The initial US centre, for example, was established in Washington, DC, in 1972. It followed the first-ever feminist 'speak-out' on rape, held in a small church in Manhattan in January 1971. Organised by feminists including Susan Brownmiller, 40 women had stood up before an audience of 300 and spoken publicly for the first time about their rape experiences.

The emerging collective projects took the brand new name of 'rape crisis centres' wherever they were established, to assist women who had been raped or sexually assaulted. Functioning (often informal) rape helplines were quickly then set up so that women could talk confidentially about sexual violence, share experiences and identify the impacts of rape. Their principal aim was to respond to the damage done to those raped or sexual assaulted. They usually had a confidential phone line, operated by a series of volunteers on a rota, switched through to the personal numbers of group members.

As more and more helplines were established in towns and cities, some groups set up actual physical centres for victims/survivors. The new feminist rape crisis lines and centres were viewed even less positively by official agencies than their domestic violence counterparts were, and were almost always operated by dedicated women, unpaid. So there they were, these brave and usually young feminists, responding supportively and often at length to sexually violated women in deep trauma. A key book on the history of rape crisis in the UK is *Rape crisis: Responding to sexual violence* (2008) by Helen Jones and Kate Cook.[3]

The centres were by no means only in Western countries. For example, the redoubtable Cape Town Rape Crisis, with whom I have had the honour of working in South African townships, was established in 1976. Back then, the women in the first rape and incest groups everywhere had nothing at all – nothing whatsoever – to guide them. Often viewing themselves as radical or revolutionary feminists, although other sorts of feminists were involved too, they were carried along by passion and commitment.

As time passed, it became more and more clear what a hard journey it was, and on what a hard issue. Rape victims continued to be viewed negatively and denied the help they needed very often. In the 1970s and 80s, violent rape by a stranger had long been a crime (initially under common law). However, if these crimes were prosecuted at all, which they often were not, this was often done in a voyeuristic way, re-victimising and traumatising for victims. Sexual assaults by men whom women knew were not taken seriously at all by the police and the criminal justice system.

The grass-roots women activists were determined to challenge this situation, to say 'no' to male sexual violence and to take on these stigmas, myths and poor responses. Feminist activists also began to develop the idea of a continuum of sexual violence against women. This continuum included rape, sexual assault, sexual abuse, domestic violence, 'honour'-based violence, pornography and all coercive and non-consensual sexual activity. It was elucidated further by Liz Kelly in her 1988 book, very influential at the time, *Surviving sexual violence*.[4]

London Rape Crisis Centre and other pioneers

London Rape Crisis Centre was set up in the mid-1970s by powerful feminist activists.[5] It was one of the first rape crisis centres of all in the UK, a strong and pioneering feminist collective for more than a decade, and a radical feminist project. It provided comprehensive training for its volunteers and also detailed, in-depth supervision, offered by more experienced members or later by paid workers to less experienced ones. As time went on, the collective took on more and more work, not only on immediate or historic rape but also on the sexual abuse of girls in families, as women phoning in spoke about them. Violence in the family and rape overlapped in these situations as women found a place where they could talk about their own youthful experiences, as well as their adult ones, and those of children, girls and grown-up women close to them.

> A volunteer with the London Rape Crisis Centre spoke of the time-consuming, but total, commitment of being part of the collective with weekly meetings and other work and supervisions in-between. When on duty she would be on call on the phone for many hours, often through the night, while also holding down a full-time job and caring for two small children. It was an exhausting schedule. She never missed or cut short a session over all the years that she was involved. It was, she said 40 years later, a crucial and defining experience of her life.

About 30 women at most volunteered or worked for London Rape Crisis, but they had to cover the whole of London, with 24/7 phone coverage, weekly collective meetings which made all the decisions, and training/supervision meetings. In its prime, it was an exemplary and pioneering example of women working together, almost round the clock. Jane Anderson, a volunteer in the 1980s for many years, contributed the following beautiful words (which describe other passionate feminist projects too): "It was like a brilliant flash moving across the sky with incredible vigour. It was too all-consuming to be sustained forever, but flashed through the sky for those years like a brilliant meteor and I am very proud to have been part of it."

Rape crisis centres evolve further

London Rape Crisis was a pioneering umbrella centre, but came to an end many years ago. As one of the originators, it leaves, like other pioneer rape crisis centres, a fine legacy. In the 1970s, other ground-breaking centres were set up in most towns and cities. In Scotland, for example, the first rape crisis centre was established in Glasgow in 1976 and in Edinburgh in 1978, with Glasgow Rape Crisis remaining the longest operational rape crisis centre in the UK countries.

Originally relying solely on volunteers, Scottish rape crisis centres, and most elsewhere too, had acquired some funding by the mid-1980s, with all the contradictions that this entails (as noted earlier for domestic violence services). The rape crisis movement in Scotland has worked tirelessly ever since to operate strong feminist centres across the country, stretching as far north as Shetland. To find out more about the pioneering women who did all this and their experiences of the early days of the rape crisis movement, you can download the wonderful *Woman to women: An oral history of rape crisis in Scotland, 1976–1991*.[6]

As time went on, rape crisis centres gradually started running more officially established Freephone helplines for those who wanted to talk about what had happened to them. Working together in a collaborative and supportive way, they offered services, irrespective of whether or not the woman wanted to report the assault to the police. Rape crisis was (and is) independent of the government and criminal justice system.

The centres were collectives, of course, and tried to do things differently. For example, they often operated flattened or non-existent hierarchies in innovative ways. Professor and rape crisis activist Nicole Westmarland described how, in the infancy of the movement and for many years after, women working and volunteering in the centres frequently used a common name in public interactions, to avoid 'stars' emerging and to give statutory and other agencies a contact name. Whoever answered the phone to women callers or to officials would use this name.

In a recent 2019 Master's dissertation and related academic paper, both entitled 'The Whole Place Self: Reflecting on the original working practices of Rape Crisis', Fiona Vera-Gray looked at the radical roots of rape crisis centres, compared with today.[7] She observed that, whereas most therapeutic approaches concentrate on individual issues, rape crisis recognised cultural, social and structural factors, as well. They framed their work, she suggested, not as counselling, but as conversation, as what she names: 'relational self-encounter'.

Vera-Gray described how rape crisis, certainly in the early days, was committed to building connections, not separating the rape from the rest of a woman's life. Thus, women using services were not met with a distant professional response but with an intimate, 'whole' approach.

This radical way of working revolved around treating those who had been raped equally, with respect, and as real, whole, complex women, not solely as 'rape victims'.

Women Against Violence Against Women and Reclaim the Night

Campaigns and actions to defend the new rape services and to fight sexual violence have been necessary since the beginning – and the women's liberation movement was the pioneer. After rape crisis became established, Women Against Violence Against Women (WAVAW) was set up as a feminist organisation, fighting against sexual violence, pornography and exploitation. Established for the specific purpose of activism and campaigning in the 1980s, it was a radical and revolutionary feminist initiative in both the UK and the United States. One of the slogans it popularised was: 'All men are potential rapists'.

WAVAW was the first national feminist organisation in the US to protest mediated sexual violence against women in the media. For instance, they pressured the music industry to stop using images of violence against women in its advertising. In the UK, similarly, WAVAW campaigning groups in the 1980s fought against violent pornographic media in all kinds of ways. They often engaged with great bravery and audacity in direct action. In a few examples, they painted slogans and graffiti about sexual violence in sometimes dangerous locations for women to be in. They fly-posted slogans and posters, deliberately defiled pornographic images, and engaged in innovative guerrilla action against pornography outlets. They picketed and blocked the more sordid type of sex shops, or glued up their doors, literally pouring glue into the locks.

WAVAW also started the organising of 'Reclaim the Night' marches. The idea of these marches and campaigns was to mount a directly feminist struggle to make the streets safe from men's sexual and other predatory violence. While there had been some candle-lit women's demonstrations since about 1972, the first two specifically-named marches were probably in Philadelphia in 1975 and in Brussels in 1976, as women with candles walked through the streets at night. These pioneering actions were swiftly followed by similar ones in Germany. The Leeds Revolutionary Feminists took the initiative of holding the first UK Reclaim the Night march in 1977, building on the German and Belgian demonstrations.

The Leeds march was a very brave and defiant move in the town where the late Peter Sutcliffe, the so-called Yorkshire Ripper, was murdering women and had still not been apprehended.[8] It was deliberately routed past places where women's bodies had been found, a chilling and powerful statement. Reclaim the Night marches then rapidly happened around the UK, in North America (where they were called Take Back the Night) and elsewhere.[9] Reclaim the Night is now a global network of women's resistance to male violence and harassment on the streets. Marches are held in very many countries, including Japan, Bermuda, Canada, Italy, Poland, Germany, New Zealand, Hungary, Mexico and India. In the UK, these marches came to an end in the 1990s, but were restarted in 2004/2005 by the London Feminist Network (with some leadership from Finn Mackay who has written a comprehensive account of them in her book, *Radical feminism*[10]). Marches have been held since then especially in London, but in Bradford, Bristol and elsewhere too. In 2021, new activism after the murder of a young woman, Sarah Everard, gave rise to large-scale vigils and protests called 'Reclaim these Streets'.

While Reclaim the Night marches were traditionally woman-only, in recent years, men (in the UK and some other countries) have sometimes attended also. Elsewhere, men's marches are sometimes held. I was privileged to spend time with the African feminist woman organiser of a march against rape through a very tough South African township in the mid-1990s, not long after the end of apartheid. This march consisted solely of local Black men campaigning (exceedingly bravely in the context) against rape and the pervasive 'rape culture' in the townships.

Issues for Black and minority women

As for domestic violence services, there have been critiques of rape services as responding inadequately to women from

Black and other minority communities. This has particularly been the case, arguably, in the United States, with its unique and horrifying history of rape for African Americans. During and after slavery, the rape of enslaved women, and later their descendants, by white men was so common it was almost universal. After slavery ended, sexual violence and murder continued to be used widely to terrorise the African American population, both women and men. The lynching of Black men for supposedly raping white women (usually without evidence) then became common.

Aware of this brutal history, women of colour in the US critiqued the rape crisis movement during the 1970s and 1980s, suggesting African American women were sometimes excluded, and that their needs were not being met. After many painful conflicts, they developed strong anti-racism approaches together, which gradually informed the wider movement. This happened in the UK too, with some improvements in services for minority groups of all types. But BME specialist rape services continued to feel marginalised within the wider movement, according to women who were interviewed for this book.

A 2015 study confirmed that difficulties remained. The study was called *Between the lines: Service responses to black and minority ethnic (BME) women and girls experiencing sexual violence*, and was conducted by long-term feminist activist researcher, Ravi Thiara, with Sumanta Roy and Patricia Ng from Imkaan, which was a collaborator in the project.[11] (Imkaan is discussed in Chapter 8.) It identified that a major shift was needed in the provision of services for Black and minority ethnic survivors of sexual violence, in terms of properly understanding their specific situations, overcoming ignorance, and then responding appropriately.

Thiara and the team found some positive developments and effective projects across the country, usually women's ones in the women's independent sector. But, simultaneously, BME women and girls were still falling through the gaps generally (and even within that women's specialist provision). The second follow-up stage of the project was published in 2020 and showcased in-depth work with sexual violence survivors from BME communities and their help-seeking journeys. The study provided insights into how women from minority communities respond to sexual violence within a wider societal context of, what the study calls, 'silencing and unspeakability'.[12]

Research by Sarah-Jane Lilley Walker, Marianne Hester and others has shown that vulnerable women from all minority backgrounds who have experienced sexual violence still face discrimination in service provision, especially if they have mental health difficulties. They also point out that: 'Victims-survivors from Black and minority ethnic groups or lesbian, gay, bisexual, transgender, transsexual or queer groups are underrepresented within the criminal justice system.'[13] Further, many researchers in North America, Australia and the UK have confirmed, again and again, that disabled women are likely to be raped at twice the rate for non-disabled women, but services remain extremely patchy for disabled women across the board. There is still far to go.

Sexual violence initiatives in the UK: coming more up to date

In summary, across the world wherever they were established, the early rape crisis centres were grass-roots women-only groups. They often included survivors of rape themselves and had no buildings or funding. They were all collectives, seeing their work as radical and political. While the latter remains the case, they are, generally-speaking, no longer collectives. Both domestic violence and rape services in, for example, the US, the UK, Europe, Canada and elsewhere, tended to change in the 2000s to having Executive Directors and management boards (as discussed more fully in Chapter 7 in the Section on 'Moving on from collectives' and in Chapter 8). Almost all rape crisis centres across the UK countries became hierarchies, but generally slightly later than refuge organisations did.

The centres in London which came after the famed London Rape Crisis Centre were several. They now include North London Rape Crisis Centre, run by Solace Women's Aid, East London Rape Crisis Centre and West London Rape Crisis associated with the Women and Girls Network. Rape Crisis South London, also known as the Rape and Sexual Abuse Support Centre South London, is a pioneer service which was established back in 1984 and was the only rape crisis centre in London for about a decade. It provides advocacy, outreach and counselling, and now coordinates the National Rape Crisis Helpline. They all run services for BME women and can respond holistically, for example to immigration issues in relation to sexual violence.

From 1996, the Rape Crisis Federation was the coordinating body in England and Wales. In 2003, it was succeeded by Rape Crisis England and Wales, which joins with Rape Crisis Scotland to form the two umbrella feminist organisations in the UK. They support the work of rape crisis centres, raise awareness about sexual violence and provide coordinating services and statistics. Currently, there are 16 member rape crisis centres across Scotland. Rape Crisis England and Wales has 41 member centres in 51 locations, and a new centre has been established in Northern Ireland.

However, many previous centres have lost their funding. In 1984, there were 68 centres in the UK, but, by 2010, this number had fallen to 39. The two important reports, *Map of gaps: The postcode lottery of violence against women support services in Britain* (published in 2007 and 2009) by Maddy Coy, Liz Kelly and Jo Foord, assessed all provision, including domestic violence services.[14] For sexual violence, their reports contributed importantly to the pressure for improved funding. Scotland's funding landscape was already more generous, and coordinated through their dedicated fund and strategies. On the other hand, Northern Ireland was particularly deprived of services at the time in the surveys, and, overall, BME projects were markedly underfunded.

Another key research study by Rape Crisis and the Women's Resource Centre[15] in 2008 also demonstrated the critical need for more funding. Together with activist pressure, these moves forward resulted in the start of more sustained funding in England and Wales in the 2010s. This stabilised the movement to some extent and reversed the stem of closures, at least temporarily. Nonetheless, the majority of rape crisis centres, were, and still remain, severely underfunded, with only about 20 per cent managing to attain the full funding that they require.

The services that do exist continue to provide multiple types of support. Between them, local groups run the two Rape Crisis

National Helplines, one for Scotland and one for England and Wales (the latter hosted by South London Rape Crisis as noted). Rape Crisis England and Wales and Rape Crisis Scotland also provide detailed practice guidance and comprehensive National Service Standards which contain a particularly clear feminist vision. While some rape projects may have lost a bit of their campaigning zeal over the years and become engulfed in service provision, it can be argued that, because the sector has not been mainstreamed in the same way that domestic violence services often have, it has remained more radical as a site of feminist resistance to the patriarchal status quo. Others argue that there is not much difference.

In the UK, one in four women (24 per cent) are sexually assaulted during their lifetime, and there are about 80,000 incidents of rape or attempted rape every year, a depressing picture. However, a study by Nicole Westmarland and others in 2012 at Durham University found that rape crisis centres are highly effective in supporting women who have been sexually assaulted.[16] They might be harder to access and have sometimes lengthy waiting lists these days. Distressingly, the wait can be very many months. But they still offer free and confidential support, run by women for women, as a direct response to male sexual violence. While they have been constantly plagued by extreme funding difficulties, they have refused to go away. They always use the word 'feminist' – and often put the word 'proudly' before it.

Sexual Abuse Referral Centres, Independent Sexual Violence Advocate/Advisors and other rape organisations

Additionally, for some years, there have been SARCs, Sexual Abuse Referral Centres, commissioned by the NHS, often working with the police (in partial recognition of previous inadequate responses). The first was established at St. Mary's Hospital in Manchester in 1986. While individual SARCs work slightly differently, they all offer confidential, secure and often very good services, although not part of the independent rape crisis networks. SARCs provide legal help, liaison with the police, emotional support and, also, forensic medical examinations, when needed. They tend to cover recent cases, whereas rape crisis can also provide services responding to past rape experiences. SARCs seem to be viewed very positively by users.

There are also ISVA (Independent Sexual Violence Advocate/Advisor) teams who can provide invaluable emotional support and guidance for anyone reporting current, or historical, sexual offences, often through the criminal justice system. Created in 2005, the role of an ISVA is still, however, one that is not readily available everywhere. Originally associated with rape crisis and sexual violence activism and providing a holistic service within rape crisis centres to start with, they also now work closely with the statutory sector. Usually, risk assessments are required to access services from ISVAs and they have a set time limit. This means that victims of sexual violence can fall through the gaps. Or they might have to wait too long for services – which are then too short-lasting. But the effort is being made.

Other organisations working on rape include The Survivors Trust, an umbrella organisation, coordinating many sexual violence services. There is also Women Against Rape (WAR) founded in 1976, and associated with the English Collective of Prostitutes and Black Women's Rape Action Project. Operating separately from the other rape crisis services, they run *Against Rape*, a web resource providing support and advocacy for justice for women and girls, including asylum seekers, who have suffered sexual, domestic or racist violence. There is also support available for men experiencing rape, these days. Rape crisis centres are women-led and offer a range of services in women-only safe spaces. Over half also now provide services for male victims too, but these are kept completely separate from the women's services.

In sum

It needs to be noted that campaigns on rape including rape in war are noted in Chapter 9, as is the serious problem of attrition in rape cases (the precipitate decrease between the number of reports and of convictions). Other types of sexual violence are discussed in the section on harmful cultural practices in Chapter 8. Overall, the women's movement against sexual violence has had real victories over the years, although always fighting against inadequate funding and marginalisation, both in society and sometimes vis-a-vis the domestic violence movement.

As for domestic abuse, BMER women have had to fight for recognition in the wider sexual violence movement. And the number of rape crisis services decreased considerably in the early 2000s. Improved funding regimes have helped hugely for the moment, although they are short-term only. But the sector remains vibrant. This short history has recorded how rape crisis and other services arose and what they achieved, in parallel with the domestic violence movement, and as part of the wider effort to combat male violence. Dedicated activists and feminists led the way, then and now, and continue to carry the beacon of combatting sexual violence forward in the 2020s. They are to be supported and applauded in their painful, life-changing work.

6

A radical women's politics: the light of innovation and new ways to organise

Feminism must always be transformative. That is what feminism is.

Pragna Patel

A main aim and focus of this book is to highlight some of the transformatory understandings and wider 'politics' – most especially from the early days – that have characterised the violence against women movements in the UK and across the world. Feminism is nothing unless transformative, as Patel elucidates. And the feminist activists have always aimed to build a better world for women, but for children and men in many ways, too – in fact, for humanity.

From the 1970s on, both the rape crisis and the refuge movements in the UK's countries (and elsewhere) developed quite extraordinary ways of organising themselves, and came up with radical and innovative policies to govern their work. Many of these experimental practices no longer operate and, in fact, are in danger of being overlooked in these different times. Remembering them is important, however, to cherish and record precious feminist history. But it is also important because they can bring insights and ideas for now – and for the future. We forget them at our peril. It is to these innovations that we now turn. This is a celebration, really, of that time and of the innovative attempts at social change that the women activists made.

Focussing on domestic abuse, including sexual violence

This discussion is mainly illustrated through reference to the domestic violence movement and Women's Aid. However, the movement against sexual violence, discussed in the last chapter, also operated these sorts of policies. Like refuge organisations, rape crisis services and campaigns organised themselves as collectives. Also like refuge services, they held women-centred principles, and they tried consciously to break down power differences between the women using the services and those providing them – who were sometimes the same women. They depended, at least initially, on unpaid dedication, and they took rape services forward in new and feminist-inspired ways. After 40 years, many of them still do so.

Operating similar policies, the domestic abuse movement is the principal subject discussed here, as a kind of illustrative 'case study' of extraordinary feminist ways of organising. For myself, as author, the movement against domestic violence is, and was, a 'lived and felt' history of involvement and commitment. This account of the radical practices it pioneered is an act of retracing, of reclaiming, our feminist past. Academic analyses are available elsewhere. This, rather, is a memorialising, including some personal memoir of what we all achieved, especially but not solely in the early refuge collectives. These innovative women's policies and practice have rarely been recorded before in such detail.

The Support Group, refuge workers and ideals

The initial history of the domestic violence movement presented at the beginning of Chapter 4, described its brave stepping out into the unknown, and the way the network gradually became more firmly established as time went on. Most refuge groups in the 1970s and 1980s, operating at secret addresses, did not admit men, except as representatives of helping agencies. They were similar to rape crisis centres in that they all worked as collectives. Thus, as noted before, they were managed by a collective 'Support Group' (although in more recent times, they have developed formal Management Committees, and the Support Group is a thing of the past).

The original projects were set up and operated with endless enthusiastic work and commitment. There were years of struggle to obtain safe and secure accommodation and then to run it, all on a volunteer basis. But by the late 1970s, as discussed earlier, a Women's Aid group would usually employ a range of both paid and volunteer workers offering support to the women, advocating for them, and organising and operating the refuge.

Often, as time passed, specialised workers would also be employed to offer follow-up for those families who had moved on (maybe, for example, by running groups for women who had left the refuge). Outreach workers were also sometimes employed, and, later, finance workers or administrators. Groups began to be established as limited companies or charities, and, as they gained in official status, many had trustees or boards. They usually also had chairpersons and treasurers to undertake the specialist tasks needed, despite their general distaste (initially, anyway) for sterile procedural ways of doing things.

Support Groups were commonly open to including any women residents who wanted to participate. Understandably of course, many did not, as they struggled with their own traumas and crises. One of the interviewees for this book was Lesley Welch, a domestic violence coordinator and feminist worker for 40 years. She pointed out that many, and probably most, of the women residents in the early refuges were looking for help, for a resolution of their personal situations, and possibly to then go home again. They almost certainly weren't thinking about trying to change the world or to build a feminist revolution.

It could be guessed that some would probably have responded to that sentence with: 'building a what?' Thus, there was often a disjuncture between what the collective believed as a whole and was trying to achieve, and what the women using the services believed and were trying to achieve. Nevertheless, the attempt was made to build something new, and some women residents joined in, and others didn't.

The Support Group would generally meet weekly in different women's houses or in an office, if they had one. Also, at least some of the meetings might be held in the refuge itself, to try and be serious about enabling residents to come along, if they wished to. There would very likely be long discussions, going on into the night, but members rarely missed a meeting. They enjoyed them usually, according to interviewees, and warm and fast friendships were often forged. It could be a pleasure, then, to meet up together once a week. Members frequently found their identity there, in the collaborative, collective, feminist group, working together in a committed and passionate way, learning from each other, and evolving together.

Members of past Women's Aid groups talked for this book about personally experiencing both growth and change in the group. They often felt that they were achieving transformative and political collective change too. At the meetings, they would discuss wide-ranging issues about the refuge, the work that needed doing each week and who was going to do it, as well as campaigning or training programmes (both for themselves and, as time went on, for professionals in the field) that they might have been conducting. They also dealt with both employment and management matters, although many of them would try not to use those words.

> The commitment of Women's Aid groups was often total and enduring. In a refuge where I worked, the joke, 35 years later, is whether any of us from the original collective can manage to pass the old refuge building (flats now for more than 20 years – nearly a quarter of a century) without turning our heads round and looking at it. So far, it seems, no one has.

What was offered?

All the paid workers, volunteers and Support Group members were able to offer emotional support. Then, as now, women using domestic violence services had frequently been physically, sexually and psychologically traumatised and had left behind not only their male partners, but also their communities, homes, families, friends and possessions. They were often in the most severe crisis of their lives. The workers, together with other women living in the refuge or using related services, usually offered as much support as they could, and became very skilled at dealing with the painful experience of domestic violence.

One thing that was almost always done, as recalled by several interviewees who had worked in refuges in the past, was going to get the woman's possessions. Brave workers, together with the woman, would go back to her home, often with police officers attending. In the 1970s, these officers tended to be less than helpful, but by the 1980s, after some training, the police to their credit sometimes helped a lot. However, if the police could not come, the women would go anyway.

Trying to ascertain if the violent partner could be there might take some detective work, but then the house would be entered, and the woman would take her children's and her own belongings. Workers would cart heavy bags, or even pieces of furniture, out onto the street and take everything back to the refuge. Sometimes, they would use a project minibus (which many refuges had after a few years) or their own private transport, or women-driven vans which other women's collectives, at the time, might operate. An argument could extremely easily be made that this was foolhardy with insufficient attention to physical safety, as well as to the general 'health and safety' of employees, but it was routinely and cheerfully done, nonetheless.

If the partner was there, angry scenes might ensue. Sometimes, in my own experience, the workers might mediate to calm the man down, as possessions he probably regarded as his – not to mention his former family life – were removed from in front of his eyes. And his wife or partner disappeared into the unknown, with a group of strange women. There might be tears and screaming, as well, on all sides, or sometimes physical belligerence and tussles over possessions. Obviously, there was real danger too.

This is rarely done these days when risk issues, together with health and safety regulations, tend to reign supreme. All the Women's Aid federations offer helpful online guidance for survivors, including advice on leaving home and safety planning. Practically, some train companies now offer free tickets so survivors can move areas (as is often recommended) to find safe refuge. Looking back to those earlier 'do-it-yourself' days though, the way women's belongings were brought to the refuge shows the commitment of the collective members.

It also shows the risks which they were all willing to take to help women survivors. We/they were determined to do things differently from what traditional or statutory agencies would do. It turned out, though, as Lesley Welch and others recollected, that occasionally statutory workers would help way beyond the call of duty too, particularly (but not solely) if the worker had experiences of violence herself.

Another example was the common practice of one or two workers going to meet somewhere with a woman and children who were escaping violence. They might meet them at a bus stop, for instance, scooping them up in a car and racing back to the refuge, making sure they were not being followed. Brave indeed. Of course, the violent man could be hiding round the corner and sometimes was.

At the refuge where I worked in the early 1980s, colleagues recalled a mad and dangerous chase across the city with the furious husband driving frighteningly recklessly behind them. But, even without such drama, the courage of all concerned was outstanding. First, the courage of the traumatised woman standing on the street with her children (and plastic bags of belongings perhaps), waiting to be met by ...? Well, by who? She had no idea whatsoever, usually. And then, these unknown women would whisk her away from everything that her life, until that moment, had been. Her bravery was beyond what most people could ever summon. Secondly, in the courage stakes, were the workers rushing to find her and not knowing her either, but getting her and all her children into the vehicle and away. Their bravery was staggering too, but felt normal at the time. It was just what we/they did.

One interviewee talked about the waterfall of relief she felt when, after a frightened, trembling train journey, she saw the two unknown women who were waiting for her to pick her up at the train station. She climbed into the similarly unknown car, she said, holding back tears and clasping her child's hand, throwing their fate to the winds. She said that, as soon as one of the women started to talk to her, she knew she was safe.

Women and children, arriving like this family did, would then stay in the refuge (with usually one locking room per family and communal living space) and make the best life they could there, sometimes in challenging conditions. But they usually got at least some of the support they needed from other women and the workers in the refuge. The workers also became expert at dealing with the (then) Department of Health and Social Security (then UK-wide) to access welfare benefits for the women and, later, at getting those who needed a new home re-housed in council or housing association accommodation under the 1977 Housing (Homeless Persons) Act (also UK-wide at the time).

In the mid-1970s, feminist activists had struggled to get domestic violence included in this Act as a valid reason for 'unintentional homelessness' (in the words of the legislation). This meant that the housing authority, from then on, had a duty to re-house homeless abused women in 'priority need' – for example, those with children. This was a triumph and has assisted thousands of women who have left home with their children, due to domestic abuse, to get new permanent accommodation.

Rather than being like social workers or housing officers, refuge workers instead stood firm, shoulder-to-shoulder, with survivors of violence from the refuge to advocate on their behalf with (or, sometimes, against) those social workers and housing officers. With such unwavering advocacy and emotional support offered, women and children could feel safe and secure, while their situations got sorted out. Many stayed just a short time, depending on their circumstances, but families could usually stay in the refuges for some months, if necessary, while waiting for a housing offer, or to resolve other legal, emotional or financial issues.

Statutory and other relevant agencies had to be educated to respond to abused women and their children sympathetically, and with non-judgemental respect and, crucially, belief. Often, instead, they were hostile or obstructive. Some could not have been less interested.[1] In taking them on, the feminist advocates for domestic violence survivors needed to use all their skills. I recall one early and embryonic training meeting where the relevant officers actually turned their chairs to face away from us, and responded negatively and grumpily to all our (carefully non-provocative) approaches. But gradually, the battle was more or less won. Training courses for professionals on domestic violence and its impacts started to be provided, as is routinely the case now. Refuge groups began to conduct institutional advocacy both on behalf of the survivors staying with them, and more widely. And at least some statutory agencies, including lawyers and housing officers, started responding a bit more positively and developing new policies and services.

Thus, getting into a refuge often meant not only temporary housing and emotional support, but also assistance with longer-term housing and financial help too, as well as dealing with the official agencies. An interviewee for this book, Ann Devereaux, who is happy to use her name, talked about how different it would have been for her if, instead of a refuge, she had ended up in a hostel, or social services project, or on her own with her daughter in a bedsit. Instead, she got a safe roof over their heads, deep and sustaining emotional help that continued throughout, and assistance to get re-housed after some months.

She spoke about how transformative it was, after years of isolation and coercive abuse, to meet others in the same situation and talk about the violence all had experienced. Ann described how she made deep friendships in the refuge (even though some of the families were less approachable of course). And she was provided with solid, in-depth, ongoing support by sympathetic and dedicated workers.

She explained that she doubts she would still be here in the world without the committed help of the refuge. "It was a precious stepping stone," she added. It turned her life around in every way. This offering of grounded, skilful support remains the case to a large extent today in Women's Aid member groups and other feminist-connected domestic violence services. The 'refuge way of doing things' is an important contribution to egalitarian social care, and to how to provide social services in an equal and empowering way.

Children and child support workers

As time went on in the early years, refuge services attempted to employ children's support workers to provide services for the children resident there. The provision of children's workers is now a standard part of many domestic violence organisations, sometimes funded under separate funding streams, although often the first to go when cutbacks come. Back at the beginning, they were something quite new. Support for children from families where there was domestic violence was something society had never thought of, or attempted, before.

A woman who had lived in a refuge as a child, 35 years ago, talked for this book of how much fun these children's services were then, often with exciting activities. Mothers spoke warmly of them too. Another adult survivor interviewed who had been in a refuge in the 1980s talked about the importance, as a child, of having felt safe, and of there always being a worker to talk with about how you felt. What was most important of all for her was that the child support worker would listen actively to her, more or less whenever she needed it, and make her feel special and worthwhile. Some refuges set up specific discussion groups for the children on the abuse they had experienced (although this could be hard to maintain). But children's meetings on other topics were frequently held, often very informally.

Many child residents had known very violent lives and might themselves have been subjected to physical punishment, or sometimes actual physical or sexual abuse. Workers could provide focussed help and, as time went on, refuge groups developed child protection policies. There were usually non-violence policies within the project, as well, which began in this early period, and have continued. Women were not allowed to smack or hit their children in many refuges. If they kept doing so, support (including on alternative ways of guiding children) was provided to help them stop. Workers would discuss the issues and sympathetically talk through possibilities to try to build, with the woman, a different way of parenting.

The specialist children's workers offered the children support, guidance and assistance (and continue to do so, when they have funding). They provided facilities for creative play, and represented children's interests and wishes. They also conducted advocacy work on behalf of children experiencing domestic abuse with Children's Social Services, schools and other agencies, and were committed to 'getting alongside' children in a meaningful way. When it was working well, child support workers were able – and continue to be able – to give the children a sense of security and confidence, and to provide strong emotional, practical and in-depth support.

> A previous worker remembered: "There was likely to be 'Mother Christmas' at Christmas-time, weekly swimming perhaps, games and activities which were empowering, and crazy joint holidays. These would be to somewhere like Butlin's – or camping. This was often somewhat haphazard and inefficient camping, it must be said (with some women possibly in high heels, for instance), but everyone loved it."

Another woman who now has a successful career working with survivors of sexual violence, and has transformed her life, contributed the following about her time in a refuge as a child, 30 years ago:

> When my family and I first got help, what I felt as a child was that I met this kind lady who I sensed in my gut was safe. I was about 9 or 10 years old and the kind lady was at the women's refuge that my mother had taken me to. I knew the moment we stepped in the door that we were safe. No more walking on eggshells, no more shouting, screaming, banging, bruises, lies, then sorry, and the cycle starting again. That's what the refuge meant to young me: safety and escape.
>
> For me and my family, their work is part of what saved us. Put simply, because of refuges, the world is a safer place for many, many real people. And also they pass the torch on to women everywhere (including myself) to carry on the work. And they continue to inspire new generations to carry it on. Those refuge workers didn't just work on violence against women, they sat right alongside the women and really listened and then influenced change.

Being a collective

Women's Aid and other organisations at the time, like rape crisis centres and campaigns on violence against women, attempted the very difficult task of operating as a collective. This was challenging for all concerned, but felt right politically, and led to concepts of equality, shared decision-making and the breaking down of power differentials between members. It produced an inclusive, egalitarian working environment. A variety of techniques were tried out to enable decisions to be made and work to be done collectively. Of course, there were also hidden agendas at work at times, and informal power structures (or powerful individuals) sometimes undermined the idea of being a collective. But at least the brave effort was made.

It was a journey of change being a Support Group member or a worker, almost everyone interviewed agreed. As few knew how collectives might work best, especially if they were dealing with something as painful and difficult as inter-personal or sexual violence, different ideas were tried in many groups. It is generally true that collectives need to be dynamic. They are a form of organisation that needs to grow and evolve, and not stay static or rigid. The women's movement collectives certainly fitted this requirement. Many of the refuge and rape crisis ones changed and developed all the time, as the members arrived at new ways of operating.

Being a collective did not mean that everyone did the same work. At the beginning, some groups were highly equalised with everyone doing everything. This could be difficult if someone else had already done what you had done, and if no one at all had done something else important, despite good intentions. Quite soon, most collectives refined this process. Thus, some members would do finance work, while others would offer emotional help. The women's domestic violence collectives had members fulfilling a variety of different tasks, as they developed, so that it was not a case of equal work. Rather, it was that all work was of equal value.

Everyone earned the same salary, usually. And everyone also had the same employment benefits. (These typically might include International Women's Day being a holiday.) According to three interviewees, many collectives contained women who had left-wing or socialist views, as well as being feminists, or who had strong opinions about workers' rights. Such projects would try to have generous employment strategies and benefits in place.

A few refuge groups offered 24-hour cover but many did not, on the grounds that the house belonged to the women, not the workers. Of course, the house was clearly not really the women's house, but the statement of trust was sometimes appreciated by residents. It made them feel important. On the other hand, where night-time staff cover was offered (as it often is, these days), it could be helpful, according to a woman interviewed who had worked in such a project. She said that women might open up late at night about their needs and problems, and support at any time could be provided. But this was not generally the refuge way, at least initially.

Some offered contact for women in the refuge with workers for only about 4 hours a day (although possibly including a key worker scheme). However, it is important to note that someone would certainly be on call for the rest of the time, rotated between workers, or sometimes Support Group members, using, scarcely believably these days, their personal phone numbers. A survivor interviewed who had lived in a refuge like this said that, while she understood the workers could only be there sometimes, it felt like too little time, and that it could be scary and lonely when the place was unstaffed.

The idea was that the women living there would take care of things when the workers were not on duty, and usually they did. They were adult women and often mothers, of course. They might deal with referrals and with women and children being admitted during the night, having been brought (sometimes with no notice at all) by the police, for instance. This was routinely carried out seamlessly by residents. But, sometimes, they did not wish to take on these duties or to co-operate in this way of course, and difficulties might then arise, especially around men being admitted. Looking back now, all this can sound risky (even though there was an on-call rota). What if things had gone badly wrong? But in reality, they almost never did.

A woman in a refuge in the 1980s looked around her at the scuffed paint, while chatting to a group of workers and other residents. She casually offered the insightful words,

"Well, this place is a *shit-house*, isn't it ... with a *heart of gold*."

Making decisions collectively

How to make decisions collectively in the Support Group, and also among the volunteers and workers (who might have their own meetings), was a fraught issue that many refuge groups would constantly work on. Some contained a more experienced figure who might lead the way in making important decisions, or a chairperson or small long-standing group with more power or experience who had been authorised to do so. Nevertheless, many decided to do it by consensus, however long arriving at such a consensus might take.

To try to combat some women having more power or talking all the time, techniques might be used like gently – but firmly – asking the vocal ones to give others a chance, and deliberately going round the circle. The latter meant that everyone had to speak about the issue at hand, even if they didn't really want to. With support and encouragement, those who were more silent would often learn to speak up. One woman spoke of her anguish in the group meetings as her turn to speak became closer and closer. She would feel sick in her stomach initially. It could be claimed that the technique was intrusive.

However, this women and others spoke of how so many encouraging, warm congratulations were offered that they had broken through their own barriers and become able to contribute meaningfully to collective decisions. The circle technique did enable them to become more confident and express their views, and the way that the consensus-made decisions were arrived at was improved by having everyone's input. On occasion, one interviewee said, someone who had managed to speak out about what they wanted to would be full of pleasure and pride.

Of course there were long disagreements, but there was usually, in my own experience, a careful listening to the points of view of others, with the deliberate intention, not of adversarial argument and putting the other person down, but of arriving at an agreement. After all, the project with all its traumas had to be run, come what may. This collectively-held intention carried the day usually (as far as women consulted for this book, who had been involved in making decisions in this way, could remember).

Some groups made decisions not by consensus, but by voting (verbally and informally), with the proviso that those in the minority committed themselves to do whatever the majority decided. While this is a classic, decision-making technique and democratic process in general use, it could be done, in Women's Aid, with much emotional support and caring. Sometimes, an almost therapeutic amount of attention was offered to how everyone felt about the decision made and their part in it.

Thus, the collectives were almost always more than just work groups. They tried to have a counselling and caring role in the lives of their members, according to their feminist principles. And they often saw this as an essential part of the work, not as an optional extra. In addition to weekly Support Group meetings, some refuges I knew also had weekend meetings, or longer sessions, to talk about personal issues in a more consciousness-raising format. They might discuss their mothers or childhoods, having children or not, new issues coming up in the women's movement, or each other's emotional problems. Some of these groups also had weekend meetings to educate each other about, say, new understandings of domestic violence, or social class, racism, or anti-lesbianism.

Women using the services having as equal a say as possible

One of the main ways that these experimental collectives set up by the movements against domestic abuse (and against violence against women more widely) worked was, as much discussed in this book, by involving everyone – from experienced workers to women using services – as equally as possible. The refuge and rape crisis networks, from the mid-70s on, always held that it was women who had suffered violence who were the experts on the experience, rather than professionally qualified social workers or therapists. In developing practice and policy, therefore, the views of abused women were sought, promoted, and acted on, as a matter of principle.

Women who lived in refuges usually had the opportunity, as noted earlier, to be considered as actual members of the collective (firstly with the volunteer women and, later, when workers began to be employed, with the paid workers and Support Group members). This worked well in practice a lot of the time, although women residents commonly were not interested in coming to organisational meetings. As for the wider notion of collective working more generally, it sometimes was an innovative initiative, but occasionally ran into problems and tangles. Mainly, I would suggest, though, it was a new and exciting concept in collectivity – and an honourable one.

On occasion, interviewees talked of how women in a refuge would hold the wider collective to task and state categorically that they were not being treated the same as the feminist workers/volunteers. In such a situation, class differences might come to the fore. And the women were right. Of course, it is true that the women residents could not really be equal with the workers, in a situation where the former were using services provided by the latter, and the latter had power over who came and who left. This was especially the case when the workers needed to take control to resolve difficult situations. Overall, it was they who were really running things. But, in reality, everyone was well aware of that.

In my own experience, it was not usually a case of pretence. Workers, Support Group members and women residents all understood this arrangement most of the time. What it actually meant was that the women residents and users of the services were viewed as important members of the whole, with valued experiences to share, and opinions to contribute. According to violence survivors who were interviewed, they felt that refuge workers shared their role and power in an admirable way. They said that they had never experienced anything like it in other places – even if it could not be a situation where everyone was fully equal. This experiment in equality, and its pros and cons, are also discussed in the section on: 'Was it all over-idealistic?'

Let us listen now to the words of a previous resident, Ann, quoted earlier. She explained how it was unbelievable to her that suddenly she was being taken seriously and listened to, after years of extreme coercive abuse and violence. Even if the idea was rather idealistic, it worked, she thought, in practice. She was able to build her confidence and skills, to know that she was worth something and to make friends with the women running the project. Thirty-five years later, those friendships are still in place, full of warmth, memories and mutual commitment.

She says she was helped to grow strong by other women in the refuge and by the workers. Having someone to talk to about her abuse who understood gave her a new autonomy. Being treated as an equal (as much as possible) by the workers enabled her to feel and be respected and worthwhile, and to develop a successful life. She later worked as a volunteer worker at the collective's office for some years, learning new skills, conducting administration, and participating in interviews for new workers, for example.

Children were part of the egalitarian project. They often became friends with the children of the workers who would come along to the get-togethers, too, so that they all mixed in together. There might also be parties for both women and children in worker's houses. These days, social work practice would regard this as unwise, and as not maintaining a proper professional distance between service giver and service receiver. But, back then, we didn't care. We were quite deliberately trying to make something radical and different in how women and children could interact together.

It goes without saying that some children staying in refuges might have severe problems and be difficult to handle or aggressive, in which case the mixing up with workers' own children might be curtailed. But generally it worked well. The first thing my own daughter remembered, when I spoke to her about my time working in a refuge, was 'Mother Christmas' and the Christmas parties, to which all the resident and workers' children would go.

Children's opinions were also regarded as important, and sometimes were considered as part of the wider decision-making process. In some refuges, separate children's meetings were held to make actual decisions contributing to refuge life. This could be a radical experience for the children concerned who had perhaps known little except abuse in the past. Suddenly their opinions were being viewed as important and worthwhile. There were also attempts to directly increase the power and influence of the decisions that they had come up with.

On one occasion in the same refuge mentioned above, for example, the children imposed rules on the refuge residents as a whole about not smoking in the communal rooms. (Smoking was the norm at the time, before smoking bans came into force.) These children-made rules were then discussed at the collective house meetings and the women living there agreed to abide by the children's proposals. From then on, there was no smoking and it lasted for a considerable period. The children could hardly believe that their opinions and decisions had won over everyone and that it was they – the children – who had made change happen.

Innovative employment practices in the collectives

There were other things, perhaps, that need to be remembered, revisited and celebrated about the innovations in collective working that the domestic violence movement tried out. In terms of radical and innovative contributions, some of these policies were intriguing. Support Groups and collectives, for example, were often challenged by working class members to break down both conscious and unconscious discrimination, and middle class ignorance and sense of class entitlement. As a response to these issues, working class women might well be favoured for jobs. Life experience was frequently regarded as of equal or greater importance than formal training and qualifications.

Interestingly, in most groups, there were policies that individuals could not hold employment positions for too long, in order to avoid them becoming too dominant and entrenched, and to give others a chance at the job. Typically, a couple of years was the maximum. (This was the case both in refuges and for the national workers in the federations, at the beginning.) In some projects (although not across the board), innovative employment practices, expanding this policy, were put in place. Middle class women could work at the refuge but would have to relinquish their jobs after two years. On the other hand, women from working class backgrounds (and also violence survivors) could hold their jobs for three years (or sometimes for longer).

The idea of this provision was to combat middle class and educational privilege, to open up more jobs to women who did not have such advantages, and to challenge employment discrimination. It was practised for years in some refuge groups, and was an effective innovation to strengthen working class or, sometimes, Black workers. In the 1990s to 2000s, it gradually disappeared. Keeping good workers on staff, gradually increasing the level of staff skills and training, and fulfilling funders' requirements for qualified employees, became the order of the day. As time went on, Women's Aid and other domestic violence services also developed ways of defining and setting boundaries between workers and those with employment or management responsibilities, and of providing for employment rights, including grievance and disciplinary procedures, and the like.

Abused women getting jobs and careers

Breaking down power differences led to the deliberate practice of employing ex-service users and ex-residents of refuges as paid workers. Thus, women who had lived in refuge projects, or who had experienced domestic violence, were encouraged in the 1980s and 1990s to apply for refuge jobs after they had left. The collectives at the time considered relevant life experience to be of great value in choosing workers (while also valuing specific skills and training). This belief applied both to women applying for jobs through the usual employment procedure, as noted above, but it also applied to ex-residents and other women survivors. It meant that applicants for jobs who had experience of violence did not need to have formal qualifications. Some refuge groups put in place a policy that women from the refuge who wanted, later, to apply for jobs needed to have been out of the refuge for at least 6 months, in order to achieve distance and perspective.

In recent years, Women's Aid services remain the agencies that consult domestic abuse survivors the most, and there are extensive strategies and materials through which this happens. But there has been a decrease in the extent to which refuge residents can make decisions and influence the organisation as a whole. The idea of previous residents and users of services becoming employees has lost its importance, these days, as workers are sought with qualifications and experience of the work or of, say, financial management or assessment.

It is true that a few refuge and outreach services do still operate such policies, and some Independent Domestic Violence Advisers (see Chapter 9) and other domestic violence advocates might have come through training programmes for abuse survivors. They are then likely to bring with them skills that women who have not experienced violence cannot reproduce. Women survivors can also train, and gain qualifications, through the different levels of accredited training offered by the Women's Aid (England) National Training Centre and by the other federations. But it is not the same.

Many of us from years ago regret the passing of the deliberate strategy of employing suitable previous residents. It empowered the women concerned, and gave them work experience and both life skills and professionals skills. It also reinforced a solidarity between survivors. It meant that women using refuge services were supported by 'one of their own', by other women who knew about their experiences – who knew what they were talking about. This was a strength without parallel. (Of course it could also be contradictory. An interviewee who had lived in a refuge and then become a worker talked of divided loyalties and sometimes feeling she had to cover for women residents in front of the other workers.)

It is important to remember that all this experimentation was taking place within the most painful of environments characterised by trauma and debilitating experiences of personal violence. It was a hard road, with bitter experiences all round, often of the most extreme nature – as in this sad memory. A talented woman who had lived in a refuge had later become part of the collective and was seeking employment. She was regarded as an ideal candidate for an upcoming refuge job which she was offered. She prepared for the task fastidiously, studied for the new job, and separated herself from her previous service user role.

However, just before this could take effect, she was killed by her ex-husband in 1986. Her name was Pam Cooke (Khalil). There were three editions (1993, 1998, 2005) of the book by Ellen Malos and myself, *Domestic violence: Action for change.*[2]

It is to Pam Khalil that they are all dedicated. These are the words used:

> This book is dedicated to the memory of Pam Cooke (Khalil), whom we knew and who recovered from domestic violence to build a strong new life. Pam was an inspiration to other women attempting to escape violence in the home. On 22 August 1986, Pam was killed by her former husband.

Regional and national organisation: spreading democratic decision-making

The flattening of hierarchies and the commitment to the collective ideal spread wider than individual projects. Refuges in Women's Aid were part, for example, of the regional and national organisation and structure which also aimed to work as collectively as possible. All of the federations operated a devolved structure for making collective decisions, with as many women feeding in, across regions, as possible. Member groups attended meetings with other refuge groups in their region with regular commitment. Each group was an autonomous organisation in its own right. But, after internal discussion, representatives would then feed the views of their group into the regional meeting and into wider participative debates, policy-making and campaigning.

Women's Aid in England, these days, retains a regional organisation with some national workers devolved to the regions, but the system works somewhat differently. Back then, the regional meetings made far-reaching decisions for their region and fed ideas up to the national level. An important part of this was that women residents would go along too, both to regional meetings and national ones. That meant they could represent their refuge and learn to speak in public and to negotiate issues, if they wanted to. There would be an atmosphere of solidarity as women who had been abused met other survivors from different geographical areas, and exchanged stories from far and wide. It was a fine collective effort by all concerned.

The National Women's Aid conferences in each UK country were like that too, probably to a greater extent than they are today. They would be packed with workers and Support Group (now Management) members from different refuge groups across the UK country concerned, as they still are. But women residents from all those refuges would be part of it, too. Transport and accommodation were often provided for women who lived in refuges, or who had recently done so. They could then link up with friends from other areas, feed into national debates, policies and campaigning, and take part on the national stage of the Women's Aid federations.

One women interviewed who had lived in a refuge spoke of how it had quite transformed her life, going to the national conferences of Women's Aid (England) and elsewhere. She went to places she had never even heard of before, and felt that these were some of her best moments ever. She was able to speak in discussions and to learn how things worked. And she said that new vistas were opened up for her in a way that she would never previously have thought possible. They would have been beyond her widest expectations of life.

A strong memory carried by most of us who have ever been part of those conferences (as related by two interviewees, one from Women's Aid in England) is the disco in the evenings. At some point, 'I will survive' sung by Gloria Gaynor would almost always be played, usually several times, and everyone would sing and dance. This remains the case today with passionate participation from Women's Aid member groups, a moving manifestation of the national conference and all that the movement meant – and means – to everyone.

In the earlier days, there would also be enthusiastic representation of women who were actually living in, or had recently lived in, refuges. So, there would always at the time be large numbers of women who were survivors of violence and their supporters, dancing and cheering and pumping the air joyously to 'I will survive'. They were singing the words and dancing together, in a liberated communal way within a women-only environment. They were shouting out that they would survive – and they were doing just that. It was something that, before, in their previous lives of abuse and possible control by their partners, they could never have dreamed of. And neither could the original feminist activists, starting out, back at the beginning. Abused women were building their strength together, indeed.

A concluding remembrance

The collectives have almost all gone now. But they were a wonderful, participative and challenging way to work, from the bottom up, attempting to spread equality and collaborative decision-making. Many achieved remarkable advances in how to work equally together, with participants sometimes figuring it out, as they went along. The change to hierarchies, with the expansion of the sector, is discussed at the end of the next chapter, which looks at the feminist beliefs of the domestic violence movement more broadly. But the times of the collectives were something to be remembered, to be learned from – and to be treasured.

7

Wider feminist principles and domestic violence: making a new world

This chapter moves on to discuss the wider feminist principles and innovative policies of, in the main, the domestic violence movement, but of rape crisis too. They all stemmed directly from women's liberation. The idea of these two chapters is that we can perhaps learn from these innovations, and that it is vital to preserve, to remember and to celebrate them.

Women-only

One of the most important and most basic of these principles was, and continues to be, the commitment to being women-only. Thus, most refuge groups, like rape crisis centres, were and remain, organisations of women, working with women for women, with roots in the women's liberation movement. Survivors who have suffered sometimes severe violence and violations may be intimidated by the presence of men. So, it can be particularly recuperative to leave these problems behind, to begin the process of recovery in a safe space. Women (who had previously been facing domestic violence, often in isolation and fear) living in Women's Aid refuge projects from the early 1980s on often said how wonderful it was to find out that there were other women who would help them, in a space without any men – that women could stand firm together.

The women-only principle could, however, be compromised by men gaining entry to the secretly-located premises. Abusive partners, or new or present ones, were not allowed in refuges for security reasons. But, where there were no workers on site, some women might let in their present or former boyfriends, or more rarely their abuser(s), and even have them staying overnight, which might traumatise others. To make it worse, two interviewees recalled how some of these men could be belligerent to other residents. In one refuge mentioned (and commonly), women who admitted their partners or other men would be asked to leave. To be clear, this was not a matter of anti-men ideology. At the same refuge, someone let a man (who was friendly and seemingly non-aggressive) in through the front door. He then killed his ex-partner in the hall in front of their children.

At the beginning of the Women's Aid movement, some refuge organisations employed committedly anti-sexist men as childcare workers to act as models (particularly perhaps for the boys) of how men could be gentle, non-violent and involved in looking after children. These men did their best to give children alternative ideas about male behaviour and what being a man means. They provided a careful programme of activities and many were sad and hurt, according to an interviewee, when they were told their services were no longer needed. But that is what happened. In the late 1970s, the decision was made to become a women-only organisation and to affirm the ability of women together to oppose male violence. The 'no men rule' has been, and continues to be, a strategy of empowerment, although various refuges outside Women's Aid, like some rape crisis centres, do now involve some men.

A difficult issue was when a boy started being a man. How old could boys be in order to live in women-only refuges with their mothers? Various groups allowed boys up to 16 or 17 years. Others would only take boys up to puberty or to age 11. This hard situation led to some women being unfortunately torn between seeking safe refuge and living with their sons. In many cases, sons had to be left behind. The issue continues today.

In a further hard issue concerning transgender and non-binary sexualities, sometimes distressing ongoing conflicts are in progress at the time of writing. These revolve around maintaining supportive spaces for cisgender women who are survivors of rape or domestic abuse by men, who might be traumatised by the presence of someone who was assigned male at birth. The opposing view is held by the transgender activist movement which seeks to promote rights for trans women and to ensure their access to services on domestic abuse which many experience. (A lot of refuges admit women who self-identify as women, and try to work out solutions sensitively.)

Was it all over-idealistic?

Various women who had lived in refuges spoke to me in a similar way to the survivors quoted previously in the section on 'women residents having an equal say'. The refuge was nothing like a hostel or a homeless project, they said, rather it was something new where abused women could build both their confidence and, at best, a new violence-free life. On the other hand, the views of abused women, engulfed in their own personal situations and just wanting some help, could conflict with the feminist commitment of the workers to building a new way of being for women and children, a new world. There were differential levels of power and influence, not only between workers and women using services, but also within the worker groups and wider Support Groups, with some powerful members dominating others on occasion. Ironing out these personal power differentials could be harder, in reality, than had been originally imagined.

The Women's Aid federations have changed as they have developed, but are still guided by the voices and views of survivors. However, some of the strategies from the earlier days for breaking down differences in power both within groups, and between women living in refuges and those working in them, have diminished. Survivors still form a central part of the work of domestic violence services, and everything is informed by their voices and views in organised, structured ways. But it is a different scenario.

Looking back now from the distance of years, it could perhaps be that, as Liz Kelly and myself pondered in our discussion for this book, there was a certain 'over-idealism' to the project in those earlier days, in terms of the valiant attempts made to flatten hierarchies, to work collectively and to break down power differences between women using the services and those providing them. Of course, the feminist activists had to have idealism to try any of it at all. That was a given. Their bravery was fanned by their idealism. Nothing would have evolved without it. But were they sometimes, as members of the collective, expecting too much of themselves and too much of the abused women who used the services?

Both previous workers and survivors who had lived in refuges spoke for this book of how, of course, not everyone did what the collective needed. Workers could have bitter disagreements with each other, especially as identity politics developed towards the end of the 1980s, discussed further later, although they generally tried to resolve these for the good of the work overall. Refuge residents could sometimes behave in ways which compromised everyone's ideal. Enduringly, there was, for example, the problem of men being admitted without the workers knowing.

It is probably true that activists in the violence against women movement tended to think very idealistically that, as Kelly pointed out, the women, both using services and working in them, were 'good' and would always act in the interests of the group. It could then be disturbing when they didn't! Fran Wasoff, long-term feminist family law researcher, mentioned earlier, spoke for this book of the many positives. But she also spoke of how the women residents in Scottish refuges could sometimes be racist towards, for example, South Asian Women. This was one of the impetuses for the later setting up of Shakti Women's Aid, Edinburgh's refuge for BME women, in 1986.

She also pointed out that the refuges were very short-term and temporary. There was scarcely any time for empowering change to happen in the in-out, transient situation for many women survivors, coming and going. Further, she suggested, workers sometimes under-estimated the depth of counselling and in-depth emotional support that a woman might need. Informal counselling of the type Women's Aid tended to offer at the time just might not be enough.

On the other hand, most previous residents with whom I talked disagreed strongly with the 'rather idealistic' conception of our shared past. To many of them, it had been transformative indeed, and they have never forgotten it. They were finally being taken seriously by others. They were listened to and could participate in decision-making. They were viewed as worthwhile members of something bigger, and their lives changed, often forever. Many previous workers felt the same. The radical politics and experiments in flattening hierarchies built a new and challenging way of working.

Lily Greenan, previous CEO of Scottish Women's Aid, spoke, for instance, of the truly revolutionary politics of what was attempted, and also recalled how Women's Aid and Rape Crisis in Scotland worked co-operatively together in solidarity to make a new environment for women. Most interviewees looked back with affection and some amazement at the audacity of what everyone tried to do. It mainly worked very well. And one previous resident reading a draft of this chapter wanted it to be added, loud and clear, that the 'over-idealistic' argument was absolutely the opposite of her experience. To her, the equality visions of the movement had lifted her life forever after.

In these brave attempts, a few interviewees suggested, that while the goals were a new world for women – and everyone did indeed build one in many ways – they/we were obstructed in our quest. Some of the things we were held back by were human limitation and fallibility, and by the surrounding regimes of capitalist male-dominated society and neo-liberalism. Speaking more generally, Nicola Harwin, previous CEO of Women's Aid in England, talked ironically of how: "We were building everything new but you could say we were held back by the human condition … We wanted to make a perfect world but we were working with imperfect vessels – including ourselves." We had the great ideals, but were operating in an often hostile environment, and sometimes we let ourselves down by not having the personal, political and emotional tools to achieve them.

Perhaps, the balance sheet would say that an incredible amount – in fact, an astonishing amount – was indeed achieved against the odds. As interviewees pointed out, the movement has always been characterised by strength. In fact, it was strength and idealism that fuelled the whole thing, especially at the beginning. Participants were willing to take enormous risks and did so, in a way they might not have done later. The dreams could not be reached, of course, but the members of the movement gave it their all.

Wider underlying principles

In summary, then, Women's Aid and domestic violence services, like rape crisis, were, and are, based on the principle of the value of mutual support. They strongly believed, and believe, in the central importance of the perspectives and views of abused women and children, bound (as time went on) by codes of good practice. Overall, the domestic violence movement approach was, and is, to believe women's and children's stories, make their safety a priority, and to support, respect and empower abuse survivors to take control of their own lives.

Women's Aid (then and now) recognised, and cared for, the needs of affected children. They challenged the disadvantage and social exclusion caused by the violence, and attempted to build new community. They also promoted diversity and both equal opportunities and anti-discriminatory practices. Back in the days of a refuge I myself worked for, these principles were extremely strongly adhered to. They were debated very frequently in detail at the weekly Support Group meetings which, as mentioned, often ran for many hours and which most members attended, week-in, week-out, without fail.

Domestic abuse services working within the Women's Aid federations, and related women's groups, recognised that domestic violence was a violation of women's and children's human rights. They developed the idea, along with other feminists, that personal violence was related to who has power in relationships and that it was rooted in the historic status of women. Domestic violence organisations also recognised that women and children have a right to live free from violence, and that society and the State itself have a duty to defend this right. While these ideas are more commonly accepted these days and have been achieved to some extent, at the time – as the movement against domestic violence took off – they were completely revolutionary.

Self-determination and empowerment

Self-determination and women's empowerment have always been the underlying principles of Women's Aid and of the wider movement against gender violence (including rape crisis). They have formed the foundation stones of what the movement stood, and stands, for. Domestic violence refuge organisations believed, and continue to believe, strongly in self-determination for women. They have viewed this as meaning abused women helping themselves and other women to make their own recoveries, and also the establishing of independent services to combat male violence.

They have always believed, also, in the empowerment of women and children. But empowerment can be a rather wishy-washy concept. What, after all, does it really mean? Domestic violence services have viewed it, however, as not wishy-washy at all – in any respect. They see and saw it, rather, as something only too real – as something active in terms of enabling women and children to build new lives if they wanted to. And they tried to achieve this in concrete ways. They have put down-to-earth, practical policies and actions in place to resist male control over women, and to oppose other sorts of discrimination (on the grounds, for example, of race and ethnicity, sexuality, disability, or social class).

Thus, from the start, domestic (and sexual) violence organisations attempted directly to work towards the empowerment of abused women so that they could leave behind their 'victim' status and become more powerful on a personal and psychological level – a 'survivor'. They might then be able to develop the strength and emotional resources to break away from, or to change, violent relationships, if they decided to.

The concrete existence of refuge and support services themselves was certainly part of this practical (and both lived and felt) response to women's empowerment. They were, and are, definitely real. They were, and are, made of bricks and mortar, providing women-controlled spaces, transgressive in terms of the status quo. They promoted – and promote – the solid, practical possibility for survivors and their children to make powerful changes in their lives, if they chose to. Not everyone did choose to, of course. But, overall, domestic violence services made, and make, real, tangible advances for women and children actually happen.

Importantly, empowerment has also been viewed as meaning having the economic and other resources to leave violent living situations. In many countries of the world, activists on violence against women have built economic empowerment projects to enable abused women to be able to support themselves and their children independently, further noted in Chapter 10. In the UK countries and others with some welfare benefits in place, this has also included assistance with accessing the relevant benefit provision.

Another practical empowerment outcome has always been access to permanent housing options for violence survivors. This has been much easier in countries with at least some provision of public sector or social housing, like the UK (compared with say, low income countries with no financing for such provision). It used to be fairly routine to enable families to get re-housed by the local council. In the last 30 years, however, with the selling off of council housing and the catastrophic diminishing of social and public housing options, this has become much more difficult. Forty-two per cent of people lived in council housing in the UK in 1979. Currently, the figure is just 8 per cent.[1]

Abused women and children often now stay in temporary accommodation (after their refuge stay) for some years, sometimes rotating from one accommodation to another, and in locations remote from anywhere they know. Similarly, according to a national Women's Aid interviewee, the coming of universal credit (which takes at least 5 weeks to start) has crucially decreased the ability of women and children to leave in emergencies, and also to access their share of what might have been a joint previous claim with their partner. The Women's Aid federations help with guidance on this, wherever they can.

Returning to the history, empowerment meant that refuges and domestic violence groups, from the beginning, sought to provide abused women with options and choice, rather than being trapped. The basic understanding of the refuge network has always been that survivors could come to know that they were not alone, and that they could offer each other sustenance. These seemingly simple realisations were foundational principles from the outset, which had rarely, throughout history, been put into practice for abused women previously. Well, not 'rarely' – rather 'never ever before'.

> Finding out that other women and children had been through the same thing, and that you were accepted and respected, despite everything that had happened, was crucial in survivors' transformation and confidence-building. You might then discover (after probably being isolated at home with your abusive partner) that everyone was in the same boat – and there was even the possibility of rowing that boat somewhere.

Of course, it did not happen that way all the time. Women using domestic violence services, were living in unsettling and unbalanced situations with strangers (at least initially) in the refuge. Home had disappeared. A refuge might contain a remarkable mixture of women, quite suddenly, present in the house with no warning. Women arriving at the door, or brought by the police, would be taken in with little in the way of question, if there was any space. Of course informal assessments of risk were always carried out. But women and families would be admitted straight away, then and there, without application procedures or formal risk assessments which tend to be used now.

A group of women in a refuge might contain women and children who had never left home before or who came from different ethnic heritages, classes and backgrounds. It might include women who were prostitutes escaping their pimps, women coming back for the fourth time, women who lived chaotically, in and out of contact with social services, and women and children who had never had any such experiences and were leading otherwise successful lives. It could be an unpredictable mix. As noted earlier, there were rows and disputes on occasion, often caused by the lack of privacy.

For the workers, what they did was clearly taxing and emotionally draining. Their work could result in secondary trauma and personal anguish. Workers and Support Group members might well have specific support and supervision arrangements strategically in place to help each other. In many refuge groups, these were carefully operated. But the workers and other members could still experience strong emotional traumas. Running the service could be like a hot-house of feelings for everyone. There could be disputes within the collectives, sometimes dramatic ones.

The majority of the time, however, the collectives and domestic violence services worked well and delivered dedicated services which transformed the lives of thousands of abuse survivors and their children. Overall, the affirming impact of women helping each other become strong did happen often enough to confirm the belief that women sharing together at their time of greatest crisis could indeed be empowered by the experience.

Struggling against oppression, racism and inequality

Women's Aid and domestic violence projects have tended to take strong positions on equality and diversity (although sometimes critiqued for not doing enough). A basic principle has always been to try to build services that were anti-discriminatory. By the 1980s and 1990s, inside the refuge movement, strong debates and (sometimes conflicted) attempts at change emerged around developing and operating anti-racist practice and training, alongside challenges from BME women.[2] Interviewees spoke of the commitment and efforts made within the movement, which led gradually to improvements and policy development, but not without battles and some failures. At the same time, the establishing of specialist BME projects, discussed in Chapters 4 and 8, was underway.

The following is one example of an attempt to move forward on racism and other oppressions, flawed of course, but challenging. In the mid-80s, I was involved with a refuge group trying hard to develop new practice. Encouraged by critiques from a South Asian woman who had been a worker, the group developed firm policies, deliberately and strategically to correct previous deficiencies. For example, they were among the first to bring in interpreters for South Asian women and to try to meet their possible cultural, religious and food needs.

They established a workers group of refuge, children's and follow-up workers which deliberately contained equal numbers of Black/minority ethnic women and white women, all of whom were skilled and committed to combatting domestic violence. They were also all committed to working on issues honestly and openly, and building a functioning multi-racial collective. There were many discussions and training sessions about the issue of racism and about how to evolve anti-racist practice, both in the team and with the residents.

BME workers were supported in the difficulties and racism they faced both in, and outside, the refuge. Challenging issues were brought to the fore, and everyone also had to challenge themselves. Individuals sometimes accused others of racist behaviour. Very contentious debates often took place, but the project worked overall in terms of improved practice and taking on equality. White workers had to accept mistakes made, apologise and do better in the future, and they did so. Both Black and white residents worked on living and sharing together in a better way, and they also did so.

More generally in the mid-1980s and on, conflict over racism and anti-racism, and also other forms of oppression, often erupted at local and national conferences. At the Women's Aid (England) conference, for example, there were sharp interventions by organisations like Black Women for Wages for Housework (who had members working for Women's Aid at the time), with some groups or individuals being harshly criticised. For this book, some Black workers recalled having endlessly to combat ongoing ignorance among their white colleagues and an almost automatic sense of entitlement. Some white workers recalled devastating accusations. There could be pain all round, as everyone worked on building something new in terms of combatting racism and building anti-racist services.

Since that time, anti-racism policies have been debated and committedly put into place. Various violence against women campaigns, consortiums and alliances have been formed to combat racism, especially regarding immigration, discriminatory cutbacks and the plight of violence survivors without recourse to public funds. Progress can still be slow, though, with the BME women's sector sometimes expressing dismay or anger at enduring ignorance and almost automatic expectations of privilege from majority white projects.

Black women were not alone in mounting challenges about questions of discrimination within the Women's Aid collectives in the 1980s and 1990s. In particular, both lesbians and working class women challenged the organisations in strong ways to improve their attitudes, practice and ways of interacting. Lesbianism being seen by some as the superior way forward for women could result in arguments. However, these debates, hard though they sometime were, led to open discussion and the adoption of relevant policies and improved practice, both locally and nationally. They also led to the holding of many helpful training and awareness workshops in domestic violence services on, for example, heterosexism and anti-lesbianism.

Issues for disabled women were scarcely broached at the time although the collectives were usually aware of the inadequacies of their service provision in this respect. Later, refuge and outreach services began to develop access and other policies to support disabled women. Women's Aid (England) managed the first and only national study on disabled women and domestic violence (coordinated by myself, and discussed in Chapter 8). Policies also began to be developed regarding survivors with mental health issues, learning difficulties or drug and alcohol problems, as time went on.

Class issues can reveal themselves starkly in refuge accommodation where most of the women may be working class, and some (or most) of the staff and voluntary Support Group members may be from middle class or educated backgrounds. Women's Aid was always committed to deliberately trying to break down class barriers, although this endeavour sometimes led to conflicts. In practical ways, though, Women's Aid services routinely attempted to challenge discrimination on the grounds of differing educational experiences and class backgrounds (as in the innovative employment practices discussed earlier).

Identity politics develop further

Particularly strongly-held identity politics emerged for some groups in both the domestic violence and sexual violence movements a little later at the end of the 1980s. There were some explosive arguments, as there were in other parts of the women's liberation movement. Most of the time, they were resolved, but some hurtful ongoing conflicts did arise, with distress on all sides. This could include women of particular identities feeling endlessly challenged. Those who were not part of a specific identity could feel silenced.

Women spoke for this book of having been damaged by these conflicts. Collective members could bitterly disagree, with some women leaping to claim positions of superior, feminist correctness, and then sticking to them, through thick and thin. There are some similar intense conflicts today. However, in terms of violence against women work, the disputes have thankfully largely faded into the past.

As Pragna Patel of Southall Black Sisters discussed for this book, if you are building a new humanity, it is challenging. But the idea is to learn and grow and change, rather than falling into the more extreme conflicts and antagonisms of unmediated identity politics. Such identity politics, she pointed out, is good for a beginning to 'identify' the issues. But where do you go from there? You need to use all your own humanity to work through the difficulties and move forward together with a sense of solidarity, she suggested. If everyone cements themselves into their original positions (and feels that they are the only ones who are correct and who deserve to be on the moral high ground), forward progress can be ossified, and that precious solidarity might disappear. A salutary warning.

Moving on from collectives

Things have changed for the feminist collectives. After 20 to 25 years – a quarter of a century – of stalwart collective working, many violence against women services had moved away from this way of operating by the 2000s. Now, almost all, worldwide, have a hierarchical structure with a Director or Chief Executive in post. In the UK countries, refuge groups, the National Offices of their federations, and the other women's sector projects, gradually left behind the brave politics of collective working, with the coming of more competitive work environments and increasingly demanding funders. The same is true for most of the BME projects, many of which were structured from the beginning.

The loss is greatly regretted by some women interviewed who felt that a rotation of the different tasks between collective members could still meet these increasingly stringent requirements. A few refuges and domestic violence services have continued through thick and thin operating as collectives. But not many. Mainly, the women's projects have developed hierarchical structures, offering services that are perhaps more conventional and formally 'professional', with clear divisions of roles, but still dedicated to the cause. (For more information on the practical sequence of what happened, see the section on 'Women's Aid in the 2000s' in Chapter 8.) Of course, the change has meant, also, that concomitant differences in pay were introduced. Women didn't all earn the same anymore.

Overall, the coming of Chief Executives and Directors to coordinate services may have been inevitable, according to the majority of women interviewed, as services were pushed towards the mainstream. Some suggested that there is a limit to the size a collective can be to work effectively, and that, come what may, long-term collectives need to have structures of management and performance assessment, together with employment protection. They described how a structure with a Director can still operate as collectively as possible – as, for example, Southall Black Sisters tries to do – with the hierarchy flattened, and both workers across the board and women survivors of violence still feeding into decision-making as equally as possible.

A final word

This account of the experiments in working practice that feminist activists tried out, especially in the earlier days, has mainly concentrated on the development of refuge services. The innovative practices, discussed in the last two chapters, were brave – and sometimes stunning – in their challenge to the status quo. They have many lessons to teach us which may have been almost forgotten. It is worth cherishing both the memories and the innovativeness, perhaps. I would like to make a plea for us not to forget – in fact, instead, consciously to celebrate, talk about and preserve – the radical practices that were espoused. Revisiting those times and their passion can give us some inspiration in these different days, as in the following poem – some light to shine on our long struggle.

> The following poem was written after a one-off reunion of the Collective of Bristol Women's Aid (active from the mid-70s onwards), as a celebration. The reunion included refuge, children's and follow-up workers, collective and support group members, women who had lived in the refuge and a daughter, who was eight at the time, but is now nearly 40. The poem mentions Ellen Malos. The first Bristol refuge and first Women's Centre were both in her house.

Memories of Bristol Women's Aid: a reunion 2017

We met once again, a one-off reunion.
We who had sat so many times before
In a circle in that same room.
We remembered the workers' meetings,
the collective meetings …
Laughed at how we never missed one.
Arguing it out till past midnight often.

Sometimes we'd meet for a whole day
Just to build our closeness.
We were dedicated, all of us,
Standing firm for the refuge.
Making something new and brave.
We were lucky as well – given
All those health and safety violations.

We remembered together
The children's and follow-up work,
The fights with the Council,

The Support Group meetings,
The policies of Women's Aid,
The togetherness, the struggle,
The excitement of that early politics.

Arguments and traumas too.
But those days transformed us all.
It turns out that, even now,
Everyone remembers them.
Even though it's been 30 or 40 years.
We can't forget those days.
The passion and zeal we shared.

So we met together again.
We brought food to share.
Read out messages, shared stories
Of how we made all decisions collectively.
Exchanged news about collective members.
Talked of women in the refuge,
and what had happened to everyone.

Remembered their bravery so often.
Those who had lived in the Big House
Spoke of the security and safety it had given.
Enabling them to change everything.
We talked, too, of how some of the women
Ran rings around the workers sometimes,
And no doubt found it very funny.

We spoke of the garbage and the outings,
The parties, the house meetings
And the Brother typewriter
renamed Sister in felt-tip pen.
But we also spoke of the woman
Whose husband pushed her out
through a third-floor window.

We celebrated those we have lost
Remembered what they gave.

Talked of the first refuge at Ellen's,
Thanked her for starting it all off.
We recalled how we
Tried to do it all differently.
Were part of that wider movement,

That movement of sustenance, strength.
We parted proud
At what we had made together –
How, throughout our lives,
We have been, always,
Women who stand strong
For women, against violence.

8

As time went on: the movements on domestic violence and harmful practices grow

We return now from the often inspirational ways of working, discussed in the last two chapters, to focus on the organisation and history of the domestic violence movement, mainly in the UK's countries. This was covered in Chapter 4 up to the end of the 1980s. This chapter moves forward to look at policy and service issues in the movement since that time.

More services in the 1990s

The domestic violence and abuse sector was well established by the 1990s. The early days of the white-heat of women's movement activity at its peak were over (although the movements remained active). The phase of figuring out what to do from scratch and how to do it were long gone. Services had diversified as time had passed. They included refuges, support and outreach projects, BMER services, legal campaigns and policy work. In 1993, there were 275 refuge groups in England, many running more than one refuge. Welsh Women's Aid, Scottish Women's Aid and Women's Aid Northern Ireland coordinated 37, 35 and 9 refuge groups, respectively.

In all, refuge was offered to about 40,000 women and children, and assistance to a further 100,000 annually. Workers and activists continued to work tirelessly, and the domestic violence sector, including the Women's Aid federations and BME women's initiatives, were innovative in constantly moving the sector forward. Domestic abuse services conducted advocacy widely with agencies and institutions, and domestic violence training courses began to be provided across the board in the 1990s to educate professionals, stemming often from the independent women's services.

The sector began to liaise more closely (if, often, more in opposition than not) with government. Governmental departments like the Home Office and Department of Health sometimes commissioned research and policy development on violence against women. And the Women's Aid federations, rape crisis and others initiated research themselves, which took off more and more in this decade. After a two-year consultation with Women's Aid members and national interest groups on how to improve its diversity, equality and effectiveness, the management body of Women's Aid (England) changed its legal structure in 1995 to a charitable company with a Council of Officers. These officers had specific designated responsibilities for specialist areas of work, including posts to represent the interests of Black women, of lesbians and of disabled women, elected through electoral colleges of all women in those groups who were working in, or using, the services.

Further developments across the board included an increased emphasis on the impacts on children of experiencing domestic violence. Importantly, child contact issues in cases of domestic abuse began to gain wider attention. Multi-agency work on violence against women started at this time. Also in the 1990s, publicity and awareness-raising became quite widespread, run by Women's Aid, Refuge and many others. The most important publicity campaign was Zero Tolerance, a pioneering and revolutionary poster campaign on violence against women, set up in Edinburgh in 1992. Zero Tolerance still continues in Scotland in a wider format, focussing on primary prevention of violence by tackling gender inequality. (Other campaigning organisations sometimes use the same name.) Some of the other diverse services that were set up 25 or more years ago included one-stop shops providing multiple services under one roof, and dedicated outreach projects. Examples of initiatives established then, and still thriving, include Next Link, the main provider of domestic abuse services across Bristol (set up after Bristol Women's Aid ended). A large women-only organisation, it also provides mental health, sexual violence, and forced marriage services, as well as refuge space. In a further example (of many), WAITS (Women Acting in Today's Society), has provided, since 1993, a range of holistic services on domestic violence across Birmingham. Throughout this period, the movement and sector, overall, expanded. Projects were vibrant and embedded, but still always fragilely funded.

The Black women's movement and specialist Black and minority ethnic services

This included BME(R) services. Into the 1990s and 2000s, the Black women's movement continued to set up projects and campaigns in response to what sometimes looked like foot-dragging or lack of attention from the general movement. Meanwhile, various Women's Aid projects also set up specialist refuges or support projects for BME women under their rubrics or, alternatively, BME services decided to become Women's Aid members. In the late 1990s, Women's Aid in England operated a No Recourse to Public Funds initiative to provide funding to assist migrant women in this situation who were experiencing domestic violence and abuse. This fund continued for ten years or more. Refuge services also offered them free places where, and if, they could (and still do).

BME or BMER projects set up in the 1990s included BAWSO, the Black Association of Women Step Out, in Cardiff. Established in 1995, it has been, ever since, an all-Wales project providing practical and emotional support services for BME women on domestic abuse, trafficking, forced marriage, female genital mutilation (FGM) and 'honour'-based violence. In another example, the Ashiana Network in London was expanded as an independent project 20 years ago and now runs three specialist refuges for Asian, Turkish, Iranian and Middle Eastern women which can also offer dedicated beds to those without recourse to public funds or, for example, at risk of forced marriage.

Importantly, in 2004, Imkaan was set up as an umbrella support project in London. It was, and remains, a specifically

Black feminist 'second tier' organisation, the only one in the UK addressing violence against Black and (in the term they favour) minoritised women and girls. Directed for many years by acclaimed activist Marai Larasi, the organisation has worked for nearly two decades on violence against women and girls, including domestic violence, sexual violence and harassment, forced marriage and 'honour'-based violence. It has established itself as key within the sector. Overall, the BME and minority sector on violence against women and girls has grown considerably (but often precariously) for both domestic and sexual violence.

One example of the latter is the specialist sexual violence BME work of the Women and Girls Network in West London. For many years now, there have also been Jewish women's projects, Chinese and African women's groups, and others, working on gender-based violence. For example, Jewish Women's Aid has offices in London and Manchester, having started out back in the 1980s in London and Leeds. It currently has 22 members of staff and runs support services for Jewish women experiencing domestic violence and abuse, and the Dina Service to support Jewish survivors of sexual violence.

Latin American Women's Aid was founded back in 1987. It has run the only two refuges in Europe run by, and for, Latin American women and children fleeing gender-based violence for 30 years. In another few examples of many, Sahara in Manchester was established in 2014 to provide support services to BME women and children as part of Manchester Women's Aid. In 2015, the Iranian and Kurdish Women's Rights Organisation (IKWRO) opened in London the first specialist refuge specifically for Middle Eastern and North African women. The refuge aims to accommodate and support vulnerable women at risk of 'honour'-based violence, forced marriage, female genital mutilation and domestic violence. In 2020, the pioneering 'Faith and Violence Against Women and Girls coalition' was set up in London by Huda Jawad through Standing Together Against Domestic Violence (discussed in the next chapter). Many more general domestic violence services have, for years, also offered a specialist BMER service as an integral part of their wider provision.

Two pioneers among many: Asian Women's Resource Centre and Southall Black Sisters

An important project has been the Asian Women's Resource Centre (AWRC), set up 40 years ago. It was, and is, a specialist women's organisation based in Brent in London, providing independent and dedicated support services to abused BME women and children, including refugees and asylum seekers. The AWRC provides a range of services, ensuring a holistic and needs-led response. These include domestic abuse outreach and advocacy, safety planning, working across a spectrum of risks, and supporting women to recognise abuse. The Resource Centre works to build women's self-esteem and confidence through group-work and advice/information services on welfare benefits, homelessness, debt and immigration. For many years, they have supported women who have no recourse to public funds, and they also lead on two major partnership projects in London, discussed below in the section on harmful practices.

The wide-ranging holistic and empowering support services that AWRC offers BMER women, and particularly women of South Asian descent, have often been lifesaving, guided for very many years by their totally dedicated Director, Sarbjit Ganger. This long-standing project has transformed the lives of generations of survivors of violence, and has had a pioneering role in the development of services for BMER women in Brent and across London.

Similarly, Southall Black Sisters (SBS) emerged in the late 1970s as one of the first Black feminist campaigning groups in the UK to work specifically on violence against women and to challenge both racism and sexism at the same time. In the early 1980s, together with other pioneering projects (like the AWRC and the then-called Newham Asian Women's Project), SBS broke the silence on domestic violence against Black women. They organised ground-breaking protests against a spate of domestic abuse-related murders of South Asian women, including those of Balwant Kaur and Gurdip Kaur, in Southall and elsewhere. In 1983, they began providing frontline advocacy services for survivors of violence of varying types, including forced marriage and 'honour'-based violence, that have since provided a lifeline for many. They have campaigned about, and publicised the stories of, individual women, burned or killed by partners and families, and published the stories and poems of violence survivors, standing firm beside them.

Southall Black Sisters have helped literally thousands of Black and minority women, across the UK and beyond, for over 40 years. They also work more broadly, campaigning against both religious fundamentalism and racism, and fighting for free speech, famously, supporting Salman Rushdie against Muslim and other fundamentalists in 1989, for instance. SBS have taken a leading role in defending the existence of specialist BME services in recent years. They have pushed for more humane immigration laws in the context, from the 2010s on, of State authoritarianism, a 'hostile' immigration environment, and deepening economic inequality.

The London 'No Recourse to Public Funds' Project assists migrant women who have experienced violence but who have no access to public funds under the immigration legislation (following on from the previous funds run by Women's Aid England and from refuges making space available). It is led by Southall Black Sisters with partners, the AWRC, Ashiana (London), Nia and Solace (a large domestic violence organisation discussed later), and funded through MOPAC, the London Mayor's Office for Police and Crime. SBS has been at the forefront of these struggles for so long, and remains, an inspiration for many. One of their passionate slogans is: 'Hate is your weapon. Courage is ours'.

Women from other minority communities experiencing domestic violence

Turning now to domestic abuse in lesbian and gay relationships, pioneering research work on these issues has been conducted in the UK by Catherine Donovan and Marianne Hester. In their 2015 work, *Domestic violence and sexuality: What's love got to do with it?*, they presented the first detailed coverage in the UK of domestic violence in same sex relationships (in comparison with heterosexual ones).[1] They analysed how domestic abuse is often shaped by gender, sexuality and age, and outlined resulting impacts, including unequal or non-existent service and policy development.

More studies have been conducted in North America, but, overall, most analyses and overviews find that abuse issues for lesbians, and also for gay men and people of other genders/ sexualities, have been generally overlooked. Further research and policy are clearly needed across the board.[2] A 2020 book by Catherine Donovan and Rebecca Barnes, *Queering narratives of domestic violence and abuse*, examines the use of abusive behaviours within LGBT+ relationships.[3] Some literary treatments also take on the issue of, for example, lesbian abuse. One of these is a powerful 2020 memoir by Carmen Maria Machado, *In the dream house*, which dissects an abusive lesbian relationship.[4]

Disabled women and women with mental health difficulties, drug and alcohol issues or learning difficulties have not always been well served in the violence against women movement in the past, although attempts have been made. One example is the Stella project which was set up in 2002 to work on domestic violence and substance misuse issues. The pioneering Beverly Lewis House in London has provided support since 1995 to women with learning disabilities experiencing domestic violence. But this is the only one. Disabled women and women with learning difficulties and mental health challenges continue to struggle to get their needs met if they leave home due to domestic violence.

I was privileged to lead in the late 2000s the only national UK study on disabled women and domestic abuse with Ravi Thiara, Audrey Mullender, Pauline Magowan, and a team of disabled and non-disabled researchers. The project was coordinated by Women's Aid in England and managed by Nicola Harwin, who had achieved the funding after several years of effort. Advised by an Advisory Group of disabled women, it found evidence of how disabled women facing abuse were in double jeopardy of the most severe kind.[5] While the abuse they had experienced was almost always of a horrendous nature, they were often unable to reach any suitable services. The services provided by the disabled people's liberation movement tended to overlook or fail abused women. Conversely, the domestic violence services tended to fail disabled women (through inadequate access, awareness and provision, despite often the best of intentions).

The study made detailed recommendations to Women's Aid and to disability projects which have led to some improvements in access and support,[6] despite the funding cutbacks of the last years. As a result of the project, Women's Aid (England) produced guidance in the 2000s and ran a national publicity campaign about the needs of abused disabled women. They continue to attempt to improve the responses of their services. But almost any disabled woman seeking help with domestic violence will tell you that services are still very often inadequate.

Services and definitions develop and change

By the 2000s, ways of understanding domestic violence had evolved, as services had developed. In recent times, comprehensive coordinated definitions have been used by refuges and domestic violence services, policy-makers, the health service, local area strategic groups, the police and the criminal justice service. Domestic violence and abuse (DVA) is more or less universally viewed, in the 2020s, as including physical, emotional, psychological, sexual and financial violence, as well as coercive control, in intimate personal relationships. Its impact on any children involved is regarded as a key part of the definitions used.

While primarily and overwhelmingly experienced by women, definitions usually note that men can also be victims (and are entitled to services and support), and that violence can occur in same sex relationships as discussed above. The Government in England and Wales defines domestic abuse or violence, as: 'any incident of controlling, coercive or threatening behaviour, violence or abuse between those aged 16 or over who are or have been intimate partners or family members, regardless of their gender or sexuality. This can encompass but is not limited to the following types of abuse: psychological, physical, sexual, financial, emotional', with a broadly similar definition used in Northern Ireland.[7]

In Scotland, there is an even more comprehensive definition of types of behaviour included, which is strategically limited to partners and ex-partners. Scottish Women's Aid uses the Scottish Government definition, expanded as follows: 'domestic abuse is a pattern of controlling, coercive, threatening, degrading and/or violent behaviour, including sexual violence, by a partner or ex-partner. Domestic abuse is overwhelmingly experienced by women and perpetrated by men. It doesn't matter how old someone is, what race or ethnicity they are, what class they are, whether or not they are disabled, or whether they have children – anyone can be a victim of abuse'[8]. Using such common definitions across services is important to their success.

Simultaneously, understandings of, and responses to, domestic abuse have become normalised and broadly accepted, with wide-ranging service provision. These advances have everything to do with the promptings, persistence, vigilance and endless work of the specialist, domestic violence sector for nearly 50 years now, ever since the early passionate days. For example, training programmes were initially set up by the domestic abuse movement, but are now widely available, across all services.

They are provided through the Women's Aid federations, SafeLives, AVA (both discussed later) and many other agencies, including activist training consultancies run by long-term trainers, like Cath Kane and Davina James-Hanman, building on years of experience and activist expertise. In the new millennium, this work has been supported by numerous awareness-raising campaigns, with many domestic violence organisations taking part. These often have a broad debt to the afore-mentioned and ground-breaking 'Zero Tolerance' campaign in Edinburgh. Government departments and statutory agencies now also run awareness campaigns.

For 25 years, domestic violence has been covered widely in the popular media, for example, in a ground-breaking story-line in (the previous) *Brookside* back in 1995, and in *Coronation Street* and *EastEnders* in the 2000s (and again in 2020). The radio serial, *The Archers*, attracted wide public attention from millions of people for its story-line on coercive control in 2016. All of these programmes took close advice from Women's Aid, and later from Refuge also, on their stories and the text used. Similarly, *EastEnders*, *Hollyoaks* and *Broadchurch* have featured sexual violence stories, with consultancy from Rape Crisis Centres, and liaison with the National Rape Crisis Helplines on increased referrals in consequence of these stories.

Women's Aid into the 2000s

In the last two decades, the four Women's Aid federations have diversified their services hugely. Women's Aid in England produced 'The Gold Book' of domestic violence services back in 1999 as the only UK-wide directory. Developing from this, the federations then together formed a partnership (administered by Women's Aid in England) to run an innovative online directory called UK Refuges Online from 2001. This online service coordinated referrals between refuge groups and recorded numbers of services. Vacancies and availability were, and are, reported daily. The service is now known as Routes to Support.

The federations campaigned widely to include women's services within the Supporting People framework (for England and Wales) from 2002 which resulted in improved funding strategies and support for domestic violence services (ring-fenced at the time, a policy which unfortunately ended, broadly-speaking, in 2008/2009).[9] Women's Aid in England has also, since the early 2000s, worked with patrons and ambassadors to represent and support their work, as have some of the other federations and domestic violence services, like Refuge and SafeLives. (For Women's Aid in England, the first patron from 2001 was Jenni Murray, who was the main presenter of Radio 4's Woman's Hour for more than 30 years, retiring in 2020.)

The federations have also changed their ways of working. Both individual refuge groups and the National Offices moved away from being collectives in the early 2000s, under the pressure of increasing demands from funders and of local authority requirements (as also discussed in Chapter 7). Scottish Women's Aid representatives talked for this book, for example, about the regulatory environment which developed from 2000 on. Governments and funders began to ask for managers to be qualified in order to access funding, and to insist on a single point of contact within the project. This meant that the collectives became harder to operate, and many groups made the change. A few refuges still exist in Scotland with the 'single point of contact' for agencies and funders being rotated among workers annually.

In the other UK countries, too, various individual refuge groups had developed hierarchical structures by 2000. They were followed by the National Office of Women's Aid in England which was a collective until 2000/2001 when it introduced a Director/Deputy Director (later Chief Executive) system. This was a result of a year-long consultation between the Women's Aid Council and national collective staff, and was agreed by a staff majority vote. It established a new Women's Aid Board to manage both the federation and the National Office, taking over from the previous electoral colleges (discussed earlier in this chapter). There was some general ongoing disagreement about whether the move from collective staff groups was the best thing for the sector, but it seemed that the writing was on the wall.

In 2004, Scottish Women's Aid National Office stopped being a collective. The National Offices of Welsh and Northern Ireland Women's Aids also moved to hierarchical structures. In this period, ever-increasing numbers of individual refuge services followed the first few in changing from collectives to having Chief Executives, under demanding pressures and requirements from funding, monitoring, commissioning and regulating bodies. But all the federations – just like in the 1970s – have continued non-stop, into the 2020s, to raise the voices of survivors, guided by their members, and continue in the 2020s to do so.

Welsh Women's Aid, for example, operates a survivors network in Wales and coordinates SEEdS (Survivors Empowering and Educating Services), a survivor participation project. Their award-winning project to celebrate their 40 years of service, 'Forty voices, forty years', recorded moving survivor stories.[10] Similarly, Scottish Women's Aid celebrated their own 40th birthday with a remarkable and also award-winning project, 'Speaking out: Recalling Women's Aid', derived from interviews with previous workers and some survivors.[11]

The Women's Aid federations in Scotland, Wales and Northern Ireland have continued as the lead domestic abuse organisations in their countries, playing a vital role for women survivors and their children, and offering a wide range of projects and assistance. Scottish Women's Aid currently has 36 members which offer specialised domestic abuse services, Welsh Women's Aid has 19, and Women's Aid Federation Northern Ireland has 9. (Not all domestic violence services run refuges.)

The Body Shop conducted a vibrant awareness campaign with Women's Aid (in England) for five years in the early 2000s, and briefly with Refuge previously. And, overall, the domestic violence services and Women's Aid federations have for many years now provided not only refuges but also complex outreach and advocacy projects. All the federations have developed online resources and specialist interactive websites, safety planning advice, domestic abuse toolkits and practice guides. They have also provided training and consultancies, and were the original pioneers of various helplines, including the National Domestic Abuse Helpline in England and the National Helplines in Scotland, Wales and Northern Ireland.

The federations have more recently participated in strategic development work on violence against women and girls (VAWG) across local and national areas. For example, Women's Aid Federation Northern Ireland were key contributors to the 2016 *Stopping domestic and sexual violence in Northern Ireland: A seven year strategy*. They also operate *See, hear, act: A strategy for children and young people (2019–2029)*. In 2020, the four federations continue to have All-Federation meetings to coordinate services and campaigns between them.

Women's Aid in England is discussed in more detail here, as it is by far the largest federation, but this is not to diminish the powerful work done by the other three which all offer comprehensive services. As the major grass-roots federation in England working to end domestic abuse, Women's Aid (England) has long had the by-line: 'until women and children are safe', important because it acknowledges the impacts on children too. In later years, it has become team-led with a Policy Team, a Media Relations and Communications Team, and so on. But still, like the other federations, it has continued to employ strong and remarkable women to take forward the Women's Aid ethos, according to various interviewees. In this, they have been guided throughout by their (written) feminist, survivor-oriented values which are integrated into all strands of work.

With about 300 local services in England, Women's Aid offered refuge support to 12,034 women in 2018 and community-based services to 136,165. For decades, they have worked strategically with central government, producing guidance and policy, while also campaigning and offering frontline support. As well as their central National Offices in Bristol and London, Women's Aid (England) has a large and well-developed regional network, with national staff assisting in the regions. Their services include their pioneering websites, *The Hideout*, specifically for children who have experienced domestic violence against their mothers, and *#LoveRespect* on healthy relationships for young people, most especially for young girls facing relationship abuse.[12]

The domestic violence sector as a whole, including in particular Women's Aid, has long struggled around the issue of child contact with violent partners and the position of the non-abusing parent, a massive campaigning thread of their work from 1987 on. Women's Aid in England, for example, conducted important research and has pushed for change in family law and justice since the 1990s (specifically in terms of the 1989 Children Act), as have the other federations in their different legal frameworks.

For many years, the English federation has published the short journal, *Safe: The Domestic Abuse Quarterly* (now an online blog). Its services, like those of the other federations, include a Survivors Forum, and a specialised survivors' website, which provide detailed guidance for women leaving home due to violence. Women's Aid also operates awareness-raising projects and campaigning (around the current Domestic Abuse Bill, for instance), and publishes the *Domestic abuse report: The annual audit*, an overview of the domestic abuse support services across England.[13]

A key resource, developed jointly with Imkaan, is the National Quality Framework, with a suite of tools to assist domestic abuse services, including Imkaan's work on Safe Minimum Standards. Women's Aid in England awards a National Quality Mark to services which meet its criteria, and offers a programme of National Quality Standards. Similar detailed National Quality Service Standards are provided by Welsh Women's Aid, Scottish Women's Aid and Women's Aid Northern Ireland, and all four federations also offer a range of accredited (and non-accredited) training programmes for survivors, staff and professionals.

The federation in England, for example, operates the Women's Aid National Training Centre providing training and accreditation courses for employees, as well as training for professionals and for domestic abuse prevention advocates. Three levels of fully accredited qualifications on tackling and preventing domestic and sexual violence/abuse are offered, and survivors of violence (and others) can gain professional learning and qualifications through these routes.[14] Welsh Women's Aid delivers the National Accredited Qualification for domestic abuse work, and also the Training the Trainers Programme on behalf of the Welsh Government.

At the time of writing, Women's Aid in England, Welsh Women's Aid (and Respect, noted later) were operating their pioneering 'Change that Lasts' project, to build long-term (rather than temporary) change for women. This had three strands, providing early intervention, training and support, positioned within a framework of feminist values, across the regions, as outlined by Teresa Parker, Women's Aid England's Head of Media Relations and Communications. The framework encompasses Women's Aid's ground-breaking 'Expert Voices' consultation project which is based on the original passion of the movement and entirely led by survivors.[15] Further, the 'Law in the Making' project[16] enables violence survivors to directly advise government, and Women's Aid continues to work with inspiring survivor ambassadors. Thus, the various campaigns and policy work undertaken are shaped by what members and survivors highlight as being the key issues.

In summary, Women's Aid says that, 'Our roots are in the women's rights' movement, and the organisation is run by women for abused women and their children. We are proud to have been at the forefront of key achievements that have increased legal protection for survivors and we have also raised public awareness.'[17]

All the federations advise government, write briefings, mount campaigns and engage in extensive policy and legislative work. This complex and wide-ranging activity is a long way from the early passionate days when services first came into existence. For example, Women's Aid (England) had 95 workers, across several offices, at the time of writing (although some of these were working on time-limited projects).

Looking back to when this all began in the 1970s, Jo Sutton was the first National Coordinator of the National Women's Aid Federation, and Jalna Hanmer chaired the very first meeting. There were usually two Coordinators at a time and they had an incomprehensibly huge job in front of them, as recalled by Kate Berry. She fulfilled the role from 1977–1978, with Judi Hodgkin, who herself added (in discussions for this book):

'From a tiny basement, we established and maintained a regional system of support and policy-making. This entailed a huge amount of travelling and coordination. On top of this, we were dealing with women needing advice and support, and working on legislation and the media. How on earth we achieved everything we did, I'll never know.'

Another previous coordinator, Elizabeth Woodcraft, described, in Women's Aid 40th anniversary celebrations, how she and Jude Stoddart took over from Jo Sutton in 1975. Their office consisted, at the time, of just a couple of boxes that one could easily pick up, and move about in search of space – or just a desk or table to put them on. Incomprehensibly far from those 95 workers of today: that was the extent of the National Office.

Refuge, Against Violence and Abuse, SafeLives and Solace

Refuge (Against Domestic Violence), with its well-established reputation and longevity, continues to provide multiple wide-ranging support services. The organisation runs refuges, and has taken on BMER issues, including 'honour'-based violence, forced marriage, woman trafficking and modern slavery. Its projects include a Vietnamese Outreach Service, an Eastern

European Advocate Service and culturally specific refuges. It also operates advocacy and community support services, and conducts research, national policy work and award-winning publicity campaigns. Refuge, a member of the Women's Aid federation in England, is the largest 'single organisation' provider of domestic violence services.

Another large organisation, Solace Women's Aid, now runs many of the London refuges that used to be independent Women's Aid projects. At the time of writing, it was operating 19 refuges, including specialist refuge spaces for women with multiple needs (and North London Rape Crisis Centre, noted in Chapter 5). It partners with the Rhea project which, since 2017, has provided good-quality accommodation to homeless abused women and children who might find it hard to access the wider network. Solace also runs the Amari Project, providing support and accommodation for women sexually exploited through trafficking or prostitution.

For many years now, the sector has included SafeLives which has an important role in training. It provides comprehensive tailored 'violence against women' training programmes extremely widely, regionally, nationally and locally, together with other services for professionals. It was set up as Coordinated Action Against Domestic Abuse (CAADA) by its original founder, Diana Barran, in 2005. Against Violence and Abuse (AVA) is also a leading independent project committed to ending violence against women. Survivors are at the heart of all they do. They provide training and campaigning across the UK's countries. AVA was formerly the ground-breaking Greater London Domestic Violence Project (GLDVP), discussed later. The London VAWG (Violence Against Women and Girls) Consortium (facilitated through the Women's Resource Centre) is the largest coalition of specialist providers working across the 32 London Boroughs, with 28 members.

Justice for Women, Centre for Women's Justice and fighting for women

In terms of pioneering projects historically, the venerable organisation Rights of Women has provided legal help to abused women, and campaigned around legal issues for very many decades. It works to improve the law for women and increase women's access to justice. Similarly, Justice for Women (whose founders include Julie Bindel and Harriet Wistrich) has been a feminist campaigning organisation since the early 1990s, including representing some women who, after experiencing years of domestic violence, have killed their violent partners. Commonly, in the past at least, women in this situation have been convicted of murder (rather than manslaughter) more frequently than men facing similar charges. Women have also traditionally received harsher sentences.

In fact, sentencing has rarely reflected, especially in the past, the fact that women are primarily victims of the men they kill, whereas men who kill their partners are usually perpetrators. A prominent example was the case of Kiranjit Ahluwalia who, in the 1980s, had killed her husband after ten years of rape, severe abuse and burnings. In 1989, she was sentenced to life imprisonment. After a campaign led by Southall Black Sisters, and supported by Justice for Women and other women's organisations, Ahluwalia's conviction was reduced to manslaughter. She was released from prison on appeal in 1992, viewed as a triumph for justice by SBS, Women's Aid, Rights of Women, and Justice for Women.

It was a turning point leading to the achieving of more just outcomes for other women who had committed such crimes. Similar successful cases involved defending women like Sara Thornton in the 1990s, and, recently, Sally Challen whose conviction for murder was reduced to manslaughter in 2019, with her later release after nine years in prison. The Challen case, which received much national publicity, was supported by a Justice for Women Campaign, and assisted by the specialist feminist lawyers of the Centre for Women's Justice, established by Harriet Wistrich in 2016 (and which has strong links to Justice for Women). This Centre was set up to hold the State to account on violence against women, bringing strategic litigation challenges, and working with the frontline women sector.

The Challen case was also supported by the American veteran activist professor Evan Stark, who attended from the US to give evidence. He had originally formulated in detail the concept of coercive control,[18] which led to the adoption of legislation on coercive behaviour in the 2010s, as discussed in Chapter 9. In another much earlier case, a young woman, Emma Humphreys, was released from prison in 1998 after a successful campaign, but sadly died subsequently. Annual Emma Humphreys Memorial Prizes for work challenging violence against women have been awarded, since then, in her memory.

'Honour'-based violence, FGM, forced marriage and harmful practices

The term harmful practices is now used for abuse like 'honour'-based violence. Much work over the years has been done by violence against women activists – and especially BMER activists – to discourage the viewing of such practices, where they occur in the UK, as aberrations of 'backward' cultures or religious practice. Rather, they can be viewed as specific manifestations of violence against women in patriarchal societies.[19] Harmful practices are considered to include forced marriage (FM), FGM, violence in the name of 'honour' (HBV), and issues like being disowned or shunned.

In recent years, there has been the development, usually under pressure from the movement, of somewhat improved legislation in the UK countries, and of detailed police and criminal justice strategies dealing with these harmful practices. DASH, short for the (snappily!) entitled 'Domestic Abuse, Stalking and Harassment and Honour-Based Violence Risk Identification, Assessment and Management Model', deals with these issues in the justice system, as well as with domestic violence. The DASH model has been used with some success by the police and criminal justice agencies since 2009 to assess risk. The improved DARA (the Domestic Abuse Risk Assessment) has been piloted but not fully rolled out at the time of writing.

These improvements (although somewhat uncertain) have been brought about through research and policy initiatives from the relevant agencies, and through the endless, focussed work of the activists. In this, they have sometimes been assisted by especially committed and dedicated police and criminal justice officers. Key official bodies involved in these steps forward include the National Police Chiefs' Council, the Metropolitan Police, and the Forced Marriage Unit of the Foreign and Commonwealth Office/Home Office. They have developed sometimes pioneering strategies, coupled with related training for relevant professionals (for example, the police). However, it is sadly true that both this specialised training and the overall implementation are often only patchily delivered.[20]

Aisha K. Gill, activist and professor, has particularly contributed to this area, both in terms of activism to change policy and also of research, along with other BME researchers, including Ravi Thiara and Geetanjali Gangoli. She has had a key role in activism on HBV, forced marriage and sexual violence and abuse, especially in the UK, as well as internationally in India, Pakistan, Iraqi Kurdistan, Libya, and Yemen. One example of useful books on HBV is *'Honour' killing and violence: Theory, policy and practice* (2014), edited by Gill with Caroline Strange and series editor, Karl Roberts.[21]

Independent organisations working on 'honour'-based violence, specifically, have been set up, usually by ground-breaking women activists and sometimes survivors from BMER communities. They include Karma Nirvana, which provides wide-ranging support and runs an 'honour'-based violence helpline. Working on forced marriage as well as honour violence, the organisation was founded in Derby in 1993 by Jasvinder Sanghera. The wide-ranging Sharan Project also provides support to women, mainly of South Asian origin, on issues ranging from 'honour' violence and domestic abuse to dowry violence and being disowned. True Honour is an organisation set up in 2015 and aiming to help and support victims of HBV, FM and FGM.

There are a variety of further dedicated BMER organisations taking on these issues, including, for example, IRKWO (the Iranian and Kurdish Women's Rights Organisation) which offers support and expert advocacy to women victims and their families. The Halo Project is a national project and also offers services on HBV, forced marriage and FGM across the North East. It partners to form 'hubs' with key universities in the area which have worked for years on violence against women, including Durham, Teeside and Sunderland.

All the women's organisations report that they welcome the strategic advances made in the legislation, in inter-agency approaches and in the criminal justice system. Just one example of strategy, training and guidance that has been developed is the *Honour-Based Violence, Forced Marriage, Female Genital Mutilation Multi-Agency Guidance* of the Safe Durham Partnership. However, the activists also point out that most local authorities and police/criminal justice services still do not understand 'honour' crimes properly in practice, or respond in a sufficiently sensitive manner. The women's agencies say little has changed in many local areas (with a few creditable exceptions). On the other hand, while the specialist strategies and trainings on these complex issues cannot reverse years of neglect and ignorance about them in the justice systems of the UK countries, some tangible advances have been made in holding perpetrators accountable and providing support services to victims/survivors.[22]

Moving on to female genital mutilation more specifically,[23] this harmful practice is experienced by many British women and by more than 200 million worldwide. In the UK, FORWARD (Foundation for Women's Health Research and Development) has been, for 30 years now, the leading organisation led by African women working to end violence against women and girls. FORWARD was founded in 1983 by the late Efua Dorkenoo, who was a pioneering figure, initiating global action against FGM. Coordinated currently by Executive Director Naana Otoo-Oyortey, it offers unique support services on FGM, including support for young women at risk, and also campaigns against child and early marriage.

Other specialist support organisations include Equality Now, founded in 1992, to use the law to protect and promote the human rights of women and girls, and now working internationally to fight domestic violence, FGM and child marriage. The pioneering organisation Daughters of Eve was established in 2010 by three BME women, Leyla Hussein, Nimco Ali, and Sainab Abdi. It works closely with young women who are at risk of female genital mutilation, raises awareness about it and signposts support services. The Black Dahlia support service, founded by Leyla Hussein and others in 2013, provides deeper therapeutic help to women who have experienced FGM in London.

It has been illegal for many years to carry out FGM in the UK, or for UK nationals to access it overseas, the maximum penalty being 14 years' imprisonment. The laws are very rarely used, however. The first conviction was in February 2019, and only four cases have ever been heard, in all. Prosecuting a hidden topic like FGM is a complex and sensitive matter, but the specialised women's projects can offer support and help. There is also a 24-hour FGM helpline (run by the NSPCC in partnership with the Metropolitan Police).

For forced marriage, this has been since 2014 a crime in England and Wales, a development strongly supported by some activist groups. However, other BMER activist women's organisations were not in favour of criminalisation on the grounds that it might deter victims reporting, and this does seem to have been the case.[24] Forced Marriage was the subject of civil law before then, under the Forced Marriage (Civil Protection) Act 2007 which provides civil orders (originally in the 1996 Family Law Act), regarded by many to be the more effective way forward. Recent briefings from Aisha K. Gill and Deborah Gould (2020) suggest that, under the newer criminal legislation, both the empowerment of victims so that they feel able to come forward and the provision of expert witnesses are of key importance.[25] The Forced Marriage Unit offers a dedicated national helpline and support service (although clearly associated with governmental officialdom). Organisations like SBS and other BMER projects have, throughout, offered help to many girls and women facing forced and early marriage over the years, and they continue to do so.

The Asian Women's Resource Centre in Brent[26] is presently leading on two partnership projects funded through the London Councils (Ascent) and the afore-mentioned Mayor's Office for Police and Crime (MOPAC) to address harmful practices against women across London. In the first of these, they have been the lead partner, since 2013, for the Ascent Ending Harmful Practices (EHP) partnership of 12 mainly BMER organisations. The partnership delivers specifically targeted services for those affected by harmful practices, like FGM, HBV, and FM, across all 32 London Boroughs.

Between 2017 and 2019, 1,258 women were supported, and they were able to reach a wide diversity of women. In November 2019, the partnership was awarded a three-year grant from MOPAC for a second project to expand on this provision across London. This is widening the support for BMER women and girls experiencing violence, including faith-based abuse, corrective rape, widow rituals and other harmful practices within the spectrum of violence against women and girls, as well as HBV, FGM and FM.

Thus, there have been real advances – but not enough. Women activists, mainly, but not solely, from the BME/BMER sector, have conducted years of committed campaigning for more efficient and sensitive recognition of these difficult issues, for better services, appropriate prosecutions, increased public and professional education, and sensitive awareness-raising. The dedicated specialist organisations, mentioned above, are joined in this work by many wider BME projects working on violence against women more generally in order, together, to build coherent responses.

The general (non-specialist) organisations also offer assistance, for example, Women's Aid, Refuge, Solace and SafeLives. It has always been a struggle to get the State and the relevant statutory agencies to take on these issues (about which they originally knew little) without victims being viewed in an 'exoticised' and stereotyped manner.[27] But the BME/BMER organisations, with redoubtable reputations and determination, and other deeply committed allies and activists dealing with violence against women in the UK, have worked on them with huge dedication.

BME women's organisations and funding cuts

Despite the growth of BME/BMER organisations working on violence against women and girls over the last decades and the challenges that the independent Black women's movement has mounted to the wider movement, Black and minority projects have been particularly vulnerable to funding cutbacks under the austerity programmes of the 2010s. While all domestic violence and abuse organisations have been badly affected, with many general refuge and domestic violence services losing financial support, BME projects have been disproportionately subjected to cuts.

In interviews for this book, it was clear that the situation has improved since the beginning when Black and other minority women sometimes felt that they were outsiders in the violence against women movement. Nonetheless, BME women's projects are still sometimes marginalised. They often continue to feel overlooked by more generic women's projects – even after all this time and all these years of effort.

A couple of interviewees suggested that, sometimes, majority white coalitions or projects – but local authorities in particular – may pride themselves on setting up strands of work led by BME projects. They often then take the credit – but without providing enough funding for the projects to be paid properly for all the work that they then do. The BME organisations, often with little power to resist, might be run ragged working to realise the project, while the local council or funder are the ones who end up looking good. (The issue of funding cuts and how they affected both BME projects and general ones is further discussed in the last sections of the next chapter.)

Struggling to change: campaigns, laws, and local and global strategies

First came campaigning and direct action, and then came legal change

Direct action has been the watchword of the violence against women and girls movement, as discussed throughout this book. Activism has been pursued with passion and energy since the beginning. Throughout this long women's history, it has always been important to mount campaigns to support survivors of domestic and sexual violence, and to both set up and then to defend the services they need. It has also been necessary to defend and support the campaigners and service providers themselves in their painful work.

Activists have constantly been attacked, as have refuges and rape crisis centres, when perpetrators find who or where they are. Physical (and now cyber) attacks have been very common from the beginning, as any worker in these services will tell you. Currently, almost all activists on violence against women, and on rape and sexual violence in particular, are exposed to social media attacks and severe trolling which are often extreme and unrelenting. In one of many examples, in 2019, a rape charity was bombarded with ceaseless, distressing, and sometimes violent racist abuse, just because a photo of its flyer offering support to victims from an ethnic minority community was posted on Facebook.[1]

More generally, there have been a large number of campaigns over the years on domestic, sexual and other forms of gender violence. Only a few can be featured here. But the foremost in the last decade or more have been coordinated by EVAW (End Violence against Women), a leading coalition of women's services, researchers, survivors and activists which mounts campaigns to end violence of all types against women and girls. Established in 2005, it has lobbied and conducted campaigning and policy work tirelessly for 15 years.

EVAW has worked at every level of government in the UK countries to improve policy, practice, and awareness of gender-based violence. Directed from January 2021 by Andrea Simon, and previously by Sarah Green, EVAW is chaired jointly by Aisha K. Gill and Huda Jawad. Long-term previous co-chairs were Marai Larasi and Liz Kelly who oversaw the campaign's growth to its leading position. It was, and is, a wide-ranging and indispensable campaigning organisation with strong contributions from BME women.

Focussing briefly here on sexual violence, in one 2018 initiative, EVAW joined with Nia (a highly respected service in London, originally Hackney Women's Aid), and with Rape Crisis England and Wales and Southall Black Sisters to intervene in a Supreme Court case in which the police and Home Secretary had argued that they should not be held to account for inadequate investigations of sexual crimes. The case concerned John Worboys, known as the 'black cab rapist' who committed more than 100 rapes and sexual assaults on women in his cab between 2002 and 2008. (Worboys was convicted and subsequently lost his appeal against this conviction in February 2021.) Back in 2018, the campaign was successful.

The landmark Supreme Court ruling which was then made was a victory for women's activism, stating that the police *must* investigate rape properly to ensure the protection of women's human rights under the Human Rights Act.[2] If the police and the criminal justice system fail to do so, then they are actually breaking the law. After the judgement was announced, Pragna Patel, Director of Southall Black Sisters said: "Today, the Supreme Court has heard our call – 'no justice without accountability'! This judgment amounts to a vindication of the rule of law itself."

Also optimistically, for a number of years, various improved criminal justice practices have been reported about the support offered to some women reporting rape, in terms of rape suites and specialist officers, partially resulting from nearly half a century of women's activism. It is also true that police forces in many regions are working to tackle rape and sexual assault offences with a series of awareness campaigns. However, attrition in rape cases remains huge with cases falling away at every stage of the criminal justice process, affected by multiple factors. In a 2017 paper, 'Rape investigation and attrition in acquaintance, domestic violence and historical rape cases', Marianne Hester and Sarah-Jane Lilly Walker provided an important overview with some historical referencing on the enduring problem of attrition.[3] Campaigning groups continue to have to battle as strongly as they can against poor service and negative trends.

In 2019, women's groups, including EVAW and Rape Crisis England and Wales, Women's Aid in England, Welsh Women's Aid, and various others, expressed huge disappointment with a series of government reports which demonstrated that, while reporting of rape has increased hugely, charging, prosecutions and conviction in rape cases have been consistently decreasing, year on year.[4] In the year up to July 2020, the situation became even worse. Of 55,130 rapes reported in England and Wales, there were only 2,102 prosecutions and just 1,439 convictions, less than half the numbers (5,190 and 2,991, respectively), three years earlier in 2016.[5] EVAW and the Centre for Women's Justice were also hugely disappointed at the failure of their case in March 2021, challenging CPS guidance on prosecuting rape which had been altered, precipitating a 60 per cent fall in prosecutions over four years to a record low.[6]

This is such a clear trend that some claim that rape is virtually being decriminalised, a deeply worrying development. This short book cannot address the complexities of rape prosecutions and the criminal justice system response, but large amounts of activist campaigning, research and policy development have been conducted. These will certainly continue, as activists, campaigners and professionals insist on holding the system to account on sexual and domestic violence, and attempt to reverse the trend in decriminalisation.[7] In Scotland, there are actually increased prosecutions and convictions, but still much needs to improve there, too.

Women's rape campaigns (in addition to the sexual violence strand of EVAW's work), include Amnesty's Right to be Free from Rape Campaign, Teenage Rape Prevention Campaigns and various campaigns operated over the years by Rape Crisis Scotland and Rape Crisis England and Wales. Such campaigns against rape have also been passionately conducted in many other countries, including India in the wake, for example, of the horrific gang rape and murder in Delhi of Jyoti Singh in 2012, which resulted in sustained action by Indian activists, and in worldwide outrage.

Thus, in summary, campaigns have been carried out, across the world, from the 1970s onwards, on sexual and domestic violence, with heritage in the early days of women's movement activity and connections to grass-roots groups. EVAW suggest that, as well as campaigning and conducting policy work, recovery and healing are also an essential part of justice.[8] Support and caring for survivors are part and parcel of trying to improve justice services.

In some further important examples, women killed by men are remembered in the Counting Dead Women campaign, developed by activist and Chief Executive of Nia, Karen Ingala Smith, and carried out each year since 2012. This is linked into the Femicide Census developed with Women's Aid and lawyer Clarissa O'Callaghan, which has become established as a leading independent record of fatal violence committed by men against women in the UK every year. Another example is the support from EVAW and other women's services offered to women in immigration detention who have been trafficked, providing them with advocacy and therapeutic support.

In London, there have been large annual Million Women Rise marches on International Women's Day since 2007. These important demonstrations, set up and coordinated by Sabrina Querishi, take over the streets of the capital each year in a huge symbolic gesture. It is the only march which focusses on violence against women as a whole. It is led by Black women and has been throughout.

International campaigns include the V Day organisation and its global campaign to end violence against women and girls, operating since 1998 and originally from the US. It is led by Eve Ensler (also known as 'V'), who wrote the enduringly popular play, *The vagina monologues*. V Day holds marches and actions in many countries as part of its initiative One Billion Rising (referring to the approximate number of women experiencing gender violence in the world).

And of course, as a result of all this activity for so long, the ground was laid for the #MeToo and #Times up movements of the late 2010s, calling out predatory men who use their power, especially in the media, over younger women for sexual exploitation. Pioneered by a Black activist and sexual abuse survivor, Tarana Burke, back in 2006, the movement took off hugely in 2017, particularly across the entertainment industries. There have been claims that Burke and other Black women leaders of the campaigns have been somewhat displaced more recently by famous women celebrities who have taken up the movement.

These celebrities have, at best, linked with activists. For example, well-known UK Black women's activist Marai Larasi highlighted the #MeToo campaign at the 2018 BAFTAs, at the invite of actor Emma Watson. These initiatives have led to activities in many countries, and have attracted considerable publicity. They have resulted in reform in, for example, film and TV, fashion, sports, and the law in different countries. The hashtag has trended in at least 85 countries, from Afghanistan to Ethiopia to Chile, and high profile successful prosecutions have taken place of serial sexual offenders. For example, the movie mogul, Harvey Weinstein, was sentenced to 23 years in prison in 2020, with worldwide media coverage.[9]

Internationally, the various loose-knit Black Lives Matter movements, resurgent in 2020, contain strands and activists working on violence against Black women. And, most importantly perhaps, the International Day of Action on Violence Against Women (or Gender-Based Violence) is held annually on 25 November. It is accompanied by a massive number of campaigns and protests. In 2019, for example, actions were held on 25 November across the world, from Argentina, to Iraqi Kurdistan to the Sudan to Panama.[10] Connected to this are the 16 Days of Activism (from the International Day of Action until World Human Rights Day on 10 December), operating globally, but particularly perhaps outside the Western countries. Powerful actions are held each year in, for example, Latin America, the Middle East, African countries, and the Global South in general, starting from 1991. These have now included at least 6,000 organisations in 187 countries.

International Women's Day (IWD) is also a time for huge demonstrations and direct action in many countries across the world. In two international examples from 2020, an amazing one million women took part in IWD actions across Chile for women's rights and against state repression.[11] Similarly in 2020, women in Mexico nearly brought the country to a standstill with huge demonstrations on the day itself, followed by a women's strike, said to have involved about half the female population.[12] In Guadalajara, women dyed the water in the city fountains red to symbolise women's blood lost through domestic violence and killings.

Very high levels of femicide (up to ten women killed per *day*) precipitated these actions. They were provoked by two particularly brutal murders, one of a 7-year-old girl and one of a 25-year-old woman, Ingrid Escamilla Vargas. This book is dedicated to her memory. She was attacked by her partner in horrific and entirely barbaric ways, too deeply upsetting to include here. There is more about the Escamilla Vargas case in the endnote.[13] The women of Mexico have taken up the challenge.

The huge 2020 demonstration in her memory in the Zocalo, Mexico City, featured a red shoes protest, following the work by artist, Elina Chauvet, from 2009 on, initiating such protests across South America and other parts of the world. (The Zocalo demonstration features on this book's cover.) The shoes, left in public places, each represent a femicide, and the red colour represents blood. Thus, the women of Mexico have taken up this distressing challenge.

Let us all take this challenge forward in the name of Ingrid Escamilla Vargas.

Global frameworks on gender-based violence and women's activism

The campaigning networks on violence against women sometimes connect to global initiatives operating through the UN and other supra-national organisations, including international women's bodies. Although remote from local struggle, often critiqued by grass-roots activists, and tending to represent a 'Western gaze',[14] these global frameworks can be of some help in providing standards and strategies to aim towards. They can be used strategically in lobbying and pressurising different governments to improve their practice. For example, they can help, if – say – the government concerned has committed their country (frequently ineffectively) to compliance with the relevant conventions, or – if they haven't – to shame them into signing up.

Almost always, these international instruments and statutes have come about, at least partially, through the dedicated efforts of feminists working in the global bodies. Their tireless input has also helped with implementation. I have worked with some of these remarkable and unsung international workers, and contend that their endless work deserves to be applauded. The relevant conventions and agreements include CEDAW (the massively important 1979 Convention for the Elimination of all Forms of Discrimination against Women). Activists on violence against women regularly contribute to the four-yearly country Reports and Shadow Reports to the CEDAW Committee.

The passing of the 1993 UN International Declaration on the Elimination of Violence against Women was a triumph for the campaigners and women's organisations who had fought for it. It states that such violence is a violation of women's human rights and a result of unequal power relations between men and women. Importantly, the UN Global (or Sustainable Development) Goals, building on the previous Millennium Development Goals, include Goal Number 5 which aims 'to achieve gender equality and to empower all women and girls'. Organisations working on these issues at the international level are myriad, including UN Women, WOW (Women of the World), Womankind Worldwide, and Women for Women

International which supports marginalised women survivors of war internationally.

In Europe, the important 2011 Istanbul Convention (in Council of Europe countries, a wider constituency than the EU) is of key importance. It represents a ground-breaking improvement in the rights of women experiencing gender violence. The UK signed, and then signalled ratification in 2012. However, the Westminster Conservative Government has been roundly condemned for still failing to ratify this pioneering pan-European convention tackling violence against women, after eight years. EVAW has accused the Government of dangerous and 'serious foot-dragging'.

Although the majority of countries have ratified, the UK in its reticence to do so shares common ground with a few other governments. In 2021, the right-wing administration in Poland, for example, is attempting to leave the Convention completely. The governments of Turkey (the site of the original convention) and Hungary (both attempting to roll back human and women's rights) are at the time of writing deciding to oppose or disrupt it, despite vehement opposition from women's groups in all three countries. (Turkey announced its withdrawal from the Convention in March 2021.) These may not be the sort of bedfellows the UK wants to be associated with.

Globally, there are key Agreements and Conventions on sexual violence and rape in place, especially in relation to war and conflict. They build on the enormously important UN Security Council Resolution 1325 (and various follow ups), and on the Global Women's Peace and Security Framework and the Global Preventing Sexual Violence in War Initiative. Activists in the various supra-national bodies have taken key roles in these advances, but they have done so alongside the more grass-roots activists. Making rape in war a war crime, as is now the case, resulted, for example, from worldwide campaigning over years, especially, but not solely, in the Global South.

Legislation in the UK on domestic abuse and gender violence

In the UK, the Women's Aid federations, Refuge, AVA, Rights of Women, Rape Crisis, Justice for Women and the more recent Centre for Women's Justice have together directed much campaigning energy towards the legislature. Improving legal responses to violence against women remains one of the important streams in building a multi-stranded approach to women abuse, although on its own it can achieve little (without simultaneous campaigning, service provision, policy work, awareness-raising and training).

The difficulties of getting fair outcomes for women from the legal process have been highlighted many times, including in Jackie Barron's 1990 book, discussed below, revealingly entitled *Not worth the paper ... ?* to indicate the lack of effectiveness of legal protection for abused women. Barron's work, key at the time, reported on the 1980s. Thirty-three years later, in 2013, Susan Edwards, long-term writer on domestic violence issues in relation to the police and the law, contributed the latest update of her book on continuing and unremitting gender discrimination in the legislative system, *Sex and gender in the legal process.*[15] Inadequate legal provision for women continues, despite some improvements.

It is important to note that the law takes different forms in the four UK countries. Scotland, for example, generally has different legislation to England and Wales. In a few examples (mainly but not solely from England and Wales, and not, by any means, a complete list of laws passed), the Women's Aid federations were extremely instrumental in the drafting of vital legislation from the 1970s on. These included the Domestic Violence and Matrimonial Proceedings Act, 1976, the Domestic Violence and Magistrate's Courts Act, 1978, and the Housing (Homeless Persons) Act, 1977 (now much modified). They were followed by the very useful Matrimonial Homes (Family Protection) (Scotland) Act, 1981, which enabled occupancy rights to be granted to women (and their children) in Scotland to stay in the matrimonial home.

The 1976 and 1978 Acts in England and Wales also introduced pioneering civil law improvements for abused women which were of key importance. However, these were often ineffective or poorly implemented, as documented by Barron in her influential book from the period, noted above and commissioned by the WAFE Legal and Research Group of the 1980s.[16] Leading on from this and from the recommendations of the Parliamentary Home Affairs Select Committee Report 1992, improvements in civil law injunctions, and the attachment to them of a mandatory power of arrest, were introduced in the important Part 4 of the Family Law Act, 1996. However, these improvements only came about due to a long struggle to be heard by Women's Aid and others, and to the work of sympathetic women in the judiciary.

In 1991, rape in marriage became illegal in England and Wales after a long fight and much dedicated work by rape crisis and feminist activists. Rights of Women, the Women's Aid federations, Rape Crisis and WAVAW had joined forces with other feminists and violence survivors to exert coordinated pressure. Remembering this vibrant history, Liz Kelly spoke for this book about linking with survivors of rape in the passionate campaign which led to this historic change and which included ground-breaking consciousness-raising type discussion of sexual violence in marriage. In Scotland with its powerful women's advocates and separate legislature, the precedent was set much earlier in 1982, confirmed in 1989. The 2003 UK Sexual Offences Act was also key and was passed after a huge feminist effort, especially around rape and around the definition of consent. It was followed by the 2009 Act in Scotland.

In the 2000s, the UK domestic violence legislation was improved with the Domestic Violence, Crime and Victims Act, 2004 (applying to Wales, Northern Ireland and England), the largest overhaul in 30 years, passed with the violence against women sector fully participating in consultations and draftings. One of these reforms was the introduction of Domestic Violence Homicide Reviews which have been important since then. This law has been followed by further legislation on forced marriage and on other violence against women issues, as noted earlier.

In 2020, the Domestic Abuse Bill (applying mainly to Wales and England), which had been on a stop-start journey through parliament due to the Brexit negotiations of 2019, was brought back into the parliamentary schedule. Rights of Women, Women's Aid in England and Wales, Refuge, SBS, survivors groups and other women's organisations have been tireless in their work on amendments to this Bill, demonstrating the role that women's movement activists can have in influencing the law. They continued to pressure the government in early 2020 to improve the Bill further in terms of more effective protection overall, and to fill gaps, for example the lack of protection for migrant women and children in its provisions. The Bill represents a milestone in improving domestic violence legislation including introducing a new statutory definition. It was passed by the House of Commons in July 2020. However, the amendments to support migrant women and those without recourse to public funds were not passed. The Bill continues to fail women in these situations who face almost insurmountable barriers in escaping violence.

The campaigning group 'We can't consent to this', together with influential researcher Susan Edwards and others, have worked to improve legal responses to the deaths of women killed during so-called rough sex, who are presented as having consented. There has been an alarming increase in the use of the 'rough sex defence' by men who have killed their intimate partners. This work has resulted in the very welcome introduction of a 'no defence for consent to injury' clause into the Domestic Abuse Bill in 2020.

Crucially, the activists on domestic violence and abuse have argued strongly (but unsuccessfully at the time of writing) for the Bill to include increased and ring-fenced funding for support services, presently suffering from years of cuts. They point out that, however excellent the legislation, it cannot work if it is accompanied, as in UK Conservative policy from 2010 till at least 2021, by cutbacks, underfunding and, in some cases, naked attacks on the independent support provision which protects and supports thousands of women and children daily.

A key piece of legislation in Scotland has been the Domestic Abuse (Scotland) Act, 2018, which establishes the offence of domestic abuse and is a pioneering law all round. Marsha Scott, the CEO of Scottish Women's Aid, points out that the Act has a consistent message about gender and reflects a feminist analysis, which have also been notable distinguishing elements of the Women's Aid movement in Scotland over the last ten years, and are not unrelated to the relative progressivism of the Scottish Government.

Recent innovative pieces of legislation across the UK, and accompanying statutory guidance, have focussed on coercive control in intimate relationships. The Domestic Abuse (Scotland) Act includes coercive and abusive behaviour. And, as part of the Serious Crime Act, 2015, the Westminster Government's coercive or controlling behaviour offence can also now bring perpetrators to justice. These Acts built on ground-breaking work on coercive control, and its role in abuse for many women.

The concept was originally developed by Evan Stark (as noted in relation to the case of Sally Challen). For this book, he contributed this extract from his evidence to the Challen case to explain the concept more clearly:

> Many of the tactics used in coercive control could seem relatively harmless if considered separately and only take their legal significance from their role in the overall pattern designed to subordinate a victim. Taken together, with the more overtly criminal behaviors, they create an experience of entrapment that is hostage-like. The rights and liberties denied in coercive control are fundamental to personhood, autonomy, dignity and citizenship. (Evan Stark, 2019)

To bring this brief discussion to a close, it is important to celebrate how tenaciously and powerfully the activist organisations have struggled. Nicola Harwin recalled for this book the huge efforts on legislation made by the violence against women movements since the 1970s. She talked about how hard Women's Aid (England), herself personally, and others had worked to build their research and policy profile and to influence the legal process, in particular, for example, personally drafting multiple amendments to the Family Law Act, Part 4, to strengthen it. Activists and campaigners have worked on VAWG issues nonstop. She and others noted, too, how key civil servants and individuals in government agencies often fulfilled a pivotal role in getting policy or legal changes through, which might not otherwise had happened without their committed assistance.

Allies in high places have been useful to feminists engaging in legal reform work. Particularly helpful women MPs, judges and officers include (of many) three redoubtable pioneers, Lady Brenda Hale, Helena Kennedy and Vera Baird. Let us also take a moment to remember and celebrate the late Jo Richardson who was an amazing support in the early days and who died in 1994.

Wider collaborations, strategic development and multi-agency coordination

This account is geared towards the history of the movement against domestic violence, rather than developments in policy and legislation. It is important to note, however, that government commitment and funding have been key over the years (although sometimes problematic). In this context, Scotland and Wales have, as noted throughout, provided more sympathetic government environments for the development of gender violence services, compared with the government in England, as pointed out by both Scottish and Welsh Women Aids, and by consultants for this book, Fran Wasoff and Lily Greenan from Scotland, and Eleri Butler from Wales. Their smaller size also means that 'violence against women' activists and government officers often know each other. Apart from immigration and welfare, all other elements of work on violence against women and girls are devolved in Scotland. This has meant greater strategic cohesion and more generous funding regimes. There is similar devolution in Northern Ireland, complicated by the wider political situation there.

An important development over the last 30 years, nationally and internationally, has been the initiation of inter-agency collaborations. These have aimed to support women experiencing domestic violence, often bringing together services, or pioneering new practice in criminal justice or health. For example, the IRIS initiative, with inter-agency liaison between the Health Service and the independent women's sector, aims to enhance identification and referral procedures for domestic abuse in the NHS (across the UK countries) and to provide practical interventions for assisting doctors and health practitioners.

Vital in these developments has been the evolution of more formalised multi-agency collaboration to bring together voluntary and statutory agencies. Pioneered initially through the violence against women movement, innovative multi-agency forums were first set up in the early 1990s in Leeds, Nottingham, Islington, Hammersmith and Fulham, and elsewhere, with input and some leadership from Women's Aid, including from Nicola Harwin. Key figures included Andrea Tara-Chand in Leeds, Davina James-Hanman in Islington and Robin Holder in Hammersmith. Many other forums were then established including Greenwich, coordinated by Janet Bowstead, which followed the example of Islington and others in recruiting a 'Domestic Violence Coordinator' from a feminist voluntary sector background, with a wide-ranging role to engage voluntary and statutory sector agencies and develop shared priorities, rather than statutory dominance.

Domestic Violence Coordinators, from then on, began to be employed to coordinate multi-agency work in local areas across the country. Examples of particularly innovative inter-agency practice also evolved in Derby and (then-called) Cleveland in the mid-1990s. This early, exciting work was documented in *The multi-agency approach to domestic violence: New opportunities, old challenges?* (1999), edited by Nicola Harwin, Ellen Malos and myself.[17] Inter-agency forums and partnerships dealing with violence against women and girls have been established across the country ever since, with representation, usually, from specialist domestic violence organisations. These have, more recently, fed into both local and national multi-agency 'strategic developments' across regions.

Often, initiatives of this type broadly derive from the ground-breaking Duluth Abuse Intervention Programs (known as the Duluth model) in Minnesota, developed by my friend, the wonderful Ellen Pence, who was endlessly humorous and one of the great innovators of the violence against women movement.[18] What she pioneered is the 'coordinated community response' to domestic abuse, which brings together all relevant agencies in a locality. Such responses now operate in many countries in different forms. Ellen died in 2012, leaving a huge void.

Coordinated community responses are, ideally, led by shelter/ refuge organisations and women's activists (although in reality the large statutory agencies tend to be more dominant). The idea was, and remains, to build a seamless and co-operative response across a local area. Within this world-leading effort, ideas about power and control in relationships were famously first articulated to a wider audience in the Duluth Power and Control Wheel,[19] developed by Ellen and the Duluth Project. A simple diagrammatical representation of power in relation to experiences of abuse, it is now used, in different forms, all over the world.

A number of Specialist Domestic Abuse Courts now exist in the UK (as in some other countries, for example, the US) to deal with domestic violence cases, a development usually evaluated positively. However, the long-term domestic abuse organisation Standing Together Against Domestic Violence (a UK charity working for 20 years to bring communities together to end domestic abuse) and its coordinator, Beryl Foster (now retired), have proposed that these specialist Courts and other criminal justice initiatives can only really be effective if they are part of a wider coordinated initiative. (The Government also stated this in their commissioning framework.) Standing Together has always pointed out how, when it really works, the coordinated community response brings services together to ensure local systems truly keep survivors safe, hold abusers to account, and prevent domestic abuse in a measurable way.

From the 1990s onwards, coordinated community responses in the UK were often developed as part of Crime and Disorder Partnerships within local authority areas. These partnerships frequently then employed Domestic Violence Coordinators in a more formal, structured way to work strategically across localities. At least initially, these Coordinators were almost always connected in some way to the wider women's movement. Such developments referred back in some ways to the Greater London Council of the 1980s, which had instigated Women's Committees (as had many Labour-controlled councils), who then funded women's projects. (Some feminist activists at the time, though, viewed these developments as sapping vibrance from the movement and co-opting the women's groups involved.)

Coordinated community responses and strategic partnerships now exist widely. It must be said, though, that in a major national research study on this approach in the 1990s, conducted by Ellen Malos and myself, we found that it was difficult to avoid statutory agencies dominating and to ensure that the work was informed by survivor voices.

> The study found that, while such inter-agency responses can be very helpful, they can also act as smokescreens – or as face savers – which make the local area look good, but disguise the lack of real change.[20]

Greater London Domestic Violence Project

An important development in London from 1997 showed what could be achieved, with a dedicated champion with experience of the violence against women movement to drive the work forward (Davina James-Hanman), a sympathetic Labour-controlled Council (the Greater London Authority) and a helpful Mayor (Ken Livingstone). The wide-ranging domestic violence work that they developed was also made possible by being embedded in a somewhat enabling environment provided by the Labour Government from 1997, and its crime and disorder measures which gave a green light to work on domestic abuse.

The GLDVP assisted in developing key action plans, strategies and policies in all 32 London Boroughs as a pioneer in attempting coordination across the whole of the capital. The project had an open door to the Metropolitan Police (which, like many police services, had put domestic violence units in place in police stations to assist victims). Coordination services and policies proliferated. The *London Domestic Violence Strategy* (from 2001) was also entirely pioneering, and a model of good practice. All this enabled access to the central Westminster Government and widespread policy development across the capital. Incredibly, when Boris Johnson (as London Mayor) and the Conservatives were elected in 2008, one of the very first things done, literally in the first *week*, was to end this world-leading project. It then became the independent charity, AVA, which continues coordination and strategy work.

Domestic violence and abuse strategies and partnerships multiplied across localities from the 2000s onwards, often called by names like Violence against Women and Girls (VAWG) Strategies. The Government for England has provided its own national *Ending Violence against Women and Girls Strategy* (for example, from 2016–2020). In Scotland, there is *Equally Safe: Scotland's Strategy to Prevent and Eradicate Violence against Women and Girls* (2018). Meanwhile, with a more sympathetic regime back in power in London under Mayor Sadiq Khan, at the time of writing, funding and coordination projects have been forthcoming under the *Mayor's Violence against Women and Girls Strategy 2018–2021*.

Helplines and men's projects

All the Women's Aid federations and Refuge have for many years run helplines, and continue to do so, as do local domestic violence or rape services in their own areas. The 24-hour National Domestic Abuse Helpline (on 0808 2000 247), set up by WAFE, as noted before, has been of key importance. It was operated jointly in England by Women's Aid and Refuge for many years, and now by Refuge. Women's Aid and other projects also operate confidential online live chat-lines (which can be used more easily by disabled women or by those who are phone-averse). As noted earlier, the other UK countries set up their own National Domestic Abuse Helplines, which are Live Fear Free Helpline in Wales, the 24-Hour Domestic and Sexual Abuse Helpline in the North of Ireland (now in the hands of Nexus NI which runs sexual violence services), and Scotland's Domestic Abuse and Forced Marriage Helpline, run by Scottish Women's Aid. They are complemented by the Rape Crisis National Helplines in Scotland and in England and Wales.[21]

For decades now, programmes for perpetrators of domestic violence to deal with their violent behaviour have been provided, sometimes as part of coordinated community responses. These programmes vary widely in type, from those situated within the criminal justice service to those with voluntary attendance. They generally offer support to women partners simultaneously, and some have input from violence against women activists. For instance, the well-thought-of feminist and pro-feminist organisation, Respect, provides accreditation guidelines for working with perpetrators, and a Respect toolkit for professionals doing so. They operate the Respect Phone Line for male perpetrators to seek help. They provide support and training, too, and offer a programme of work with young people who use, or experience, violence in personal relationships.

Services also exist for men who have been abused. Respect run another helpline, the Men's Advice Line for male victims. Dedicated Helplines for abused men include those provided by, in Scotland, the 'Abused Men in Scotland' organisation, and, in Wales, the Dyn project which offers support to heterosexual, gay, bisexual and trans men who are experiencing domestic abuse from a partner. There is also the Mankind Initiative offering support to men experiencing domestic violence across the UK, and the National LGBT Domestic Abuse Helpline.

Recent years: commissioning, mainstreaming and fighting back

Of course, the women's movement does not now exist in the same way that it did. In the wider frame, feminism itself has had to change, coping with hostility and backlashes, and with diversity in approaches to the liberation of women. In the last 15 years, funding has become a key issue with new projects being commissioned through complex tendering and commissioning frameworks in which organisations compete with each other to provide services, and also compete in term of budgets and regulatory control. These budgetary and commissioning issues now often override concerns about responding to domestic abuse in a transformative way.

Throughout the 2000s and 2010s, domestic violence projects on violence against women and girls have continued to diversify. Manchester Women's Aid, for example, is a large organisation with many component projects, including Sahara for BME women. However, the sector has suffered not only because of competitive commissioning, but also because equality policies in local areas have changed. Previously, they had specialist streams, each combatting a different type of inequality, for example, racism or discrimination towards disabled people. But, in recent years, local authorities have lumped all these type of inequality together in the interests of being 'generic'. Southall Black Sisters took this policy head-on in their Campaign to Survive (2008/2009).

What happened was that the local Council decided to fund general, non-specialist services in the supposed interest of equality for all, and tried to take away funding from specialist BME services. SBS fought back, not only for themselves, but to assist other less powerful BME services in the same position. And they convincingly won the struggle and regained funding. It ended up being about the meaning of equality itself, according to Pragna Patel, and the need to counteract disadvantage with specialist, focussed input, *before* you can start thinking about getting to an even 'generic' playing field.

However, despite this victory for small independent Black, minority and other organisations, some large housing associations more widely have often taken over services and set up 'empires', providing domestic violence projects principally as housing provision. These housing association projects have frequently operated with few social care staff and without the support that the refuge movement traditionally has offered. This has all brought new challenges to feminist activists.

To help refuge organisations with these complexities, 'On Track' is the Women's Aid case management monitoring programme which can assist with measuring outcomes and both monitoring and standards. Also, in response to commissioning and budgeting frameworks, some domestic violence services have joined up together in powerful umbrella organisations, with many members. These larger organisations have sometimes displaced smaller projects. Solace Women's Aid, for example, offers wide-ranging therapeutic and refuge services in London, as noted earlier.

Large conglomerations like this may well provide good services and take an active part in the wider movement for change on violence against women, as Solace itself tries to do, participating with commitment in campaigns and consortiums on harmful practices, for example. But then again (as suggested in interviews in regard to some other powerful groups and housing associations), such large organisations may not.

> Southall Black Sisters and others suggest that when service provision becomes all there is, and is cut off from the founding politics and belief systems, it is like the coming of a classic neo-liberal approach. This presently dominates social and economic policy more broadly. But it has recently spilt over into the organisations of the women's community sector. This means the advent of bitter competition for funding, target-driven marketisation and empire-building by some, leading to a loss of feminist solidarity, and cutback in the welfare state. This is precisely what the violence against women sector has experienced in recent years.

Emphasis on risk assessment

A further issue is that there has been an increasing emphasis on 'risk'. In the last decades, the Multi-agency Risk Assessment Conference (MARAC)[22] system has been developed as a statutory information–sharing and risk management provision. This system assesses risk to victims, and coordinates specific support between relevant agencies, provided to those designated as at most risk. The first MARAC was tried out in Cardiff in 2003, and the scheme was rolled out from 2006/2007 by the Home Office, first to areas with specialist domestic violence courts, and then across the board. As a key part of the approach, Independent Domestic Violence Advocates/Advisors, IDVAs, address the situation of victims at highest risk of harm to secure both their safety and that of their children. IDVAs are trained by various organisations, including, importantly, SafeLives. Sometimes survivors themselves, they can at best offer grounded, realistic support to the women and children concerned.

These initiatives help many women, and the MARAC scheme can be successful as good practice in protecting very vulnerable victims and their children. However, the use of MARACs and of statutory power can work against women's rights, privacy and dignity. They can interfere in the lives of survivors in ways which are sometimes prescriptive and unhelpful, and can even be seen as secondarily abusive. Moreover, the emphasis on high risk, above all else, means that other issues are perforce overlooked. Assessing risk and complex form-filling may take away valuable time in helping a victim of violence.

Funding is then funnelled accordingly, so that women not designated as at 'high enough risk' lose out. Together with the dominance of commissioning and tendering frameworks, of large housing associations (and others) taking over the work, and of restrictive government funding policies, these trends in the VAWG sector have resulted in cutbacks and project closures, especially in BME services, and have threatened service advances in many cases.

Davina James-Hanman, long-term activist and previous Director of the GLDVP and AVA, writes that:

> Professionalising turned out to mean depoliticising the women's anti-male violence movement and burying them in paperwork. It meant reshaping services so that they met less of survivors' needs and looked more like those provided by the State. 'Professionalising the sector' was targeted solely at voluntary sector organisations ... It invariably resulted in putting agency objectives – especially those of the criminal justice system – at the centre rather than the needs of survivors. With many parts of the women's movement reacting in equal parts of frustration and outrage ... to poorly drawn-up contracts that favoured costs over quality of service, a vacuum was created into which generic service providers eagerly stepped. (Davina James-Hanman)[23]

To support smaller projects disadvantaged by having to survive in such a competitive marketplace with the large, powerful organisations, Imkaan and Women's Aid operate a Sustainability Partnership.[24] This offers training and support to build the resilience of these independent domestic violence services to cope with funding battles and the serious hardship that the most marginalised and vulnerable of them experience.

Then come project cutbacks and closures

Despite such efforts, these wider trends, together with increasingly competitive and target-driven demands, have badly affected many of the autonomous, independent women's projects. Small, feminist and often gutsy, projects may not be able to compete in fundraising terms with the larger organisations and may be marginalised in their own field – when they have been the ones doing the work for decades. Feminist projects working at the grass-roots have always been the backbone of the violence against women movement. Seeing some of them pushed to one side by more powerful players is both a tragedy and travesty.

Many specialised projects on violence against women and girls have been cut back or closed down since the austerity period started in 2010. As one example, the previously important Poppy Project, a unique service supporting and helping trafficked women, together with the more broadly-focussed Eaves Housing for Women of which it was a part, tragically lost their funding (in 2015).

Within this wider inhospitable funding environment, Black and minority domestic violence and abuse projects, as noted, have suffered disproportionately. A particularly important example is the situation at the time of writing of the London Black Women's Project (LBWP), the long-standing former Newham Asian Women's project. LBWP, a specialist and dedicated organisation for Black and minority ethnic women and girls, has been a leader among BME services on violence against women in London, with an unsullied reputation across the field for 32 years.

Recently, they lost the contract to provide their services, including five specialist refuges across Newham, to a much larger non-specialist organisation. In November 2019, the project was given a year's reprieve, after a fierce campaign, but the future remains uncertain. The Executive Director of Imkaan, Baljit Banga, stated, after one of the protests: "You have small, grass-roots organisations bidding against organisations that are twenty times their size." Apparently, 22 BME refuge services across the country have had their funding cut or have been taken over by larger organisations in the past years. This is an extraordinary and distressing number.

More widely and despite the overall advances of the sector, domestic violence services and the Women's Aid federations state that many refuges and services have suffered serious cuts. In December 2019, Women's Aid in England reported back on a study that they had conducted which demonstrated that an additional £393 million per year is needed to properly fund the sector. The study found that a large percentage of abused women were not able to access the refuge they needed, with only one quarter accommodated in suitable refuge space.

Women's Aid (England) stated that:

> 60% of refuge referrals were declined last year, and an estimated one in ten refuges and one in five community-based services receive no local authority funding at all. Services led 'by and for' Black and minority (BME) women have been disproportionately impacted by local budget reductions and competitive tendering processes which too often favour larger-scale, general services but not the quality and expertise women need.[25]

They added that what continues, in 2020, to be required is:

1. Ring-fenced funding within the settlement for the 'by and for' expert sector.
2. Availability of a full range of service types.
3. Effective and sustainable funding of the wider support sector.
4. Provision for women with no recourse to public funds (NRPF).
5. Availability of housing benefit to cover housing costs for refuge services.
6. Funded coordination and oversight/monitoring.

Conclusion

The various factors discussed in the last sections have sometimes jeopardised broader feminist dreams and hopes around violence against women. And those long-held dreams have tended to get pushed towards a back seat. It is vital to celebrate and remember the feminist heritage of struggle and passionate innovation, at the same time as charting the changes.

These changes include the fact that, despite the cutbacks, the variety of the sector and its size is now beyond dispute, immeasurably dwarfing the early days. It provides interlinked services, policies, strategies and activist campaigns, including specialist provision, which are still, of course, inadequate, but which are now wide-ranging. At the time of writing, they are tackling the crisis of the COVID-19 pandemic, with the 2020 and 2021 lockdowns leading to rates of domestic violence worldwide increasing hugely, and even doubling.

Overall, the violence against women movements continue across the world. In the UK countries, the movement is complex and multi-layered, pushing forward the fight for abused women – despite mainstreaming, marketisation, the rigid demands of commissioning frameworks, others sometimes appropriating the work, and debilitating cutbacks. The sector is more structured in the 2020s, as it celebrates nearly 50 years of work. Some enter the field now as a career path without knowing or caring about its redoubtable feminist roots.

However, the landscape in terms of provision addressing violence against women and girls has been transformed. Developments have been way beyond what the early activists of Women's Aid, rape crisis centres and refuges could ever have visualised – even in their most extreme imaginings. The wide-reaching movement they started has led to huge (though still sometimes fragile) achievements in terms of provision. It might not seem like it sometimes, but we have indeed come further than you might think.

Perhaps, in all this, the work has lost some of its organic, holistic approach. But, as Teresa Parker of Women's Aid in England commented for this book, Women's Aid and the sector are still driven by the passionate values of (second wave) feminism and the women's movements of the world, and by the views of survivors. Sometimes she said, with a warm smile, the magical moments are still there.

Activist responses, justice and shelters (refuges) across the world

International initiatives to work with the police

Turning now to international activist responses, these have often revolved specifically around justice issues. It is true that the original feminist movements against domestic violence in many countries were full of passion. They were commonly suspicious of the police and the criminal justice system, and unenthusiastic about working closely alongside them.[1] Back in the early days, responses almost everywhere by the police to women reporting violence (of all types) were poor, and the issue was not taken at all seriously.[2] The police tended to assume in most countries that a man's home was indubitably his castle. These difficulties led, as time went on, to women's projects grasping the nettle. Sometimes reluctantly at first, there began to be attempts by women across the world to challenge inadequate criminal justice and other statutory responses.

The violence against women activists in many countries have since worked with determination on police and justice issues over all these years, through training, policy development, campaigning and lobbying, with some (often fragile) successes. Passionate movements for change and strongly fought-for advances have occurred, for example, in the varying activist contexts of India, Brazil and elsewhere.[3] Some of these are highlighted here.

As a first example of international activist innovations, the Special Cell for Women and Children in India was, and is, a unique and astonishing programme, aimed at eliminating violence against women, especially domestic violence. It has long provided strong gender violence activists and social workers to support women victims of violence, actually within local police stations.[4] Such a milieu can be challenging, demanding grit and courage from the women activists. One of the principals of the Special Cell initiative is a clear understanding that it is the responsibility of the State to prevent violence against women.

It was established in 1984 as a strategic collaboration between Bombay Police and the Tata Institute of Social Sciences, in Bombay/Mumbai, led originally by Anjali Dave of TISS, and now by Trupti Jhaveri Panchal, to both of whom my thanks are due for friendship and liaison. This has been a pioneering feminist project in the Indian context, which has been rolled out across India (sometimes using different names). There are currently 144 Special Cells across police stations in Maharashtra alone. Amazingly, there are more than 300 nationwide.

Paying tribute to the Special Cell for Women and Children

The Special Cell approach has worked against the odds for more than 35 years to embed itself, and to establish violence against women as a serious issue requiring public and police attention across rural and urban India. The author has had the opportunity to work with the employees of the Special Cell, who offer immediate support, advocacy and counselling to women victims right inside police stations. They also provide training to professionals. During our several days together, these professionals from across Maharashtra interspersed every meeting with rousing activist songs, engendering enthusiasm and infectious laughter to kindle the fire and the spirit.

The history of challenging violence against women in different countries has varied. However, there are other projects across the world in which feminist activists have established services to work directly in police stations. They include Domestic Violence

Matters in Islington, UK, set up in 1993, and positively evaluated by Liz Kelly and her team in 1999.[5] The evaluation found that proactive responses to domestic violence survivors worked best in these circumstances, rather than waiting for referrals.

Domestic Violence Matters was an adaption of a Canadian project, the Family Consultancy Service in London, Ontario, which was set up to work directly with women who had experienced domestic violence incidents in which the police were involved. This ground-breaking project, extremely positively regarded since the late 1970s, was a pioneer in locating a team of skilled civilian crisis interveners within the police service to follow up police responses.[6] It continues to operate.

Overall, London, Ontario, in Canada, has been regarded for decades as offering models of excellent practice.[7] The London Coordinating Committee to End Woman Abuse has provided a long-standing, multi-agency, coordinated community response, smoothly integrating local agencies. It has worked with various pioneering local domestic violence services. These include its refuge/shelter (transition house in Canadian terms), the famed London Women's Community House. This outstandingly successful shelter stands proudly at a widely known and public address. A beacon in the Canadian domestic abuse sector, it has struggled more and more to keep up with demand in the 2010s.[8] More recently, the Women's Community House has merged with the Sexual Assault Centre London to form the organisation, Anova, whose resounding aim is to move towards: 'An inclusive world of shared power where everyone lives freely without fear of violence.'[9]

A further much-lauded project is the London Abused Women's Centre, previously the London Battered Women Advocacy Centre. They have provided proactive support, counselling and advocacy services on an outreach basis, and from a well-developed feminist activist perspective for 40 years, and operate their 'Shine the Light on Woman Abuse Campaign'. If you want to learn about domestic violence services which are an inspiration, check out London, Ontario.

In Brazil, and also in other countries such as Mexico, there have long been women's police stations to deal with violence against women, providing specialist women officers.[10] In the early 1980s, the social movement of women in Brazil was successful in pressuring the (then) military regime to consider establishing these provisions. Staffed by women, they worked alongside 'normal' police stations specifically to assist women experiencing abuse, including domestic and sexual violence. As with many women's policy innovations across the world, these initiatives emerged as a direct impact of protest and campaigning by women, and further developed as Brazil emerged from military rule in the second half of the 1980s.[11] The original ground-breaking station, set up in São Paulo in 1985 with activist input, was the first such initiative anywhere in the world, and continues to function. There are now about 250.

The women's police stations have sometimes provided rather bureaucratic responses, and have been somewhat marginalised within the wider police service, but have been an innovative police response, perhaps worth replicating elsewhere. Brazil has developed a wide range of services on violence against women including 'reference centres' which support victims/survivors. But, at the time of writing, these are being substantially attacked under the extreme right-wing Government of Jair Bolsonaro, according to discussions between the author and activist women who prefer not to be named.

More optimistically, coordinated community responses on domestic abuse (briefly discussed in Chapter 9), like the world-leading models in Duluth, Minnesota, and London, Ontario, have been set up in many countries. They have all attempted, in different ways, to bring agencies together, including the police, social services and any independent women's services that exist. These wide-ranging initiatives, which have had varying degrees of success (although positive more often than not), have attempted to reform the criminal justice system from a feminist perspective, and to build new coordinated ways of responding.

Women's movements have also worked without pause in many milieus and countries to promote concrete legal changes and to push for specialised legislation. Usually, these laws, as for one of the best known, the Violence against Women Act in the US, have been passed mainly (but not solely) as a result of grass-roots women's activism. Domestic Violence Acts have been passed in various Western countries and also in the 'Majority World', including in Uganda, Zimbabwe, Iraqi Kurdistan, South Africa and India. Since 2007, there has been the pioneering Maria da Penha Law in Brazil, named to honour a well-known activist, made paraplegic after murder attempts by her husband. Commonly though, with all these varying laws, there are problems with inefficient or uncommitted implementation.

Overall, resources remain minimum in most countries and inadequate across the world. Nevertheless, attempts at change for women are being made everywhere. Activists have given the impetus to the development of these various legal, criminal justice, educational and community innovations in many countries. Of course, in almost all Western countries, the key original activist response to domestic violence has always been the provision of shelters/refuges (together with legal, education and policy change). However, this has not been the case in many non-Western countries.

Are activist-inspired shelters a Western concept? Controversy and context-specific projects

How much, then, are domestic abuse shelters/refuges a Western idea? Although they now exist in many countries globally, it is true that there has been controversy about their usefulness in 'Majority World' economies. Called shelters rather than refuges in this chapter, as common throughout much of the world, there have been suggestions in the past that they represent a Western solution which should not be imposed in other regions. Some activists in 'Majority World' countries have viewed them as fitting in with Western concepts of individualism and personal freedom above all else. But they have pointed out that shelters can be viewed as definitely *not* fitting in with different family structures and cultural ways of life in their countries of the Global South.[12]

Difficulties, for example, may include the near impossibility of keeping domestic violence shelters or safe houses out of the public eye in rural communities in many areas and cultures.[13] In such areas, people are likely to know each other, the family is often of enormous importance, and it may be very hard for women to survive independently of male kin. The renowned

Musasa Project in Zimbabwe has previously cautioned against removing abused women from their social and economic links with their extended families and communities. There is also a widespread argument that it is not women who should be separated from their networks and 'shut away' in shelters. Rather it is men who should leave or be made to control their violent behaviour. A further argument is that funding may not exist in many countries to provide shelters, and that scant or limited resources would be better spent in other ways, seeking collective rather than individualised solutions.[14]

Rebecca and Russell Dobash, the well-respected Western researchers, quoted throughout this book, usefully suggested in 1992 that there were four types of shelters. These were: a) professional and bureaucratic projects, b) philanthropic and religious services, c) therapeutic models, and d) activist (or feminist) projects.[15] In India, for example, shelters (called shelter homes there) tend to be set up by religious, charity or State institutions, so can be classified as types a) and b), although there are a few more activist-based shelters, type d).

Shelter organisations, where they exist in 'Majority World' countries, have tended to slide between these categories, and have often adapted themselves to culturally specific contexts. They have then tailored their services directly to their communities in creative ways (perhaps taking on extended family or HIV issues, for example). Some non-Western shelter projects in the 21st century have not identified themselves publicly as 'feminist' – a word which can be associated with Western or previous colonial enterprises. They have also sometimes been part of a network of local women's services.

Thus, this latest generation of non-Western shelter services,[16] in various African, Asian, Middle Eastern and Latin American countries, has comprehensively adapted the Western model and has attempted to create unique, indigenous projects, usually community-based, like, for example, the long-running NISAA in Lenasia, South Africa. Musasa itself set up a refuge for up to 27 women at the end of the 1990s, with support and empowerment sessions offered to the women.[17] They now also run several pioneering community shelters in rural areas, set up after community conversations and with the support and involvement of local, rural leaders. In 2014, Musasa established a one-stop centre in Harare.

A huge variety of shelters: examples that I have been privileged to interact with

- A secret shelter for rape survivors in an African country, comprehensively hidden due to the dangers it faces, in a way that Western shelters could not imagine.
- A shelter on a First Nations Reserve in Canada at a public address because it would be too shaming for the men to be seen going near it.
- Someone's house in a remote Northern community for women to hide in, while waiting for the small plane out once a week.
- Seven 'first-ever' shelters in Tunisia set up after the Arab 'Spring' revolution from 2010.
- A shelter with heavily armed male guards and security officers in a Middle Eastern country which women never go out of.

In a few further examples of many, there are now shelters for indigenous women in Bolivia and some other South American countries. In Egypt in 2006, Beit Hawa (the House of Eve) was founded as the first comprehensive women's shelter in Egypt (and much of the Arab world). In Ethiopia, there are about 12 pioneering shelters. AWSAD (the Association for Women's Sanctuary and Development), for example, runs four women-only shelters, setting up the first in 2006 in Addis Ababa. The shelters operate from a holistic and empowering perspective. Secret refuges exist in Iraq, Kurdistan and other Middle Eastern countries. In Jordan, Morocco and Lebanon as well as Tunisia, there are culturally specific crisis centres, set up in the late 2000s and 2010s.[18]

In a final expanded example, MIFUMI[19] is a Ugandan development NGO and women's rights organisation. It is the largest grass-roots agency in Uganda providing domestic violence services, and globally leads the campaign on reforming bride-price. About ten years ago, they established the first shelter in Uganda, purpose-built, as part of their diverse domestic violence services. The shelter, at a known location in a small town (where it is to be expected that people know each other and have wide-ranging, multiple family connections), featured the visible presence of workers, outdoor communal cooking, and careful security.

It has always been over-subscribed, but has tended to be used as an absolute last resort, not, as often in the West, as a first response. MIFUMI's frontline services are, rather, advice centres, providing basic services, legal and medical help, support, advocacy and assistance. These services aim to strengthen the woman and improve her position, given that she is likely to later return to her marital home. MIFUMI has since established four more shelters across Uganda, all women-only safe spaces.[20]

Overall, it seems to be the case that, even in communities where family networks are the foundation stones of society and women rarely live without male relatives, many women's projects now consider that at least a few emergency shelter places are needed.[21] This has been the case over the last 20 years, even for NGOs and activist groups previously opposed to the way in which Western consultants and visitors have seemed, in the past at least, to be wedded to the idea of shelters.

Women's empowerment may be developed, however, in a variety of other ways too. For instance, economic empowerment projects for abused women enable them to support themselves independently of male relatives. Examples include baking and sewing women's co-operatives in South Africa, and women's loan schemes in many countries such as India and Uganda. Such projects aim to enable financial self-sufficiency, but they may also retain some access to temporary safe space as well. More widely for some activist responses, the 'space' provided (so that women experiencing domestic violence can work out their options) may not even be physical space. Thus, complex routes to empowerment, possibly with a collective element, but still under the 'shelter' rubric, have been developed, rather than necessarily establishing private physical spaces. This means that sheltering is being regarded in a wider more holistic and culturally specific way in these newer projects.

The World Conference of shelters

Bringing together activist domestic violence projects and shelters has sometimes been tried in regional or country-wide networks (for example, the National Network on Violence Against Women in South Africa, WAVE in Europe, or the National Coalition Against Domestic Violence in the US). However, there have only been occasional attempts to hold larger international activist shelter get-togethers. In a pioneering development in September 2008, the First World Conference of Women's Shelters, named 'Discovering the Common Core: Practical Frameworks for Change', was held in Edmonton, Canada, the first such gathering that could be seen as global.[22]

It was attended by 800 representatives from over 60 countries, including many trying to establish domestic violence services in difficult economic and political situations (who were financially supported to attend by Canadian organisations). Although there were a large number of North American delegates, participants also attended from Armenia, Australia, Botswana, China, Ecuador, Egypt, many European countries, Georgia, Ghana, Guatemala, Honduras, Iceland, India, Israel, Kenya, Kyrgyzstan, Mexico, New Zealand, Nepal, the Palestinian Territories, the Philippines, Russia, Serbia, South Africa, Ukraine, and Vietnam.

Aiming to exchange, and provide evidence of, good practice internationally, ideas were presented from 150 projects. They established both the Global Network of Women's Shelters, and the Global Shelter Data-Count initiative. The latter collects data internationally to create a worldwide picture of the work that shelters do, and to identify existing shelter networks. A second World Conference was held in 2012 in Washington, DC, and a third in The Hague in 2015, organised by the new Global Network. The fourth was in Taiwan in 2019, attended by 1,500 participants, and offering a forward-looking programme, reflecting the key issues facing the shelter community and the broader movement to end violence against women today.[23]

To conclude

Overall, focussed attempts both to set up women's support projects and to pressure governments and agencies into providing justice, legal and other responses have been made in many countries. A few further examples include Australia, Bangladesh, China, Kenya, Malaysia, New Zealand, Pakistan, and many other Latin American, Asian and African countries. However, such responses only work where there are at least some services, resources and commitment. Even in many richer Western countries, such services remain fragile under climates of privatisation or cutback. They can appear impossibly ambitious in many societies where resources are scarce and services thin on the ground – which is most places across the world.

Nevertheless, activists everywhere have made social change wherever they can, often against massive odds, and sometimes in dangerous situations. They have set up services, campaigned and lobbied their governments. One example is Iraqi Kurdistan, where I have been honoured to work with Nazand Begikhani, long-term Kurdish gender violence activist, academic and internationally-known poet, and with others, on pioneering new developments for women. The poem that ends this chapter pays tribute to these brave Kurdish activists.

Over many years now, women activists in different world regions have campaigned around domestic violence, femicide, rape, dowry and bride-price in relation to abuse, FGM, HBV, and so on, depending on the situation in their country. They have worked without pause on relentless sexual violence in conflict zones to assist its women victims. Their collective story is one of transformation, bravery, struggling for a better world and standing strong with survivors of abuse and violence. In different ways in different places, from the 'Majority World' to Western countries, the women activists have built inspiration, hope and collective resilience.

The following poem contains distressing images. It is set in a Middle Eastern country, but of course 'honour'-based and other forms of gender violence occur widely and are in no way confined to the Middle East, or to any particular religion (for example, Islam). The poem by myself is dedicated to all survivors and victims of violence in the name of 'honour', and to the brave women activists working to combat it.

A girl and a boy

A girl and a boy
She leads the play in a sweet way.
He follows her, with adulation in his eyes,
giggling and tumbling together.

They don't know yet.

They don't know that in the future
she will probably have to obey him,
her younger male relative,
rarely enter public spaces,

uphold family honour at all costs,

never go out at night
unless with male kin,
do whatever – whatever –
her husband demands.

He will probably have free range.

Things are better in the cities.
In some places, she could still be killed
in the name of 'honour'.
Young girls burned to death by their families.

We met a wife whose nose had been cut off,

spoke with women mutilated,
imprisoned, unable to walk
after attack by beloved brothers,
forced to marry and serve their rapist.

Not anymore though.

Things are on the move.
A new type of woman won't stand for it.

Old ways are being challenged
through their courage, their vigilance,

these fine women activists.

Many have fought
as freedom fighters,
for the liberation of their homeland.
exposed war, genocides and gassings.

Now, they challenge 'honour' killings.

They have to keep going
despite death threats.
Despite public 'dishonouring' by name,
in their traumatised country, sprouting anew.

Despite religious fatwas against them,

They have pushed through a change
in the law that used to say murder
of women for 'honour' was
not murder.

Now they make more progress.

They campaign against beatings, shamings.
They set up some services.
A few shelters with guards are opened.
The government says it will make changes.

The TV calls 'honour' violence dishonourable.

The authorities are forced to act.
A new consensus begins to emerge.
The courageous women
stand firm as tigers.

Sometimes they cry at night.

But they are making something fresh.
A curve of change that can't be stopped now.
Perhaps that girl and that little boy
will be able to walk free.

Hope has arrived.

For now,
she leads the play in a sweet way.
He follows her, with adulation in his eyes,
giggling and tumbling together.

11

Expanding the movements, gaining the evidence: feminist research and transnational action

We turn now to another previously-unprecedented development, stemming out of women's activism: feminist research. This sort of research on social issues has been evolving, in both Western and 'Majority World' countries, since the late 1970s, with much new theory and practice developed. A ground-breaking paper by Marcia Westcott in 1979 elaborated such feminist contributions.[1] They were, she suggested, like strands that viewed social knowledge as: 'open, contingent and humanly compelling', as opposed to 'closed, categorical and human controlling'. 'To attend to the feminist criticism,' she suggested, 'is to open the Social Sciences to both the feminist challenge and its hope.'[2]

Powerful words indeed. The idea was gradually developed, along 'the challenge and the hope' lines, that feminist research could be used as a tool for social change.[3] New feminist challenges developed regarding, for example, avoiding essentialism in regards to viewing women as a single 'category'. The idea that social research could be entirely objective and value-free was also much questioned. It was argued (not only by feminists, but by many radical movements and critical theorists, too) that belief in total objectivity, akin to that in some sorts of scientific research, may not be possible in the social sciences.[4] On some subjects, it could seem as if the gaze of so-called 'total objectivity' could be a (heterosexual) male one (as elucidated, in one example, in the famous film studies work from 1975 of Laura Mulvey[5]). It could also be a gaze that was oblivious to, or unconscious of, other perspectives, which might have given a different view (say, that of minority women).

There was much debate as to what it actually meant to say you were doing feminist research. Perhaps the strongest feature identified was that it was research that served the cause in some way, research as an activist endeavour, as the Dobashes proposed in 1988.[6] This type of research could be seen as research 'for women', that advanced or improved women's lives, and that, where possible, both broke down power differences and was collaborative.[7] Feminist research could thus become an emancipatory enterprise (in its broadest sense), and one that could also take on other issues of oppression (including, for example, on grounds of class, poverty, heterosexism, and racism).

Feminist research methods on violence against women

Research specifically on violence against women scarcely existed 35 years ago. There was research in the 'family violence' school on child and wife abuse, but studies by feminists were only just beginning. And the importance of it was slow to be realised by the activist movement. By the 1980s, though, it gradually began to be understood that research evidence was needed to support the women's movements challenging violence against women. It was needed in order to provide evidence as to what women's experiences of violence were in different contexts, and to investigate who committed the violence and how extensive it was. Then, it was needed to assess what campaigns, policies or practices could be set up to counteract the impacts. Later, it was needed to conduct evaluations of these new policies and to come up with new theorisations – in other words new ways of understanding and thinking – about gendered violence.

From the latter part of the 1980s on, important research along these lines on violence against women has been conducted in Western countries, like the US, Canada, European nations and Australia, with many superb and well-known researchers. More recently, further research has taken place in non-Western countries like India, China and South Africa (where the first survey by activist academic Shahana Rasool of the extent of violence against women was as early as the mid-1990s[8]).

In the UK, exciting and new contributions about how to do research on gender-based violence with a feminist base were made, under the influence of the women's movements, rape crisis and Women's Aid.[9] Initially, this research was often (but not always) qualitative, raising the voices of survivors and trying to construct new knowledge together. But, over the years, it has expanded to use all available methods: quantitative and qualitative, participatory action, surveys, evaluation research, and so on.

> What defines feminist gender-based violence research is less which methods are utilised, and more the uses to which it is put. Thus, it cannot be contained in a 'feminist ghetto', a single 'methodological box'. Rather, it floods out to make use of whichever research methods are best suited to the project at hand.

The idea has been to do research that was robust. This meant that it was reliable, replicable research. It wasn't something flimsy, driven by anti-male sentiments and assumptions, as some researchers from other schools of thought had originally suggested, often in a patronising way. Feminist research on violence against women was research that could stand up in comparison with traditional research methods, was unbiased in its conduct, but could serve the cause of abused women and children by providing sound evidence and findings.

In the past, criticisms were sometimes made that this kind of research tended frequently to be small-scale and actively to avoid quantitative methods.[10] This challenging work, however, was with 'hidden populations' of abused women on 'sensitive subjects' (in the research parlance often used). In such difficult research, it was often impossible to use methods like random control trials or large, representative surveys. More recently, though, such methods have been widely adapted to gender-based violence subjects.

This has been especially the case for survey methodologies on violence against women which have developed considerably.[11] A key piece of work in 2005, for example, was the *WHO multi-country study on women's health and domestic violence against women* assessing levels of violence in many countries.[12] In this and other studies, though, feminists have wanted to ensure, almost always, that survivor voices were represented in everything they did, including quantitative work.

Gradually, over time, more and more studies were conducted which began, also, to take on issues of diversity. These might include research on the needs of abused women from BMER communities, on issues for the children of abused women, or on sexual violence against girls, same sex abuse, whether programmes for violent men could work, or how schools should react. The studies done began to be respected, asked for and – increasingly frequently – acted upon, by agencies, women's projects, services and governments. New funding streams began to open up by the 1990s.

The difficulty of getting this sort of research established, and the criticisms that traditional researchers sometimes mounted, have muted over time, as the feminist research canon on violence against women has grown and grown. Expertise has increased (say, in statistical, quantitative methods and so on), and this new canon has gained embeddedness and prestige.

Collaboration as a principle and making something new

While feminist gender-based violence research is now well established, the initial excitement of it has perhaps diminished. Funding sources have widened, but have also become harder to get, as more researchers have emerged and criteria have tightened. In the past at least, before competition for grant-funding became as acute as it is now in the UK, feminist violence against women researchers often engaged in egalitarian collaborations with researchers in other institutions. They still do, whenever they can.

The idea from the beginning was to subvert traditional or sterile academic ways of acting. These were characterised somewhat ironically, by Liz Stanley and Sue Wise in 1980, as the 'uncharitable academic three-step'.[13] In this, forward development and new knowledge are spurred by seeking to criticise the arguments of others, sometimes through stereotyping them, the better to demolish them, and then replacing them with one's own 'correct' argument.[14] The feminist gender violence researchers have tended to challenge this. They deliberately tried to replace such competition with collaboration, and to make research as equal as possible.

Equality also tended to be promoted within the research teams, where the study might be done collaboratively with a flattened hierarchy between principal investigators and research assistants. Feminist researchers frequently tried, as well, to break down power differentials, where they could, between themselves and the women taking part in any given study. The idea was to treat women research participants with respect, and to involve them in the research (after their interviews), if they wanted.

Data collection methods which were developed included more sympathetic and equal ways of interviewing respondents than had traditionally been the case.[15] They also included careful privacy and confidentiality, protection of safety, and according the woman some control over her contribution. These approaches attempted to avoid the researcher being seen as a remote authority, and the research respondent as 'the researched'. It was a matter, rather, of joining in the project together.

From the beginning, feminist researchers on violence against women tried, like the rest of the women's movements, to make something new. The idea was to build a fresh sort of knowledge, to engender social change, and to contribute to a new world for abused women. The researchers attempted, also, to fulfil the wider principles of feminist methodologies discussed above. They saw the need for transformative research, as well as transformative services.

The new researchers set up centres

The first feminist research on gender-based violence in the UK began in the late 1970s/early 1980s and was conducted by game-changing researchers like Jalna Hanmer, Rebecca and Russell Dobash and Liz Kelly, all giants in the field. They were joined in the early days by others like Fran Wasoff and Jill Radford. The contributions of these original pioneers cannot be over-emphasised. They were, in turn, joined a little later, from the mid-1980s on, by others like Audrey Mullender, Betsy

Stanko, Ellen Malos, Lorraine Radford, Marianne Hester, Susan Edwards, and myself.*

After a while, centres began to be established to bring researchers together and develop joint projects. These centres included CWASU (the Child and Woman Abuse Studies Unit) in London, the Centre for Gender and Violence Research in Bristol, SWELL (the Centre for the Study of Safety and Wellbeing) in Warwick, and various other important centres like the current Durham University Centre for Research into Violence and Abuse. Key sites of gender-based violence research have included Bradford, Leeds, Teesside, Leicester, Manchester and other universities, which have all developed and changed over the years.

As time passed, researchers from minority communities emerged who took research on issues for BMER and other minority women (as well more general studies) forward. They paid attention to matters like forced marriage and 'honour'-based violence which general researchers had previously been slow to take up. These pioneering early researchers on BMER issues included, among many, (the afore-mentioned) Aisha K. Gill, Geetanjali Gangoli and Ravi Thiara, since joined, in just a few examples of many, by researchers like Nadia Aghtaie, Nazand Begikhani, Sumanta Roy, Sundari Anitha and Khatidja Chantler.

The Child and Woman Abuse Studies Unit

The Child and Woman Abuse Studies Unit, CWASU, originally named CASU, was established within the (now-named) London Metropolitan University in 1987. It has been one of the pioneers

---

* A very incomplete list of further prominent UK violence against women researchers who have been of key importance includes Jan Pahl, Linda Regan, Sheila Burton, Jackie Barron, Cathy Humphreys, Sylvia Walby, Sue Griffiths, Lynne Harne, Tina Skinner, Claudia Garcia-Moreno, Janet Bowstead, Gene Feder, Jean Ramsey and Loraine Bacchus. And later, Nicole Westmarland, Donna Chung, Nicky Stanley, Catherine Donovan, Emma Williamson, Hilary Abrahams, Melanie McCarry, Jane Ellis, Fiona Vera-Gray, Maddy Coy, Louise Livesey and many, many others. Pioneering researchers from BMER backgrounds are named in the text.

of the field for nearly 35 years, conducting independent feminist research. The unit has particularly developed innovative methodologies, working nationally and internationally, changing the face of the work. CWASU has often directly instigated new research on violence against women, rather than responding to requests for studies coming from the movement (although of course they have done this, too).

While working on all aspects of violence against women, CWASU have especially conducted research on sexual violence. They also conducted the crucially important 'Map of Gaps' surveys of the mid-2000s (discussed in Chapter 5) and, for many years, have run a ground-breaking MA Degree on Women and Child Abuse. CWASU's Director, Liz Kelly, elucidated for this book that the Unit has provided a reflective space to research and promote good practice, and to evaluate or pioneer new developments. Like much feminist research on violence against women, CWASU sits between the women's services, the academic world and other stakeholders like government, not being fully integrated into any of them. Kelly calls it 'working in-between' and operating a critical engagement, not only with the statutory sector and government, but with the women's sector too.

The Violence Against Women Research Group (now Centre for Gender and Violence Research)

The Violence Against Women Research Group in Bristol, UK, of which the author was a co-founder, is discussed here in a bit more detail as a case study of feminist gender violence research. It was established in 1989/1990. But the idea emerged before that, from meetings of the Women's Aid Legal and Research Group, set up by Nicola Harwin in 1987. This was the only such national group, bringing together researchers and activists on violence against women from across England, to work up research agendas and to discuss the development of (specifically at the time) the domestic violence movement.

In 1989, Ellen Malos and myself set up the original Domestic Violence Research Group. This was from an idea of Ellen's to try to establish a grant-funded research unit through the University of Bristol, which could also work closely with the Women's Aid Federation (England). Then still called WAFE, their headquarters had not long moved to Bristol. We could then conduct research, alongside them, which they needed. Since that time, though, the Group has expanded its reach across the whole sector, including rape services, as well as working with governments and a wide variety of funders and stakeholders.

Back in 1990, the first study was on the housing options open to women who had left home due to domestic violence. This was funded by the Joseph Rowntree Foundation, which was particularly generous in funding policy research, including on violence against women, at the time. Even with this support, though, the Group was marginalised, and other academics often failed to take it seriously. One male professor explained to me in the early 1990s with earnest seriousness that studying violence in general was fair enough, but studying violence against women was most definitely not. Overall, it was a challenging journey for the Group to make its mark and to be accepted as important.

Members have worked specifically as feminist researchers since that time and have, like CWASU, attracted feminist-inspired graduate students from around the world who want to study violence against women. The Centre has conducted a broad variety of research projects. From 2003, it was named the Violence Against Women Research Group and, from 2009, was set up as the Centre for Gender and Violence Research (CGVR). Thirty years after its foundation, it contains a large group of dedicated researchers and PhD students, with projects (often in partnerships) in progress in many countries, ranging from China to India, Iran and Chile.

It links with the Domestic Violence and Abuse Health Group (Centre for Academic Primary Care), also at the University of Bristol, and led by Gene Feder. With the two Centres working together, the latter group has pioneered unique research and practical initiatives, specifically in the Health Service, such as IRIS, an intervention for health workers (noted in Chapter 9), currently being rolled out nationally. Both Centres offer research, training, teaching and consultancies on all aspects of gender-based violence. Whenever they can, they link their work to activism, and raise the voices of abused women.

The CGVR, like CWASU, has always aimed to stand strongly with survivors of violence, to raise their voices, and to link with women's movements. It also aimed to break down power differences where possible, to work collaboratively (with other researchers, within the research teams and with women and children participants), and to take on diversity. It has attempted to provide an example of feminist research, conducted in an activist vein and aiming towards social change for women. And it has continued, throughout, to provide robust research evidence in the service of women's empowerment and of ending abuse. I am thrilled to have been one of the founders.

The Centre has produced some 'first of its kind' research, leading to policy change, new practice, evaluations, and the introduction of innovative methods, including participatory action and transnational projects. Marianne Hester, present Centre Head, explains that "Over the years, we have joined with other feminist researchers in the UK and elsewhere, and worked closely with organisations tackling violence against women, to provide the evidence needed to shift policy and practice and to underpin activism."

Studies by the Centre have addressed the needs of disabled women, lesbians, LGBT+ communities, girls, South Asian women and women from other BME communities experiencing abuse. Research subjects have included multi-agency work, children, mothering and domestic violence, survivor participation in policy-making, forced marriage, 'honour'-based violence, criminal justice responses to rape and to domestic violence, and so on.[16] The Centre hosts the key journal in the field, the *Journal of Gender-Based Violence*, and members have produced many books.[17]

The British Sociological Association Violence against Women Study Group

The British Sociological Association (BSA) Study Group on Violence against Women has been of key importance to researchers on gender-based violence across the UK, over the years since 1985. It was (and remains) a lifeline for many feminist researchers, PhD students and activists. The Group has always valued equality as a matter of principle, so that PhD students and full professors would all be there on equal terms. In the day-long meetings, especially in the 1990s and early 2000s, there would be an exchange of support and ideas about the research that each participant was engaged in, and usually there would be a stimulating main input from someone.

In the early days, the Study Group would meet in the building well-known to feminists, in Featherstone Street, London, which has been packed with women's projects since the 1970s (currently hosting Imkaan, for example). It has produced a series of helpful books, over 20 years, edited by key gender violence researchers, like Jalna Hanmer, Betsy Stanko, Marianne Hester and Jill Radford (and fully listed in the endnote).[18]

The BSA Study Group has had an important role in supporting the development of activist research and feminist action, and in assisting isolated PhD students. Guided by its current coordinator, Louise Livesey, it continues to share concepts, innovative or new feminist research methods, study findings and discussion (frequently these days online), to the great enrichment of women who are part of it. Its members have supported each other, and the violence against women research world, staunchly over all these years – 35 now, and counting.

The original gender violence research centres broke new ground

The original gender and violence research centres and the BSA Study Group tried to break new ground, in terms of academic research on women and abuse that aimed to be activist-based and to feed into the social movement of women. It would be almost impossible to establish the centres now. We were set up 'in the margins'. But such margins, in the marketised and intensely competitive, and often over-worked, academic world of today, scarcely exist anymore. Still though, an exhilarating range of studies and PhD projects in various countries takes place, and sometimes these have enabled the establishment of services or research in those countries for the very first time.

In the 1990s and on, Black and minority ethnic researchers enabled diversification of the work. And the world of gender-based violence research has expanded, changed and become more mainstreamed. But, between us, violence against women feminist researchers and centres have made more positive impacts than can be enumerated for abused women and children in many contexts and places around the world.

Transnational action, research and partnerships

Combatting violence against women is a worldwide effort, and multi-national networks have frequently been established in the last 25 years. Women activists and researchers in various countries have often attempted joint work together across borders and regions, with partnerships between Western and low income countries being set up and tending to focus on social action. Such initiatives are frequently exciting developments for abused women, but they can be hard to manage, especially if the partners involved are deliberately trying to avoid dominance from the West. This type of activist-oriented work is usually known by the term 'transnational', preferred by women activists from the Global South, over, say, 'global feminism'. The latter is commonly used by global initiatives, for example, through the UN (as noted in Chapter 9) which may be uncritically (or inadvertently) led and dominated by players from the powerful Western, mainly white, nations and the previous colonial powers.[19]

Of course, Western funders are where the funding tends to come from. And entrenched domination from the West has been hard to shift in the history of the violence against women movement (as it has been in general). (Of the 30,000 women from 189 countries at the 1995 Beijing World Conference of Women, for instance, nearly a third came from one country – the United States.[20]) Both gender violence consultants from the West and NGOs (sometimes with Western connections) are to be found everywhere in Global South countries, which can work out very well.

But it can also mean the imposition of Western feminist ideas and an overlooking of grass-roots activism and cultural complexities. Also, the gender consultants come and go. The local organisations concerned are often sucked into advising governments (that they may disapprove of), and may find themselves having to overlook both community involvement and direct social change – a phenomenon sometimes called 'NGO-isation'. However, there is now the idea of 'transnationalism from below' as regards who controls it and whose voices get heard most – or at all.[21]

Transnational feminist work and ideas are often no longer uni-directional (i.e. from richer nations to poorer), and there can then be the possibility of creatively combining in the struggle against violence and abuse. Attempts at such transnational activism have been made since at least the period between the World Wars.[22] More recently, the concept of transversalism has been developed, originally by Italian feminists in the 1990s. Nira Yuval-Davis has insightfully described this as feminist coalitions building bridges between women of different cultures and backgrounds, rather than being immobilised by difference.[23]

Transversalism talks of 'rooting' and 'shifting', in order for participants to make alliances and engage in social action together. There are also efforts across previously colonised countries to 'decolonise' agendas (popularised in 2020 through the Black Lives Matter movements). For example, the Social Work Department, in the University of Johannesburg, has been engaged in decolonisation for some years, reforming the whole curriculum from top to bottom to remove unwanted ideas from the colonial past and to Africanise programmes, including in terms of social work and gender-based violence.[24]

Transnational feminist research/projects on gender violence consist of multi-country partnerships, sometimes as part of wider research programmes, to challenge aspects of violence against women. In these partnerships, Western-based partners may bring resources, prestige, kudos and wider 'weight' to collaborations, while local partners bring expertise, knowledge, embeddedness and cultural appropriateness (as has been my experience working in violence against women partnerships in India, African countries and in the Middle East). But it can get difficult to work against dominance from the richer Western partners, which is sometimes upfront – but often more hidden and subtle. Even where all involved have brought with them commitment, empathy and respect, and everyone is trying, it remains a complicated, multi-layered enterprise. Ways of thinking from the powerful West tend to creep in, come what may.

I have worked in such partnerships in various countries, and I know that ideas about Western strategies being the best in combatting violence against women need to be resisted at all times. Otherwise, they accidentally find their way in, almost unconsciously. Of course, if ideas for practice, research or policy-making on gender-based violence from the richer countries are specifically requested by 'Majority World' partners, then they must be carefully shared. But sometimes there is a sense of entitlement, or even superiority, that the Western partners bring. At best, such assistance can be provided, instead, in a way which does not indicate that Western feminists have all the answers, and which enables information to be respectfully offered, shared both ways, and culturally adapted to the situation at hand.

Structures can also be put in place to govern the transnational project: for example, leadership and control coming from the non-Western partners, or being gradually passed to them as expertise and, essentially, support and training are built in. Gene Feder, at the time of writing, is involved in a project developing interventions on violence against women in Palestine, Nepal, Sri Lanka and Brazil. He explained:

> Funding from the UK Global Challenges Research Fund (and other resources from the Global North) has allowed us, as UK 'domestic violence and abuse' researchers, to support and collaborate with partners in low and middle income countries. Starting with what could be called a neo-colonial economic power imbalance and our own Anglo-Saxon academic hegemony, we work towards challenging this, and towards genuine co-production and co-leadership of research programmes that respond to the needs of survivors of violence against women.[25]

This initiative is currently delivering specifically-tailored practical health responses in each country.

On a general level, such partnerships can have a transforming role. On the other hand, the activists concerned may have differing cultural methods of working, and varying organisational relationships to time and work requirements across far-flung locations. Steadfast accountability, protections and safeguards for all sides may be necessary, including for those controlling the budget. But with effort and care, all involved can make at least an attempt at righting past injustices, pain and imperial exploitation, and at building a safer future for abused women and children. I have been privileged to engage in this transnational work as someone from a previous colonising nation, and seen it work.

As an example, from 2008–10, a collaboration of Kurdish women's groups and activist researchers, Nazand Begikhani, Aisha K. Gill (both mentioned earlier) and myself, conducted the first study of 'honour' killings and violence, in Iraqi Kurdistan (funded by the Kurdistan Regional Government). The project produced the first-ever detailed, multi-stranded, Action Plan in the Middle East on combatting 'honour'-based violence.[26] Later, following up one of the strands of this Plan, Nazand coordinated setting up the first Gender and Violence Studies Centre in the Region at the University of Sulaimaniya, Iraqi Kurdistan, from 2011. She suggested for this book that:

> Equality and injustices in the world cannot be separated from the historic processes of imperialism, colonialism, industrial capitalism and globalisation. Hence, transnational feminist theories and methodologies are necessary to analyse social and political realities for women. Feminist discourses can then have strong impacts on policy and practice, not only to challenge structural power relations, but also to transform our realities.[27]

In a project in Uganda run by MIFUMI from 2008 to 2009, the UK participants included Ravi Thiara, long-term gender violence researcher, and myself. The local partners in the research teams were both MIFUMI workers and also, crucially, local village people who engaged fully in the participatory action methods used. This involved collectively designing and conducting the research, planning the methods and analysing the data – all together. It led on to drawing out themes – all together – and then working out ways forward and 'strategies for action' – also all together. The idea of these strategies was to lead to change, based on what we had found. For me, it was the greatest privilege to work in this way alongside people from rural villages, to learn from them, to collectively evolve what was to happen and to convert decisions to action.

At the same time, it was vital to remain aware of the gulfs in power between us, as we flew in on expensive planes with all our privileged resources, and the researchers walked from their villages. But together we made something special. Ravi and myself listened and learned, as well as contributing our own expertise when relevant, passing control to the local participants where possible, and trying to combat any tendency to think we knew better. We almost always didn't.

The enrichment for me included learning from Ravi, as well as from our other collaborators. For me, the project was more nourishing than I can say. But I'd suggest, and others have confirmed, that the enrichment for almost everyone at a deep human level was considerable and powerful. The project which was on bride-price in Uganda, and its possible connections to domestic violence and to impoverishment for women, was the first of its kind, and led to direct practical initiatives.[28]

I would strongly suggest that, if the issue of more powerful Western voices dominating partnerships on violence against women is to be avoided, what is required is humility. And not just humility, but humility of the most profound type. It means the deepest humanity, too, from all involved. It needs to be felt and lived and breathed – with enduring compassion and vigilant self-scrutiny. In my experience, it cannot be done at a superficial level. It cannot be faked or pretended, and it means the Western partners putting aside self-confident views and assertion. Rather, it means learning as humans together, taking on the cultural and power differences, and meeting the other activists and violence survivors eye-to-eye as equally as possible (but not hiding the differences in power, history and resources). While not sweeping difficulties under the carpet, we are talking about engaging in deep respect and deep human recognition, as we together battle violence against women.

In the bride-price project, the participation of, and guidance from, the pioneering and inspiring MIFUMI organisation were what made it possible. Atuki Turner, the Executive Director of MIFUMI contributed for this book that:

> My deepest learning and insight into bride-price has come from the survivor living with the violence and oppression in the community. It is where I get my inspiration and commitment. Most Western donors and partners do not have this insight, and hence their appreciation of the problem remains shallow. Partnerships and donors will work best with Southern partners only where both partners are valued equally. It was a pleasure working on the bride-price project because it was a collaborative effort where MIFUMI's experience and knowledge was valued, yet we gained so much from the expertise of the international partners.[29]

To conclude, this is a poem of tribute to the sensational village women activists with whom we worked, used with their permission. Jane Rose and Immaculate have agreed to their names being used.

To the women, and to Jane Rose and Immaculate

These women from remote villages,
each one spread out over miles,
they live a subsistence life
exactly where they always have.
They fight domestic violence with deep courage
beyond what most of us can start to imagine.
Living and breathing what they believe.

And what they believe is
that they **must** stay strong
and help any woman in trouble.
Give them some of that strength.

They take violated women into their homes,
to sleep in their one room on the mud floor.
Go with them to the hospital.

Shield them at the door if the men come.
Sit some of these men down.
And give them a stern talking-to.

Yes, often you are in danger,
in case hostile individuals beat or stab you.
You offer solace to those who come,
beaten, distressed, raped,
some with HIV, with raped babies,
possibly on the edge of starvation.
They need you to stand firm with them.

And you always do.
To give some power to the women.
To take some power from the men.
The men tend to do what they can to stop you.
This is gender equality work at its most testing.
'Power and control' that we endlessly speak about
in the domestic violence movements of the world.

But don't always practise.
You are doing it without being able to read
any of the famous books.

Dear Jane Rose and Immaculate.
Thank you for agreeing to let me speak of you.
You are dedicated beyond belief.
Hundreds of women and children have benefited
from your committed, thorough, powerful work.
Taking women in, strengthening them,
Sharing everything you have with them.

Sometimes you dare not buy food
From your local male traders for fear of poisoning.
Activists on domestic violence elsewhere
could learn much from your courage and commitment.
What a gift and an inspiration indeed.
Please know that you are heroes and beacons
to all around you.

Thank you deeply from all of us
who struggle to end domestic violence,
not only in Africa, but across the world.

12

End word

This book has offered a journey through the history, since the 1960s, of the movements combatting violence against women, especially domestic violence, mainly in the countries of the UK, but in other countries too, with some emphasis on transnational activism. The coverage has been brief, and, inevitably, issues have had to be left out or abbreviated. It has been impossible to fit everything in.

The book has highlighted the bravery and tenacity of those who made these women's struggles. And it has celebrated the passion and dedication that gave rise to services on domestic and sexual violence, and to the later developments. It has aimed to valorise these achievements and the individual activists who made them, sometimes by name (although many others, equally deserving of recognition, have regretfully had to be left out). The idea has been to tell the story of how it all started and developed – in order to remember it for the future. A few poems and anecdotes have, hopefully, enriched the mood, while not detracting from this distressingly painful subject.

In the last 50 years, a loose network of activists across almost every country in the world has arisen, and they have not shrunk from reacting to domestic violence, sexual violence, 'honour'-based violence, femicide, psychological violence, coercive control, rape in war and conflict zones, sexual slavery, terror against women, and so much more. The book has aimed to showcase the transformations that have been achieved, from which we can learn as we go forward. There is a danger of overlooking them – of not remembering.

Some of the issues to recall – and, perhaps, indeed to learn from – include the power and exhilaration of collective working and ideas for how to make it effective. They include the possibility of reclaiming, and using, the political organising techniques of consciousness-raising. Raising the voices of abuse survivors and informing everything with their views have been enduring principles to which we need always to return. And we can learn, too, from the thrill of being part of a dynamic social movement which must be one of the greatest human experiences.

The book especially tells the story of the innovative, early days of the domestic violence (and rape crisis) movements in this country. This is becoming forgotten women's history – the passion and radical innovation of those days. They are discussed here in some detail to recall them, while many of those who made them are still here - and for the future too. They were transformative times. Let us remember and preserve them.

Within this history and from that time on, dealing with intersectional, BMER, transnational and equality issues, challenging hurt and oppression, campaigning for resources and funding, refusing to allow gender-based violence to be belittled and ignored: these have been, and remain, key as we move forward into the different political climates of the future.

Times have changed for us all as we face the challenges of the 21st century. As abuse survivors, feminist activists, service providers, campaigners, policy-makers, lawyers, researchers and activist academics, we have a responsibility to go on building the challenge to male violence now that the subject is in the public domain in a way which we would not have believed possible in days gone by. Let those of us who are activists in our different countries wish each other continued success – and possibly luck – as we go on putting our energies into changing the world for abused women. Let us also celebrate our past over five decades of dedicated work. And let us especially celebrate those early violence against women projects and activists all over the world, as they started out with such bravery and resilience, from the 1960s on. They often tried to do things never done before. The intention of this book has been for their (and our) power, heady optimism and courage to shine through.

Working against violence against women is like weaving a tapestry of resistance and social change. This idea was originally put forward by Liz Kelly, and is used here (slightly adapted) with her very generous and readily-given permission. Each thread represents the work of a person, an activist, a campaign, or a project, making a difference, interlacing together with others. Together we all build it, with the threads of each person's contribution perhaps glowing out.

Sometimes, you have to undo, go backwards, untangle, start again. But, if opponents try to pull the whole thing apart, it will begin after a while to resist and knot up. It can't be pulled all the way back – not any more. We have come too far, despite the setbacks. The only way for the tapestry of challenging domestic abuse and violence against women to develop is to undo the knots and re-weave – and then re-weave again. So that it gets bigger and bigger – and bigger.

As this writing drew to a close, one of the founding figures of the movement, Jalna Hanmer, contributed these words specifically for the book. It is an honour to use them:

> We thought we were the first women to discover violence against women. Then, when we learnt something about women's history, the questions became:
> How did we forget?
> Will we forget again?

Survivors, practitioners, researchers and activists in the field are indeed sometimes forgetting, or don't know. This book has tried to reverse this process, to record this innovative history. It has celebrated all that the women's movements have tried to do, the way those involved devoted their lives to social change. Although violence against women remains a huge human tragedy, those of us committed to challenging it have tried to build something new in history. We have tried to change the world for abused and violated women in previously untried – and quite extraordinary and exhilarating – ways.

Perhaps, we can all add our own threads to the tapestry of transformation.

Notes

Chapter 1

[1] United Nations (2020); World Health Organization (2005).
[2] United Nations (2019).
[3] Hague, G. and Malos, E. (2005).
[4] UN Women (2016).
[5] Dobash, R. E. and Dobash, R. (1992); Morris, B. and Withers, D-M (2018).
[6] For example, Hester, M. (2009); Rollè, L., Giardini, G., Caldaria, A., Gerino, E. and Brustia, P. (2018).
[7] See, for example, Roychowdhury, A. (2020).
[8] For example, Burns, S. (1990).
[9] See, for example, among many: Darwin, J. (2003).
[10] Galeano, E. (1997).
[11] For information on Augusto Boal, see Boal, A. (1993).

Chapter 2

[1] Dobash, R. E. and Dobash, R. (1992), p 15.
[2] Morgan, R. (1970); Wandor, M. (1972); Feminist Anthology Collective (1981); Coote, A. and Campbell, B. (1982).
[3] Bloom. J. and Martin, W. (2013).
[4] Some examples about the movement in the United States: Evans, S. (1980); Castro, G. (1990); Davis, F. (1999); Echols, A. (1989). For movements in Canada, see Rise Up (2019).
[5] Richardson, J. (2019).
[6] Friedan, B. (1963).
[7] De Beauvoir, S. (1997), first published in two volumes in France in 1949 as *Le Deuxième Sexe*.
[8] Mackay, F. (2015), p 3.
[9] Dobash, R. E. and Dobash, R. (1992), p 17.
[10] Hanmer, J. (2010).
[11] Firestone, S. (1970).
[12] See Feminist Anthology Collective (1981); and early writings of the women's liberation movement, for example Rowbotham, S. (1969); Comer, L. (1972); Wandor, M. (1972).

[13] See Harkness. S. (1996).
[14] Zita, J. (1988).
[15] David, M. (2016).
[16] Freeman, J. (2019).
[17] Rowbotham, S. (1972); Rowbotham, S. (1973).
[18] TUC (n.d.).
[19] Hobbs, M. (1973).
[20] For example, Lazenby, P. (2011); and Tomlinson, T. (2011).
[21] Laws, S., Collins, W., Garthwaite, A. and Spellacy, M. (1984), pp 48–55.
[22] Comer, L. (1974).
[23] *Our bodies ourselves* was published by the Boston Women's Health Book collective in many editions from 1970 on.
[24] Moraga, C. and Anzaldúa, G. (1981).
[25] Lorde, A. (1984).
[26] See for example, Jeffreys, S. (2018); Chester, G. (1981).
[27] See Morris, B. and Withers, D-M (2018).
[28] Alderson, L. and Shulman, S. (1983), pp 51–56.
[29] Bryan, B., Dadzie, S. and Scafe, S. (1985).
[30] See Assiter, A. (1983).

Chapter 3

[1] See Mackay, F. (2015); Jaggar, A. (1983); Barrett, M. and Mcintosh, M. (1980); Tong, R. (1989; 1st edition, and many subsequent editions). Also Firestone, S. (1970); Jeffreys, S. (2014); Jeffreys, S. (2018).
[2] Firestone, S. (1970); Millett, K. (1970); Daly, M. (1978); Solanas, V. (1967); Rich, A. (1976); Morgan, R. (1970); Greer, G. (1972).
[3] See Jeffreys, S. (1977). Sheila Jeffreys also contributed to the key publication Leeds Revolutionary Feminist Group (1981).
[4] For further discussion of these issues, see Hester. M. (1992).
[5] Leeds Revolutionary Feminist Group (1981); see also Jeffreys, S. (2018); Frye, M. (1993), originally published 1978.
[6] O'Sullivan, S. (1982), pp 70–86; O'Sullivan, S. (1996); Chester, G. (1981).
[7] Jeffreys, S. (2018).
[8] Barrett, M. and McIntosh, M. (1980).
[9] Mitchell, J. (1971), originally published 1966.
[10] Historyireland (2012).
[11] Kelly, L. (2013), pp 135–137.
[12] See for example, among many, Nava, M. (1972), pp 36–44.
[13] Malos, E. (1980).
[14] See, for example, Wages for Housework (2020).
[15] Dworkin, A. (1976); Dworkin, A. (1981).
[16] Rich, A. (1980).
[17] Davis, A. (1983).
[18] hooks, b. (1981); hooks, b (1984).
[19] Crenshawe, K. (1989).

[20] Hill Collins, P. (1990); Hill Collins, P. and Bilge, S. (2016).

[21] For just one example, see Mirza, H. S. (1997).

[22] Walby, S. (2011).

[23] David, M. (2016).

[24] For just a few further examples, some already noted: Chodorow, N. (1978); Butler, J. (1990); Barrett, M. and Phillips, A. (1992); Harding, S. (1993); Harding, S. (1987); Hill Collins, P. (1990); Assiter, A. (2005).

[25] For example, Richardson, D. and Robinson, V. (1993).

[26] Gangoli. G. (2007); Chaudhuri, M. (2004).

[27] Nnaemeka, O. (1998), p 5.

[28] Rowbotham, S., Segal, L. and Wainwright, H. (2013).

[29] Brownmiller, S. (2000); Segal, L. (2007); Roberts, M. (2007); Nava. M. (2007); David, M. (2016); Rowbotham, S. (2019).

[30] See many writings from the women's liberation movement: for example, Mackay, F. (2015); Dobash, R. E. and Dobash, R. (1992); Kemp, S. and Squires, J. (1998); Morris, B. and Withers, D-M (2018); Rowbotham, S. (1991); Segal, L. (2007); O'Sullivan, S. (1982), pp 70–86; Campbell, B. (1980); Alderson, L. and Shulman, S. (1983), pp 51–56; Radford, J. (1994); Wandor, M. (1990); Sebestyen, A. (1988).

[31] Jolly, M. (2019).

Chapter 4

[1] Dobash, R. E. and Dobash, R. (1992), p 16.

[2] See for example, Land, H. (1980); McIntosh, M. (1981).

[3] Dobash, R. E. and Dobash, R. (1980); Hague, G. and Malos, E. (2005).

[4] Hague. G. and Wilson, C. (1996).

[5] Hague and Wilson (1996), p 33, p 37, p 39.

[6] Hague and Wilson (1996), pp 39–40.

[7] Morris, B. and Withers, D-M (2018); Hague, G. and Malos, E. (2005).

[8] Dobash, R. E. and Dobash, R. (1992), p 28.

[9] Dobash, R. E. and Dobash, R. (1992), pp 88–89.

[10] Pizzey, E. and Shapiro, J. (1982).

[11] Lewis, H. (2020).

[12] Malos, E. (2000).

[13] Dobash, R. E. and Dobash, R. (1980); Dobash, R. E. and Dobash, R. (1992).

[14] Brownmiller, S. (1975); Kelly, L. (1988); Hague, G. and Malos, E. (1993, 1998, 2005), Mama (1996); Thiara, R. K. and Gill, A. K. (2000); Jolly, M (2019).

[15] Yllö, K. and Bograd, M. L. (1988); Renzetti, C., Edleson, J. and Bergen, R. K. (2001); West, C. 2003.

Chapter 5

[1] Brownmiller, S. (1975).

[2] Radford, J. and Russell, D. (1982); Radford, J. and Russell, D. (1992).

[3] Jones, H. and Cook, K. (2008).

[4] Kelly, L. (1988).

[5] London Rape Crisis Centre (1987).

[6] Maitland, E. (2009).

[7] Vera-Gray, F. (2020).

[8] Bindel, J. (2006).

[9] Mackay, F. (2015), p 72.

[10] Mackay, F. (2015).

[11] Thiara, R. K., Roy, S. and Ng, P. (2015).

[12] Thiara, R. K. and Roy, S. (2020).

[13] Walker, S-J L., Hester, M., McPhee, D., Patsios, D., Williams, A., Bates, L. and Rumney, P. (2019).

[14] Coy, M., Kelly, L. and Foord, J. (2007 and 2009).

[15] Westmarland, N. (2008).

[16] Westmarland, N. and Alderson, S. (2013).

Chapter 6

[1] See also Pahl, J. (1985).

[2] The first of three editions dedicated to the late Pam Cooke (Khalil) was Hague, G. and Malos, E. (1993).

Chapter 7

[1] See for example, Harris, J. (2016).

[2] See Mama, A. (1996) on black abused women's experiences of both statutory and voluntary agencies at the time.

Chapter 8

[1] Donovan, C. and Hester, M. (2014).

[2] Rollè, L., Giardina, G., Caldarera, A., Gerino, E. and Brustia, P. (2018).

[3] Donovan, C. and Barnes, R. (2020).

[4] Machado, C. M. (2020).

[5] Thiara, R. K., Hague, G., Bashall, R., Ellis, B. and Mullender, A. (2012).

[6] Hague, G., Thiara, R. K., Magowan, P. and Mullender, A. (2008).

[7] Crime Prosecution Service (2020).

[8] Scottish Women's Aid (2020) *What is domestic abuse?* https://womensaid. scot/information-support/what-is-domestic-abuse/

[9] This framework provided funding for projects for vulnerable people, including survivors of domestic violence (but also imposed restructuring and complex evidencing requirements).

[10] Welsh Women's Aid (2019).

[11] Glasgow Women's Library and Scottish Women's Aid (2018).

[12] Women's Aid (2020).

[13] Women's Aid (2019a).

[14] Women's Aid (2020a).

[15] Women's Aid (2020b); see also Hague, G., Mullender, A. and Aris, R. (2003).

[16] Women's Aid (2020c).

[17] Women's Aid (n.d.).

[18] Stark, E. (2019).

[19] Welchman, L. and Hossain, S. (2005); Gill, A. K., Strange, C. and Roberts, K. (2014).

[20] Gill, A. K., Begikhani, N. and Hague, G. (2012).

[21] Gill, A. K., Strange, C. and Roberts, K. (2014).

[22] Begikhani, N. Gill, A. K. and Hague, G. (2010).

[23] Julios, C. (2018).

[24] Gill, A. K. and Anitha, S. (2009).

[25] Gill, A. K. and Gould, D. (2019).

[26] Asian Women's Resource Centre (2020).

[27] Gill, A. K., Begikhani, N. and Hague, G. (2012); Gill, A. K. and Walker, S. (2020).

Chapter 9

[1] Busby, E. (2019).

[2] EVAW (2018).

[3] Hester, M. and Walker, S.-J. L. (2017).

[4] Barr, C., Topping, A. and Bowcott, O. (2019).

[5] Topping, A. and Barr, C. (2020).

[6] Barr, C. (2021).

[7] Hester, M. and Walker, S.-J. L. (2017); see also Daly, K. and Bouhours, B. (2010).

[8] EVAW (2020).

[9] *New York Times* (2020).

[10] BBC (2019).

[11] Cuffe, S. (2020).

[12] Seymat, T. and Gaubert, J. (2020).

[13] In February 2020, Ingrid Escamilla Vargas, aged 25, was stabbed to death, and eviscerated with organs removed and some flushed down the drain, allegedly by her husband after an argument about his drinking. She was then completely skinned.

[14] Naples, N. and Desai, M. (2002).

[15] Edwards, S. (2013).

[16] Barron, J. (1990).

[17] Harwin, N., Hague, G. and Malos, E. (1999).

[18] Shepard, M. and Pence, E. (1999).

[19] Duluth Domestic Abuse Intervention Programs (2019).

[20] Hague, G., Malos, E. and Dear, W. (1996).

[21] https://rapecrisis.org.uk/

[22] Richards, L., Letchford, S. and Stratton, S. (2008).

[23] James-Hanman, D. (2017), p 331.

[24] Women's Aid (2020d).

[25] Women's Aid (2019b).

Chapter 10

[1] Dobash, R. E. and Dobash, R. (1992); Hague, G. and Malos, E. (2005); Schechter, S. (1982).

[2] See Edwards, S. (1989); Dunhill, C. (1989).

[3] Hague, G. (2013), pp 1224–1245.

[4] Special Cells (2004).

[5] Kelly, L. with Bindel, J., Burton, S., Butterworth, D., Cook, K. and Regan, L. (1999).

[6] Jaffe, P. and Thompson, J. (1978).

[7] Hague, G., Kelly, L. and Mullender, A. (2002).

[8] Dubinski, K. and Duhatschek, P. (2019).

[9] Anova (n.d.).

[10] Hague, G. (2013).

[11] MacDowell Santos, C. (2005).

[12] Jung Park, Y. with Peters, R. and De Sa, C. (2000), pp 243–289.

[13] Taylor, J. (n.d.).

[14] Jung Park, J., Peters, R. and De Sa, C. (2000), pp 243–289; Dangor, Z. and Alderton, C. with Taylor, J. (2000).

[15] Dobash, R. E. and Dobash, R. (1992).

[16] Dangor, Z. and Alderton, C. with Taylor, J. (2000), pp 295–320; Mitsch Bush, D. (1992).

[17] Immigration and Refugee Board of Canada and Musasa (2001); Womankind (2016).

[18] Womankind (2016).

[19] MIFUMI as an organisation spells its name in upper case.

[20] MIFUMI (2020).

[21] International Center for Research on Women (2002).

[22] Harwin, N. (2009).

[23] TWCWS (2019).

Chapter 11

[1] Westcott, M. (1979).

[2] Westcott. M. (1979), p. 430.

[3] See for example, Kelly, L., Burton, S. and Regan, L. (1994), pp 27–48.

[4] See for example, Roberts, H. (1981); Stanley L. and Wise, S. (1983), pp 12–20; Ylló, K. and Bograd, M. L. (1988,), pp 36–39.

[5] In terms of film, see Mulvey, L. (1975).

[6] Dobash, R. E. and Dobash, R. (1988), pp 51–74.

[7] Harding, S. (1987), pp 1–14; Smith, D. (1988).

[8] Rasool, S., Vermaak, K., Pharoah, R., Louw, A and Stavrou, A. (2003).

[9] See for example, Millman, M. and Moss Kanter, R. (1975); Bograd, M. L. (1988).

[10] See the temporarily fierce debate in the journal, *Sociology*, in 1992/1993 between Martyn Hammersley and a range of feminist scholars including Caroline Ramazanoglu and Loraine Gelsthorpe. The 1992 paper by

Ramazanoglu (*Sociology*, 26(2): 207–212) was tellingly called 'On Feminist Methodology: Male Reason versus Female Empowerment'.

[11] For example, see Feder, G., Ramsay, J., Dunne, D., Rose, M., Arsene, C., Norman, R., Kuntze, S., Spencer, A., Bacchus, L., Hague, G., Warburton, A. and Taket, A. (2009); Walby, S. and Myhill, A. (2001).

[12] World Health Organization (2005).

[13] Stanley L. and Wise, S. (1983)

[14] Stanley, L. and Wise, S. (1990), pp 20–60.

[15] Oakley, A. (1981), pp 30–61.

[16] As a few examples, Radford, L. and Hester, M. (1996); Hague, G. with Harvey, A. and Willis, K. (2012); and Aghtaie, N. and Gangoli, G. (2014).

[17] These include books by Marianne Hester, Emma Williamson, Geetanjali Gangoli, Nadia Aghtaie, Lynne Harne, Nazand Begikhani, Melanie McCarry, Hilary Abrahams, Nicole Westmarland, Ellen Malos, and myself. See https://prezi.com/pqfmalrxyyzr/key-books-from-the-cgvr-and-partners/.

[18] Hanmer, J. and Maynard, M. (1987); Hanmer, J., Radford, J. and Stanko, E. (1989) (republished in 2013); Hester, M., Kelly, L. and Radford, J. (1996); Radford, J., Friedberg, M. and Harne, L. (2000). The 20th anniversary publication was Skinner, T., Hester, M. and Malos, E. (2005).

[19] Naples, N. (2002), pp 1–14.

[20] For general discussion of these issues, see Naples, N. and Desai, M. (2002).

[21] Desai, M. (2002), pp 15–33

[22] Sandwell, M. (2015).

[23] Yuval-Davis, N. (1999).

[24] See Van Breda, A. and Sekudu, J. (2019).

[25] In conversation with the author.

[26] Begikhani, N., Gill, A. K. and Hague, G. with Ibraheem, K. (2010).

[27] In conversation with the author.

[28] MIFUMI with Hague, G. and Thiara, R. K. (2005).

[29] In conversation with the author.

Bibliography

Aghtaie, N. and Gangoli, G. (2014) *Understanding gender-based violence: National and international contexts*, London: Routledge.

Alderson, L. and Shulman, S. (1983) 'Writing our own history: When lesbians came out in the movement', *Trouble and Strife*, 1(1): 51–56.

Anova (n.d.) *Anova future*, www.anovafuture.org/about-us/

Asian Women's Resource Centre (2020) *Harmful Practices Partnership to support women and girls in London*, Brent, London: Asian Women's Resource Centre.

Assiter, A. (1983) 'Woman power and nuclear politics: Women and the peace movement', in D. Thompson (ed), *Over our dead bodies: Women against the bomb*, London: Virago, pp 199–207.

Assiter, A. (2005) *Enlightened women: Modernist feminism in a postmodern age*, London: Routledge.

Barr, C. (2021) 'Legal challenge over CPS policy on prosecuting rape cases dismissed', *The Guardian*, 15 March, www.theguardian.com/law/2021/mar/15/legal-challenge-over-cps-policy-on-prosecuting-cases-dismissed

Barr, C., Topping, A. and Bowcott, O. (2019) 'Rape prosecutions in England and Wales at lowest level in a decade', *The Guardian*, 12 September, www.theguardian.com/law/2019/sep/12/prosecutions-in-england-and-wales-at-lowest-level-in-a-decade

Barrett, M. and McIntosh, M. (1980) *Women's oppression today: Problems with Marxist feminist analysis*, London: Verso.

Barrett, M. and Phillips, A. (1992) *Destabilizing theory: Contemporary feminist debates*, Stanford: Stanford University Press.

Barron, J. (1990) *Not worth the paper ... ? The effectiveness of legal protection for women and children experiencing domestic violence*, Bristol: Women's Aid Federation of England.

BBC (2019) 'Global protests denounce violence against women', BBC News, 25 November, www.bbc.co.uk/news/world-50557784

Begikhani, N., Gill, A. K. and Hague, G. (2010) *Honour-based violence: Experiences and counter-strategies in Iraqi Kurdistan and the UK Kurdish diaspora*, Farnham: Ashgate.

Begikhani, N., Gill, A. K. and Hague, G. with Ibraheem, K. (2010) *Action plan on honour-based violence and summary*, Erbil, Iraqi Kurdistan: Kurdistan Regional Government, https://research-information.bris.ac.uk/ws/portalfiles/portal/188781664/Action_Plan.pdf

Bindel, J. (2006) 'Marching to freedom', *The Guardian*, 22 November, www.theguardian.com/society/2006/nov/22/publicvoices.crime

Bloom. J. and Martin, W. (2013) *Black against empire: The history and politics of the Black Panther Party*, Berkeley: University of California Press.

Boal, A. (1993) *Theatre of the oppressed*, New York: Theatre Communications Group.

Bograd, M. L. (1988) 'Feminist perspectives on wife abuse: An introduction', in K. Yllö and M. L. Bograd (eds), *Feminist perspectives on wife abuse*, London: Sage Publications, pp 11–26.

Boston Women's Health Book Collective (1970) *Our bodies, ourselves*, Boston: Boston Women's Health Book Collective.

Brownmiller, S. (1975) *Against our will: Men, women and rape*, New York: Simon and Schuster.

Brownmiller, S. (2000) *In our time: A memoir of a feminist revolution*, New York: Delta.

Bryan, B., Dadzie, S. and Scafe, S. (1985) *Heart of the race*, London: Virago.

Busby, E. (2019) 'Rape charity hotline bombarded with "racist abuse" from Tommy Robinson supporters', *The Independent*, 16 February, www.independent.co.uk/news/uk/home-news/rape-crisis-tommy-robinson-facebook-wycombe-chiltern-south-bucks-far-right-a8782661.html

Burns, S. (1990) *Social movements of the 1960s: Searching for democracy*, Boston: Twayne.

Butler, J. (1990) *Gender trouble: Feminism and the subversion of identity*, New York: Routledge.

Campbell, B. (1980) 'A feminist sexual politics: Now you see it, now you don't', *Feminist Review*, 5(1): 1–18.

Castro, G. (1990) *American feminism: A contemporary history*, New York: New York University Press.

CGVR (n.d.) 'Key books from the CGVR and partners', https://prezi.com/pqfmalrxyyzr/key-books-from-the-cgvr-and-partners/

Chaudhuri, M. (ed) (2004) *Feminism in India*, London: Zed Books.

Chester, G. (1981) 'I call myself a radical feminist', in *Feminist practice: Notes from the tenth year*, London: In Theory Press, pp 12–15.

Chodorow, N. (1978) *The reproduction of mothering*, Berkeley: University of California Press.

Comer, L. (1972). 'The motherhood myth', *Australian Left Review*, 1(34): 28–34.

Comer, L. (1974) *Wedlocked women*, Leeds: Feminist Books.

Coote, A. and Campbell, B. (1982) *Sweet freedom: The struggle for women's liberation*, Oxford: Blackwell.

Coy, M., Kelly, L. and Foord, J. (2007 and 2009) *Map of gaps 1 and 2: The postcode lottery of violence against women support services in Britain*, London: End Violence Against Women and Equality and Human Rights Commission.

Crenshawe, K. (1989) 'Demarginalizing the intersection of race and sex: A Black feminist critique of anti-discrimination doctrine, feminist theory and antiracist politics', *University of Chicago Legal Forum*, 1989(8): 139–167.

Crime Prosecution Service (2020) 'Domestic abuse', www.cps.gov.uk/domestic-abuse

Cuffe, S. (2020) 'Feminist groups hold mass Women's Day marches across Chile', Al Jazeera, 8 March, www.aljazeera.com/news/2020/03/feminist-groups-hold-mass-women-day-marches-chile-200308192555973.html

Daly, M. (1978) *Gyn/ecology: The metaethics of radical feminism*, Boston: Beacon Press.

Daly, K. and Bouhours, B. (2010) 'Rape and attrition in the legal process: A comparative analysis of five countries', *Crime and Justice*, 39(1): 565–650.

Darwin, J. (2003) 'Britain, the Commonwealth and the end of Empire', BBC History, www.bbc.co.uk/history/british/modern/endofempire_overview_01.shtml

Dangor, Z. and Alderton, C. with Taylor, J. (2000) 'Sheltering as a tool of empowerment', in Y. Jung Park, J. Fedler and Z. Dangor (eds), *Reclaiming women's spaces: New perspectives on violence against women and sheltering in South Africa*, Johannesburg: NISAA, pp 295–320.

David, M. (2016) *Reclaiming feminism: Challenging everyday misogyny*, Bristol: Policy Press.

Davis, A. (1983) *Women, race and class*, New York: Ballantine Books Inc.

Davis, F. (1999) *Moving the mountain: The women's movement in America since 1960*, Chicago: University of Illinois Press.

De Beauvoir, S. (1997) *The second sex*, London: Vintage Classics, first published in two volumes in France as *Le Deuxième Sexe* in 1949.

Desai, M. (2002) 'Transnational solidarity: women's agency, structural adjustment and globalization', in N. Naples and M. Desai (eds), *Women's activism and globalization: Linking local struggles and global politics*, New York: Routledge, pp 15–33.

Dobash, R. E. and Dobash, R. (1980) *Violence against wives: A case against patriarchy*, London: Open Books.

Dobash, R. E. and Dobash, R. (1988) 'Research as social action: The struggle for battered women', in K. Yllö and M. L. Bograd (eds), *Feminist perspectives on wife abuse*, London: Sage Publications, pp 51–74.

Dobash, R. E. and Dobash, R. (1992) *Women, violence and social change*, London: Routledge.

Donovan, C. and Barnes, R. (2020), *Queering narratives of domestic violence and abuse*, London: Palgrave.

Donovan, C. and Hester, M. (2014) *Domestic violence and sexuality: What's love got to do with it?*, Bristol: Policy Press.

Dubinski, K. and Duhatschek, P. (2019) 'Ontario's largest women's shelter is struggling to keep up with service demands', CBC, 11 June, www.cbc.ca/news/canada/london/thousands-of-women-turned-away-from-shelter-due-to-lack-of-beds-anova-says-1.5169732

Duluth Domestic Abuse Intervention Programs (2019) *Understanding the power and control wheel*, www.theduluthmodel. org/wheels/understanding-power-control-wheel/

Dunhill, C. (ed) (1989) *The boys in blue: Women's challenge to the police*, London: Virago.

Dworkin, A. (1976) *Woman hating: A radical look at sexuality*, New York: Dutton.

Dworkin, A. (1981) *Pornography: Men possessing women*, New York: Putnam.

Echols, A. (1989) *Daring to be bad: Radical feminism in America, 1967–1975*, Minneapolis: University of Minnesota Press.

Edwards, S. (1989) *Policing domestic violence*, London: Sage.

Edwards, S. (2013, 4th edition) *Sex and gender in the legal process*, Oxford: Blackwells.

EVAW (2018) 'Supreme Court rules police failings in Worboys breached women's human rights', www. endviolenceagainstwomen.org.uk/supreme-court-rules-police-failings-in-worboys-breached-womens-human-rights/

EVAW (2020) 'Recovery and healing are an essential part of justice', www.endviolenceagainstwomen.org.uk/ supporting-women-and-girls/

Evans, S. M. (1980) *Personal politics: The roots of women's liberation in the civil rights movement and the new left*, New York: Vintage Books.

Feder, G., Ramsay, J., Dunne, D., Rose, M., Arsene, C., Norman, R., Kuntze, S., Spencer, A., Bacchus, L., Hague, G., Warburton, A. and Taket, A. (2009) 'How far does screening women for domestic (partner) violence in different health care settings meet criteria for a screening programme? Systematic reviews of nine UK National Screening Committee criteria', *Heath Technology Assessment*, 13(16): 137–147.

Feminist Anthology Collective (1981) *No turning back: Writings from the women's liberation movement, 1975–80*, London: Women's Press.

Firestone, S. (1970) *The dialectic of sex: The case for feminist revolution*, New York: William Morrow & Co.

Freeman, J. (2019) 'The tyranny of structurelessness', www. jofreeman.com/joreen/tyranny.htm

Friedan, B. (1963) *The feminine mystique*, New York: Norton.

Frye, M. (1993) 'Some reflections on separatism and power', in H. Abelove (ed), *The lesbian and gay studies reader*, New York: Routledge, pp 91–98.

Galeano, E. (1997) *Open veins of Latin America: Five centuries of the pillage of a continent*, New York: NYU Press.

Gangoli. G. (2007) *Indian feminisms: Law, patriarchies and violence in India*, London: Routledge.

Gill, A. K. and Anitha, S. (2009) 'The illusion of protection: An analysis of forced marriage legislation and policy in the UK', *Journal of Social Welfare and Family Law*, 31(3): 257–269.

Gill, A. K., Begikhani, N. and Hague, G. (2012) 'Honour-based violence in Kurdish communities', *Women's Studies International Forum*, 35(2): 75–85.

Gill, A. K., Strange, C. and Roberts, K. (2014) *'Honour' killing and violence: Theory, policy and practice*, London: Palgrave Macmillan.

Gill, A. K. and Gould, D. (2019) 'The role of family coercion, culture, expert witnesses and best practice in securing forced marriage convictions', *Journal of Gender-based Research*, 4(1): 89–105.

Gill, A. K. and Walker, S. (2020) 'On honour, culture and violence against women in black and minority ethnic communities', in S. Walklate, K. Fitz-Gibbon, J. Maher and J. McCulloch (eds), *The Emerald handbook of feminism, criminology and social change*, Bingley: Emerald Publishing Limited, pp 157–176, https://doi.org/10.1108/978-1-78769-955-720201014

Glasgow Women's Library and Scottish Women's Aid (2018) 'Speaking out: Recalling Women's Aid in Scotland', https://womenslibrary.org.uk/discover-our-projects/speaking-out/

Greer, G. (1972) *The female eunuch*, London: Paladin.

Grierson, J. (2020) 'Domestic Abuse Bill fails to protect children and migrant women', *The Guardian*, 3 March, www.theguardian.com/society/2020/mar/03/

Hague, G. (2013) 'Learning from each other: The Special Cell and domestic violence activist responses in different contexts across the world', *Violence against women*, 19(10): 1224–1245.

Hague, G. and Malos, E. (1993, 1998, 2005, in three editions) *Domestic violence: Action for change*, Cheltenham: New Clarion Press.

Hague. G. and Wilson, C. (1996) *The silenced pain: Domestic violence, 1945–1970*, Bristol: Policy Press.

Hague, G. with Harvey, A. and Willis, K. (2012) *Understanding adult survivors of domestic violence in childhood: Still forgotten, still hurting*, London: Jessica Kingsley Publishers.

Hague, G., Kelly, L. and Mullender, A. (2002) *Challenging violence against women: The Canadian experience*, Bristol: Policy Press.

Hague, G., Malos, E. and Dear, W. (1996) *Multi-agency work and domestic violence*, Bristol: Policy Press.

Hague, G., Mullender, A. and Aris, R. (2003) *Is anyone listening? Accountability and women survivors of domestic violence*, London: Routledge.

Hague, G., Thiara, R. K., Magowan, P. and Mullender, A. (2008) *Making the links: Disabled women and domestic violence. Action Plan*, Bristol: Women's Aid.

Hanmer, J. (2010) 'Jalna Hanmer discusses consciousness-raising', British Library, www.bl.uk/collection-items/jalna-hanmer-consciousness-raising-groups

Hanmer, J. and Maynard, M. (1989) *Women, violence and social control*, London, Macmillan Press.

Hanmer, J., Radford, J. and Stanko, E. (1989) *Women, policing and male violence: International perspectives*, London, Routledge.

Harding, S. (ed) (1987) *Feminism and methodology: Social science issues*, Milton Keynes: Open University Press.

Harding, S. (1987) 'Introduction', in S. Harding (ed), *Feminism and methodology*, Milton Keynes: Open University Press, pp 1–14.

Harding, S. (1993) 'Rethinking standpoint epistemology: what is "strong objectivity?"', in L. Alcoff and E. Potter (eds), *Feminist epistemologies*, London: Routledge, pp 49–82.

Harkness. S. (1996) 'The gender earnings gap: Evidence from the UK', *Fiscal Studies*, 17(2): 1–36.

Harris, J. (2016) 'The end of council housing', *The Guardian*, 4 January, www.theguardian.com/society/2016/jan/04/end-of-council-housing-bill-secure-tenancies-pay-to-stay

Harwin, N. (2009) 'First world conference of women's shelters: Discovering the common core, practical frameworks for change', *Safe: The Domestic Abuse Quarterly*, 28: 4–7.

Harwin, N., Hague, G. and Malos, E. (1999) *The multi-agency approach to domestic violence: New opportunities, old challenges?* London: Whiting and Birch.

Hester, M. (1992) *Lewd women and wicked witches*, London: Routledge.

Hester, M. (2009) 'Who does what to whom?', *European Journal of Criminology*, 10(5): 623–637.

Hester, M. and Walker, S.-J. L. (2017) 'Rape investigation and attrition in acquaintance, domestic violence and historical rape cases', *Journal of Investigative Psychology and Offender Profiling*, 14(2): 175–188.

Hester, M., Kelly, L. and Radford, J. (1996) *Women, violence, and male power: Feminist activism, research, and practice*, Milton Keynes: Open University Press.

Hill Collins, P. (1990) *Black feminist thought*, New York: Routledge.

Hill Collins, P. and Bilge, S. (2016) *Intersectionality*, Boston: Polity Press.

Historyireland (2012) 'The Price sisters', www.historyireland. com/20th-century-contemporary-history/the-price-sisters/

Hobbs, M. (1973) *Born to struggle*, London: Quartet Books.

hooks, b. (1981) *Ain't I a woman: Black women and feminism*, Boston: South End Press.

hooks, b. (1984) *Feminist theory: From margin to center*, Boston: South End Press.

Immigration and Refugee Board of Canada and Musasa (2001) *Zimbabwe: Musasa Project including the protection/services it offers women who are victims of domestic violence, the effectiveness of the program, state funding, and whether it obtains sentences against abusive husbands before the courts*, 1 June, ZWE37085.E, www.refworld. org/docid/3df4becc4.html

International Center for Research on Women (2002) *Domestic violence in India: Exploring strategies, promoting dialogue: Women-initiated community level responses to domestic violence*, Washington, DC: International Center for Research on Women.

Jaffe, P. and Thompson, J. (1978) 'Family Consultant Service with the London (Ontario) police force', in J. Eekelaar and S. Katz (eds), *Family violence: An international and interdisciplinary study*, Ontario: Butterworths, pp 216–224.

Jaggar, A. M. (1983) *Feminist politics and human nature*, Rowman & Littlefield.

James-Hanman, D. (2017) 'Whose movement is it anyway? Reflections from the field', in S. Holt, C. Øverlien and J. Devaney (eds), *Responding to domestic violence: Emerging challenges for policy, practice and research in Europe*, London: Jessica Kingsley Publishers, pp 325–340.

Jeffreys, S. (1977) 'Revolutionary feminism', *Spare Rib*, 58.

Jeffreys, S. (2014) *Beauty and misogyny: Harmful cultural practices in the West*, London: Routledge.

Jeffreys, S. (2018) *The lesbian revolution: Lesbian feminism in the UK, 1970–1990*, London: Routledge.

Jolly, M. (2019) *Sisterhood and after*, Oxford: Oxford University Press.

Jones, H. and Cook, K. (2008) *Rape crisis: Responding to sexual violence*, Dorset: Russell House Publishing.

Julios, C. (2018) *Female genital mutilation and social media*, London: Routledge.

Jung Park, Y. with Peters, R. and De Sa, C. (2000) '"More than simply a refuge": Shelters for abused women in South Africa', in Y. Jung Park, J. Fedler and Z. Dangor (eds), *Reclaiming women's spaces: New perspectives on violence against women and sheltering in South Africa*, Johannesburg: NISAA, pp 243–289.

Kelly, L. (1988) *Surviving sexual violence*, Cambridge: Polity Press.

Kelly, L. (2013) 'Changing it up: Sexual violence three decades on', in L. Appignanesi, S. Orbach and R. Holmes (eds), *Fifty shades of feminism*, New York: Hachette, pp 133–137.

Kelly, L., Bindel, J., Burton, S., Butterworth, D., Cook, K. and Regan, L. (1999) *Domestic violence matters: An evaluation of a development project*, London: Home Office.

Kelly, L., Burton, S. and Regan, L. (1994) 'Researching women's lives or studying women's oppression', in M. Maynard and J. Purvis (eds), *Researching women's lives from a feminist perspective*, London: Taylor and Francis, pp 27–48.

Kemp, S. and Squires, J. (1998) *Feminisms*, Oxford: Oxford University Press.

Land, H. (1980) 'The family wage', *Feminist Review*, 6(1): 55–77.

Laws, S., Collins, W., Garthwaite, A. and Spellacy, M. (1984) 'Writing our own history: working for the women's liberation movement: Starting *WIRES*', *Trouble and Strife*, 1(2): 48–55.

Lazenby, P. (2011) 'Britain's unions face a battle for survival', *The Guardian*, 27 June, www.theguardian.com/commentisfree/2011/jun/27/unions-30-june-strike

Leeds Revolutionary Feminist Group (1981) *Love your enemy? The debate between heterosexual feminism and political lesbianism*, London: OnlyWomen Press.

Lewis, H. (2020) *Difficult women: A history of feminism in eleven fights*, London: Vintage Books.

London Rape Crisis Centre. (1987) *Strength in numbers: Report of research by the London Rape Crisis Centre on women's experiences of rape and sexual assault*, London: London Rape Crisis.

Lorde, A. (1984) *Sister outsider*, Berkeley: The Crossing Press.

Machado, C. M. (2020) *In the Dream House: A memoir*, London: Serpent's Tail.

MacDowell Santos, C. (2005) *Women's police stations: Gender, violence and justice in São Paulo, Brazil*, New York: Palgrave.

McIntosh, M. (1981) 'Feminism and social policy', *Critical Social Policy*, 1(1): 32–42.

Mackay, F. (2015) *Radical feminism: Feminist activism in movement*, London: Palgrave.

Maitland, E. (ed) (2009) *Woman to woman: An oral history of rape crisis in Scotland, 1976–1991*, Scotland: Rape Crisis Scotland.

Malos, E. (1980) *The politics of housework*, London: Allison & Busby.

Malos, E. (2000) 'Supping with the devil? Multi-agency initiatives on domestic violence', in J. Radford, M. Friedberg and L. Harne (eds), *Women, violence, and strategies for action: Feminist research, policy, and practice*, Milton Keynes: Open University Press, pp 120–136.

Mama, A. (1996, 2nd edition) *The hidden struggle: Statutory and voluntary sector responses to violence against black women in the home*, London: Whiting and Birch.

MIFUMI with Hague, G. and Thiara, R. K. (2005) *Bride-price, poverty and domestic violence in Uganda*, London: British Academy.

Millett, K. (1970) *Sexual politics*, New York: Ballantine Books.

Millman, M. and Moss Kanter, R. (eds) (1975) *Another voice: Feminist perspectives on social life and social science*, New York: Doubleday.

Mirza, H. S. (1997) *Black British feminism: A reader*, London: Routledge.

Mitchell, J. (1971) 'Women: The longest revolution', in J. Mitchell, *Women's estate*, London: Penguin, pp 75–122.

Mitsch Bush, D. (1992) 'Women's movements and state policy reform aimed at domestic violence against women: A comparison of the consequences of movement mobilization in the US and India', *Gender and Society*, 6(4): 587–608.

Moraga, C. and Anzaldúa, G. (1981) *This bridge called my back: Writings by radical women of color*, Watertown: Persephone Press.

Morgan, R. (1970) *Sisterhood is powerful: An anthology of writings from the women's liberation movement*, New York: Random House.

Morris, B. and Withers, D-M (2018) *The feminist revolution: The struggle for women's liberation*, Washington: Smithsonian Press.

Mulvey, L. (1975) 'Visual pleasure and narrative cinema', *Screen*, 16(3): 6–18.

Naples, N. (2002) 'Changing the terms: Community activism, globalization and the dilemmas of transnational feminist praxis', in N. Naples and M. Desai (eds), *Women's activism and globalization: Linking local struggles and global politics*, New York: Routledge, pp 1–14.

Naples, N. and Desai, M. (2002) *Women's activism and globalization: Linking local struggles and global politics*, New York: Routledge.

Nava, M. (1972) 'The family: A critique of certain features', in M. Wandor (ed), *The body politic: Writing from the women's liberation movement in Britain*, London: Stage 1, pp 36–44.

Nava. M. (2007) *Visceral cosmopolitanism: Gender, culture and the normalisation of difference*, London: Bloomsbury.

New York Times (2020) 'Harvey Weinstein's stunning downfall: 23 years in prison', 11 March, www.nytimes.com/2020/03/11/nyregion/harvey-weinstein-sentencing.html

Nnaemeka, O. (1998) 'Introduction: Reading the rainbow', in O. Nnaemeka (ed), *Sisterhood, feminisms and power: From Africa to the Diaspora*, Asmara: Africa World Press, pp 1–38.

Oakley, A. (1981) 'Interviewing women: A contradiction in terms?', in H. Roberts (ed), *Doing feminist research*, London: Routledge, pp 30–61.

O'Sullivan, S. (1982) 'Passionate beginnings: Ideological politics, 1969–72', *Feminist review,* 11(1): 70–86.

O'Sullivan, S. (1996) *I used to be nice: Sexual affairs*, London: Cassell.

Pahl, J. (1985) *Private violence and public policy: The needs of battered women and the response of the public services*, London: Routledge & Kegan Paul.

Pizzey, E. and Shapiro, J. (1982) *Prone to violence*, London: Hamlyn.

Radford, J. (1994) 'History of the women's liberation movement in Britain: A reflective personal history', in G. Griffin, M. Hester, S. Rai, and S. Roseneil (eds), *Stirring it: Challenges for feminism*, London: Taylor & Francis.

Radford, L. and Hester, M. (2006) *Mothering through domestic violence*, London: Jessica Kingsley Publishers.

Radford, J. and Russell, D. (eds) (1992) *Femicide: The politics of women killing,* Milton Keynes: Open University Press.

Radford, J., Friedberg, M. and Harne, L. (2000) *Women, violence, and strategies for action: Feminist research, policy, and practice*, Milton Keynes: Open University Press.

Ramazanoglu, C. (1992) 'On feminist methodology: male reason versus female empowerment', *Sociology*, 26(2): 207–212.

Rasool, S., Vermaak, K., Pharoah, R., Louw, A. and Stavrou, A. (2003) *Violence against women: A national survey*, Johannesburg: Institute for Security Studies.

Renzetti, C., Eldeson, J. L. and Bergen, R. K. (2001) *Source book on violence against women*, New York: Sage.

Rich, A. (1976) *Of woman born: Motherhood as experience and institution*, New York: W.W. Norton.

Rich, A. (1980) 'Compulsory heterosexuality and lesbian existence', *Signs: Journal of Women in Culture and Society*, 5(4): 631–60.

Richards, L., Letchford, S. and Stratton, S. (2008) *Policing domestic violence*, Oxford: Oxford University Press.

Richardson, D. and Robinson, V. (eds) (1993) *Introducing women's studies*, London: Macmillan.

Richardson, J. (2019) 'Women in SNCC', https://snccdigital.org/our-voices/women-in-sncc/

Rise Up (2019) 'Rise up: A digital archive of feminist activism', https://riseupfeministarchive.ca/

Roberts, H. (ed) (1981) *Doing feminist research*, London: Routledge & Kegan Paul.

Roberts, M. (2007) *Paper houses: A memoir of the '70s and beyond*, London: Virago.

Rollè, L., Giardina, G., Caldarera, A. M., Gerino, E. and Brustia, P. (2018) 'When intimate partner violence meets same sex couples: A review of same sex intimate partner violence', *Frontiers in Psychology*, 9: 1506, https://doi.org/10.3389/fpsyg.2018.01506

Rowbotham, S. (1969) *Women's liberation and the new politics*, Nottingham: The Spokesman, 17.

Rowbotham, S. (1972) *Women, resistance and revolution: A history of women and revolution in the modern world*, London: Verso.

Rowbotham, S. (1973) *Hidden from history: Rediscovering women in history from the 17th century to the present*, London: Pluto Press.

Rowbotham, S. (1991) *The past is before us: Feminism in action since the 1960s*, Boston: Beacon Press.

Rowbotham, S. (2019) *Promising of a dream: Remembering the sixties*, London: Verso.

Rowbotham, S., Segal, L. and Wainwright, H. (2013) *Beyond the fragments: Feminism and the making of socialism*, London: Merlin Press.

Roychowdhury, A. (2020) 'Explained: Why a capital 'B' in 'Black' is culmination of very long journey', *The Indian Express*, 4 July, https://indianexpress.com/article/explained/why-a-capital-b-in-black-is-culmination-of-very-long-journey-6485691/

Russell, D. (1982) *Rape in marriage*, New York: MacMillan.

Sandwell, M. (2015) *The rise of women's transnational activism: Identity and sisterhood between the World Wars*, London: Bloomsbury.

Scottish Women's Aid (2020) *What is domestic abuse?* https://womensaid.scot/information-support/what-is-domestic-abuse/

Sebestyen, A. (1988) *'68, '78, '88: from women's liberation to feminism*, Bridport: Prism.

Segal, L. (2007) *Making trouble: Life and politics*, London: Serpent's Tail.

Schechter, S. (1982) *Women and male violence: The visions and struggles of the battered women movement*, London: Pluto.

Seymat, T. and Gaubert, J. (2020) '*Mexico: Women stay at home to protest femicide*', EuroNews, 10 March, www.euronews.com/2020/03/10/mexico-women-stay-at-home-to-protest-femicide

Shepard, M. and Pence, E. (eds) (1999) *Coordinating community responses to domestic violence: Lessons from Duluth and beyond*, Thousand Oaks: Sage Publications.

Skinner, T., Hester, M. and Malos, E. (2005) *Researching gender violence: Feminist methodology in action*, Devon: Willan Publishing.

Smith, D. (1988) *The everyday world as problematic: A feminist sociology*, Milton Keynes: Open University Press.

Solanas, V. (1967) *SCUM manifesto*, New York: Olympia Press.

Special Cells (2004) *Executive summary of the 'Evaluation of the Special Cells'*, Mumbai: TISS.

Stanley L. and Wise, S. (1983) *Breaking out: Feminist consciousness and feminist research*, London: Routledge & Kegan Paul.

Stanley, L. and Wise, S. (1990) 'Method, methodology and epistemology', in L. Stanley (ed), *Feminist praxis*, London: Routledge, pp 20–60.

Stark, E. (2019) *Coercive control: How men entrap women in personal life*, Oxford: Oxford University Press.

Sutton, J. and Hanmer, J. (1984) 'Writing our own history: A conversation about the first years of Women's Aid between Jo Sutton and Jalna Hanmer', *Trouble and Strife*, 4: 55–60.

Taylor, J. (n.d.) *Organising women around the issue of violence against women: A Southern African perspective*, Paper No 18, Harare: Musasa Project.

Taylor, J. and Stewart, S. (1991) *Sexual and domestic violence: Help, recovery and action in Zimbabwe*, Harare: Musasa project.

Thiara, R. K. and Gill, A. K. (eds) (2000) *Violence against women in South Asian communities: Issues for policy and practice*, London: Jessica Kingsley Publishers.

Thiara, R. K. and Roy, S. (2020) *Reclaiming voice: Minoritised women and sexual violence*, London: Imkaan and University of Warwick.

Thiara, R. K., Roy, S. and Ng, P. (2015) *Between the lines: Service responses to Black and Minority Ethnic (BME) women and girls experiencing sexual violence*, London: Imkaan and University of Warwick.

Thiara, R. K., Hague, G., Bashall, R., Ellis, B. and Mullender, A. (2012) *Disabled women and domestic violence*, London: Jessica Kingsley Publishers.

Tomlinson, T. (2011) 'Trade union membership has fallen further than ever before', Resolution Foundation, www.resolutionfoundation.org/comment/trade-union-membership-has-fallen-further-than-ever-before/

Tong, R. (1989) *Feminist thought: A comprehensive introduction*, London: Routledge.

Topping, A. and Barr, C. (2020) 'Rape convictions fall to record low in England and Wales', *The Guardian*, 30 July, www.theguardian.com/society/2020/jul/30/convictions-fall-record-low-england-wales-prosecutions

TUC (n.d.) 'Dagenham women's strike: How Ford's striking women drove the Equal Pay Act', https://tuc150.tuc.org.uk/stories/dagenham-womens-strike/

TWCWS (2019) 'About the 4th World Conference of Shelters', https://fourth.worldshelterconference.org/en/about

United Nations (2019) *Conflict-Related Sexual violence*, Geneva: UN.

United Nations (2020) 'A staggering one-in-three women', https://news.un.org/en/story/2019/11/1052041.

UN Women (2016) 'Facts and figures: Ending violence against women', www.unwomen.org/en/what-we-do/ending-violence-against-women/facts-and-figures

Van Breda, A. and Sekudu, J. (eds) (2019) *Theories for decolonial social work practice in South Africa*, Oxford: Oxford University Press.

Vera-Gray, F. (2020) 'The whole place self: Reflecting on the original working practices of Rape Crisis', *Journal of Gender-based Violence*, 4(1): 59–72.

Wages for Housework (2020) 'Wages for housework and social reproduction: a microsyllabus', 27 April, www.radicalhistoryreview.org/abusablepast/wages-for-housework-and-social-reproduction-a-microsyllabus

Walby, S. (2011) *The future of feminism*, Cambridge: Polity Press.

Walby, S. and Myhill, A. (2001) 'New survey methodologies in researching violence against women', *British Journal of Criminology*, 41(3): 502–522.

Walker, S.-J. L., Hester, M., McPhee, D., Patsios, D., Williams, A., Bates, L. and Rumney, P. (2019) 'Rape, inequality and the criminal justice response in England: The importance of age and gender', *Criminology & Criminal Justice*, https://doi.org/10.1177/1748895819863095

Wandor, M. (1972) *The body politic: Writings from the women's liberation movement in Britain, 1969–1972*, London: Stage 1.

Wandor, M. (1990) *Once a feminist: Stories of a generation*, London: Virago.

Welchman, L. and Hossain, S. (eds) *'Honour': Crimes, paradigms and violence against women*, London: Zed Books.

Welsh Women's Aid (2019) 'Forty voices, forty years', www.welshwomensaid.org.uk/2019/11/forty-voices-forty-years

West, C. (2003) *Violence in the lives of Black Women*, Oxford: Routledge.

Westcott, M. (1979) 'Feminist criticism of the social sciences', *Harvard Educational Review*, 49(4): 422–430.

Westmarland, N. (2008) 'The Rape Crisis', *New Statesman*, 18 March, www.newstatesman.com/politics/2008/03/rape-crisis-centres-women

Westmarland, N. and Alderson, S. (2013) 'The health, mental health, and well-being benefits of rape crisis counseling', *Journal of Interpersonal Violence*, 28(17): 3265–3282.

Wilson, E. and Weir, A. (1986) *Hidden agendas: Theory, politics, and experience in the women's movement*, London: Tavistock Publications.

Womankind (2016) *Womankind report: More than a Roof*, www.womankind.org.uk/policy-and-campaigns/resources/more-than-a-roof

Women's Aid (2019) 'Campaign with us: The Domestic Abuse Bill', www.womensaid.org.uk/what-we-do/campaigning-and-influencing/campaign-with-us/domestic-abuse-bill/

Women's Aid (2019a) *The domestic abuse report*, www.womensaid.org.uk/research-and-publications/the-domestic-abuse-report/

Women's Aid (2019b) 'Women's Aid report says £393 million a year is needed', www.womensaid.org.uk/womens-aid-report-says-393-million-a-year-is-needed-to-fund-domestic-abuse-services-in-england/

Women's Aid (2020) www.thehideout.org.uk and www.loverespect.co.uk

Women's Aid (2020a) 'Our qualifications', www.womensaid.org.uk/what-we-do/training/qualifications/

Women's Aid (2020b) 'Expert voices', www.womensaid.org.uk/our-approach-change-that-lasts/expert-voices/

Women's Aid (2020c) 'Law in the making', www.womensaid.org.uk/what-we-do/campaigning-and-influencing/campaign-with-us/law-in-the-making/

Women's Aid (2020d) 'Sustainability partnership', www.womensaid.org.uk/what-we-do/sustainability-partnership/

Women's Aid (n.d.) 'History', www.womensaid.org.uk/about-us/history/

World Health Organization (2005) *WHO multi-country study on women's health and domestic violence against women*, Geneva: WHO.

Yllö, K. and Bograd, M. L. (1988) *Feminist perspectives on wife abuse*, London: Sage Publications.

Yuval-Davis, N. (1999) 'What is transversal politics?', *Soundings*, 12: 94–98.

Zita, J. (1988) 'Review essay: A critical analysis of Sandra Harding's "The science question in feminism"', *Hypatia* 3: 157–68.

Index